Lobbyists at Work

Beth L. Leech

Apress®

Lobbyists at Work

ISBN-13 (pbk): 978-1-4302-4560-5

ISBN-13 (electronic): 978-1-4302-4561-2

President and Publisher: Paul Manning
Acquisitions Editor: Robert Hutchinson
Editorial Board: Steve Anglin, Mark Beckner, Ewan Buckingham, Gary Cornell, Louise Corrigan, Morgan Ertel, Jonathan Gennick, Jonathan Hassell, Robert Hutchinson, Michelle Lowman, James Markham, Matthew Moodie, Jeff Olson, Jeffrey Pepper, Douglas Pundick, Ben Renow-Clarke, Dominic Shakeshaft, Gwenan Spearing, Matt Wade, Tom Welsh
Coordinating Editor: Rita Fernando
Copy Editor: Kimberly Burton-Weisman
Compositor: SPi Global
Indexer: SPi Global
Cover Designer: Anna Ishchenko

Distributed to the book trade worldwide by Springer Science+Business Media New York, 233 Spring Street, 6th Floor, New York, NY 10013. Phone 1-800-SPRINGER, fax (201) 348-4505, e-mail orders-ny@springer-sbm.com, or visit www.springeronline.com. Apress Media, LLC is a California LLC and the sole member (owner) is Springer Science + Business Media Finance Inc (SSBM Finance Inc). SSBM Finance Inc is a Delaware corporation.

For information on translations, please e-mail rights@apress.com, or visit www.apress.com.

Apress and friends of ED books may be purchased in bulk for academic, corporate, or promotional use. eBook versions and licenses are also available for most titles. For more information, reference our Special Bulk Sales–eBook Licensing web page at www.apress.com/bulk-sales.

Any source code or other supplementary materials referenced by the author in this text is available to readers at www.apress.com. For detailed information about how to locate your book's source code, go to www.apress.com/source-code/.

For my students

Contents

About the Author

© F. Araga 2012

Beth L. Leech is an associate professor of political science at Rutgers University. She teaches, researches, and publishes on interest groups, lobbying, and policymaking. She is the co-author of several books, including the APSA award-winning *Lobbying and Policy Change: Who Wins, Who Loses, and Why* (University of Chicago Press, 2009) and *Meeting at Grand Central: Understanding the Social and Evolutionary Roots of Cooperation* (Princeton University Press, 2012). Professor Leech is a widely consulted expert on interviewing methods in the social sciences. Before embarking on an academic career, she was a newspaper editor. She holds a bachelor's degree from Northwestern University's Medill School of Journalism and a PhD in political science from Texas A&M University.

Acknowledgments

This book quite literally would not have been possible without the busy lobbyists and policy advocates who gave their time to speak with me and answer my many questions. If not for their good humor and willingness to explain, this would be a much shorter and duller book. My sincerest thanks go out to all of them.

Thanks also to my editor, Robert Hutchinson, who first approached me with the idea for the book and encouraged me through the process, keeping me amused with his wit and wordplay. I also thank coordinating editor Rita Fernando, who kept the project running smoothly throughout.

Several colleagues helped me along the way with ideas, introductions, and feedback on chapters: thank you to Frank Baumgartner, Jeff Berry, Lee Cronk, Ben Dworkin, David Kimball, Marie Hojnacki, Timothy LaPira, Bert Levine, and Christine Mahoney.

Finally, thank you to Lee, Lauren, and Cooper for putting up with me as I scurried to meet deadlines and for making me happy.

Introduction

In the popular view, the word "lobbyist" is often taken to be synonymous with "special interest" and "corruption." Media stories assume that lobbyists twist arms and force government officials to do things that they otherwise would not. Campaign contributions are equated with bribery.

Professors who study the topic, however, have learned that lobbyists are more likely to spend time with government officials who already share their views. Dozens of studies have discovered that, on average, organizations that give more campaign contributions succeed in their policy goals no more often than we would expect by mere chance. And only about a third of the thousands of interest groups active in Washington even have a political action committee with which to give campaign contributions. The other two-thirds of the interests give zero dollars to candidates.

Why, then, are there so many interest groups and so many lobbyists? There are more than 12,000 registered lobbyists in the nation's capital, but the legal definition of a lobbyist is narrow, and so that number vastly undercounts the number of people who do policy advocacy as part of their daily jobs. During a single year—2011—interest groups in the United States reported spending $3.33 billion on lobbying and advocacy efforts not related to campaign donations.

One reason for the large numbers is that lobbying is part of a political arms race. Research that four of my political science colleagues and I have conducted showed that moneyed interests did win more often when there was an extreme imbalance of resources between the two sides of an issue.[1] It was just that such an imbalance didn't happen very often—only in about 10 percent of the cases.

Another reason for the large numbers of lobbyists is that government today is involved in so many things. In Chapter 8, for example, Christina Mulvihill, an in-house lobbyist for Sony, talks about how many different federal agencies regulate a television set. And mostly the numbers are so big because, even without twisting arms, sometimes the alliances that lobbyists have built, the

[1]Frank R. Baumgartner, Jeffrey M. Berry, Marie Hojnacki, David C. Kimball, and Beth L. Leech, *Lobbying and Policy Change: Who Wins, Who Loses, and Why* (University of Chicago Press, 2009).

arguments they have made, the information they have collected, or the stories they have told can indeed make a difference in the policies that affect our lives.

In selecting the sixteen political advocates profiled on these pages, I have tried to provide a broad overview of the profession. Perhaps the most important distinction is between in-house lobbyists, who work directly for a company or nonprofit, and contract lobbyists (so-called "hired guns") who work for one of Washington's many lobbying firms. Five of those interviewed are the founders of or partners in a lobbying firm. In the first chapter, Howard Marlowe is president of his own lobbying firm specializing in representing local governments in Washington. In Chapter 2, Robert Walker is a former member of the US House of Representatives with a fascination with aerospace who for more than fifteen years has been a partner in a prominent Washington lobbying firm that bears his name. In Chapter 3, Nicholas Allard, a partner in the world's largest lobbying firm, Patton Boggs, is a lawyer who has spent time in and out of government and who today is the dean of Brooklyn Law School. In Chapter 6, the career of Lyle Dennis begins in state government, transitions to Washington, and eventually into the lobbying firm where he now is a partner. In Chapter 7 we hear the story of Dale Florio, who founded what is now the largest state-level lobbying firm in the country.

In-house lobbyists in Washington may work for a company—like Christina Mulvihill in Chapter 8—or they may work for a trade association—like Danielle Her Many Horses in Chapter 11. Her Many Horses represents Native American tribes involved with casino gambling, but there is an enormous range of trade associations in Washington representing virtually every category of industry or business, from cell phones to frozen pizza to medical device manufacturers. Other lobbyists work for professional associations and unions. Doctors have the American Medical Association, political scientists have the American Political Science Association, and lobbyists themselves have the American League of Lobbyists, a professional organization that Howard Marlowe discusses in Chapter 1. In Chapter 12, Timothy Richards of the Fraternal Order of Police talks about the role of his organization, which can act as a union at the local level but in Washington takes on the role of professional organization as it advocates for policies to help law enforcement.

Many governmental entities, including a majority of the states, have their own lobbyists in Washington. Lyle Dennis (Chapter 6) spent a year of his career lobbying for the State of New Jersey. Large institutions like hospitals, museums, and universities also often have their own in-house lobbyists. Mark Burnham in Chapter 10 describes what it is like to lobby for a large research university, Michigan State, given the importance of federal research dollars and federal aid to students.

Six of the chapters deal with the world of nonprofit citizen advocacy. These advocates sometimes fit the legal definition of lobbyist—like Laura Murphy of the American Civil Liberties Union (Chapter 5) or Craig Holman of Public Citizen (Chapter 15). In other cases, the interviews are with policy advocates who are not required to register as lobbyists because they spend relatively little time directly contacting members of government and more time providing information to their members, the media, and the public. Leslie Harris in Chapter 9 and Jonathan Schleifer in Chapter 13 have been registered lobbyists in the past, but today have shifted roles. Harris runs a nonprofit organization devoted to Internet freedom. Schleifer directs a nonprofit organization in New York that advocates on education policy. In Chapter 4, Julie Stewart has never been a registered lobbyist, but the nonprofit she founded works ceaselessly to get media, congressional, and legislative attention directed at the problem of unfair prison sentences. Chapter 14 features a discussion with two Washington interns—Angela Guo and Faith Shapiro—as they talk about what it is like starting out in the world of advocacy.

As a career, political advocacy has been a growing field because of the expansion of government. The Washington, DC, economy emerged relatively unscathed from the economic downturn of recent years. But as the career paths of most of the political advocates in this book show, it is relatively unusual for someone to go directly into lobbying as a profession. Most begin with at least a few years working in entry-level positions within government or nonprofits, and some spent many years rising through the ranks before transitioning into lobbying. As many of the chapters advise, would-be lobbyists should follow their passion and do what most interests and motivates them, be that law or policy in general or some specific topic like civil liberties or education. The career path to advocacy extends from the experiences and knowledge built in those early years.

About half of the interviews for this book were conducted by phone and the other half in person, in the lobbyists' own offices. My goal was to interrupt with questions as infrequently as possible, to get each person talking, telling his or her own story in his or her own words. Many of the central questions are the same throughout: How did you become a lobbyist? Tell me about a recent issue that you worked on. Describe an "average" day. What advice can you offer to those who are interested in lobbying as a career? But in all of the interviews I tried, above all, to just let the conversation flow. The interviews provide insight into what motivates these advocates and what made them want to enter a career that has such a negative connotation in the public view. Why did they want to be lobbyists? And now that they are lobbyists, what are the rewards that they find in following their policy passions?

CHAPTER

1

Howard Marlowe

President, American League of Lobbyists

President, Marlowe & Company

***Howard Marlowe** is, quite literally, the lobbyists' lobbyist. In his role as president of the nonprofit American League of Lobbyists (ALL), he speaks on behalf of his profession before government and in the news media.[*] The League of Lobbyists provides training and networking opportunities for its members and has advocated for greater disclosure and stricter ethics requirements for lobbyists. At the time of this interview, Marlowe was in the midst of a lobbying campaign to convince Congress to revise the Lobbying Disclosure Act of 1995.*

When he is not volunteering for ALL, Marlowe's job is being president of Marlowe & Company, a "boutique" lobbying firm on Washington's K Street that he started in 1984. The firm has nine employees and, in 2011, it reported billings of $1.4 million, lobbying on behalf of more than 40 clients, most of them coastal cities and towns throughout the United States. Its campaign contributions were modest: a mere $1,861 in the 2012 election.

Marlowe has a bachelor's degree in economics from the Wharton School at the University of Pennsylvania and a law degree from New York University Law School. He spent nine years working on Capitol Hill, first as the legislative director for Sen. Vance Hartke (D-IN) and then as a counsel on the Senate Finance Committee.

Beth Leech: You are both the president of ALL and the president of Marlowe & Company. About what percentage of your time ends up being spent with ALL, which I understand is a volunteer position?

---

[*] Marlowe was president of ALL at the time of the interview; his term ended in December 2012.

Howard Marlowe: Right now, it's easily sixty to seventy percent of my time.

Leech: Wow. And has that been true over the time that you've been in the position?

Marlowe: Yes. Although it was more at the beginning of the term. I was what I call "an accidental president." I first was president back in 1989 for two years. This time, the woman who was supposed to be president lost her job and she needed to look for another job. So I stepped in. Then, the executive director of twenty-five years passed away relatively suddenly from cancer. And the office was planning a move. My first month on the job, I started a lobbying disclosure working group and later appointed a separate working group on campaign finance. So it has been busy.

Leech: You also registered Marlowe & Company as lobbying on behalf of ALL. I've read that ALL had never previously been registered with the federal government under the Lobbying Disclosure Act—either as a client or as a lobbyist on its own behalf—because the lobbying had always been done for it pro bono, and so it wasn't required under the law to register. Why did you decide to register Marlowe & Company as lobbying on behalf of ALL?

Marlowe: I think it's embarrassing to go up to the Hill to lobby on strengthening the Lobbying Disclosure Act's registration requirements and then to say, "Oh, I don't have to be a registered lobbyist."

Leech: Although, maybe it helps make your point that the law needs to be reformed.

Marlowe: It could. Marlowe & Company has registered on behalf of pro bono clients in the past. So, it isn't anything new. I don't know why my predecessors as president of ALL didn't formally register ALL as a client, but then, there wasn't that much reason. This recent effort to reform the Lobbying Disclosure Act is the first thing that ALL has done in a long time that has required us to go up to Capitol Hill and lobby.

Leech: It is relatively rare that ALL has a major lobbying effort, because it's a professional association, and a lot of what it does is provide services to its members, right?

Marlowe: Correct. We have three things that we do: ethics, education, and advocacy. The advocacy that we've done for the last few years has consisted almost exclusively of writing letters to members of Congress: "We don't like this. We don't like that." I've done my share of that, but we wanted to be proactive.

Leech: So, right now, you are being very proactive and you're being very proactive about lobbying disclosure in particular. What's your argument? What's the problem?

Marlowe: It seems to me that there ought to be more lobbyists under the tent of registration. We need more transparency and accountability. We know that recently we've been having a loss in the number of registered lobbyists. Members of our organization who were registered lobbyists three years ago are not now, even though they still have the same position. I don't have any doubt that people are purposely de-registering. That's because of the president.

Leech: Can you explain what it is that President Obama is doing that is causing this?

Marlowe: He has constantly been bashing the lobbyists since he's been office. Allegedly, you can't go over to have meetings with the White House if you're a registered lobbyist. Staff at the White House have definitely violated that rule. I was in a meeting yesterday having nothing to do with the League of Lobbyists. Some guy who was a registered lobbyist said that he had to go over to the White House next week and somebody kidded him: "Oh, you know you can't do that," then smiled at him and added, "Well, bring cash." Lobbyists who can help the White House in some tangible way—whether it's money or whether it's making sure that the president is not losing traction with some particular interest group—those lobbyists are at the White House.

Another reason for the de-registrations is that under Obama, registered lobbyists can't serve on a Federal Advisory Committees. Those committees are important, and lobbyists often have all of the required knowledge and qualifications, but if the lobbyists are registered, they become second-class citizens and aren't allowed to serve.

There also are proposals to expand ethics rules, extending them past elected officials and political appointees to include career federal employees. Part of it is not a bad idea. Extending the congressional ban on gifts from lobbyists is no problem, but some of the proposals also discourage government employees from having any social contacts with registered lobbyists. And the term used throughout these rules and proposed rules is "registered" lobbyist, because they are ones you can identify. You can't identify the unregistered lobbyists.

Leech: So it's encouraging some people to try to find a way not to register, even though they really are lobbying.

Marlowe: Yes. The rules encourage hypocrisy and it doesn't do any of us any good. I have nothing to hide about what I do as a lobbyist. All of the other lobbyists that I know have nothing to hide. I suspect all of the registered lobbyists have nothing to hide except, perhaps, the fact that they are lobbyists. And many of them can hide the fact that they are lobbyists through what I call the "twenty percent loophole."

Leech: They aren't required to register under the law because they spent less than twenty percent of their time doing direct lobbying.

Marlowe: Yes. One thing ALL wants to do is to close that loophole. Under ALL's proposals, a firm like Marlowe & Company, which is a for-hire firm, would have zero percent tolerance. As soon as we got hired and made one lobbying contact, we'd have to register. For an association of corporations, the cutoff would be ten percent of their time. If someone in the association spent ten percent of their time on lobbying activities, then that association would need to register and to list that employee as a lobbyist.

Leech: So, we're talking four or five hours a week. Under ALL's proposal, if an employee spends four hours a week making lobbying contacts or doing writing and research to prepare for those contacts, then that employee should legally be considered a lobbyist. Under current law, the employee would have to spend eight to ten hours a week doing those things to be considered a lobbyist.

Marlowe: Yes, and currently the law is self-enforcing, so we also recommend that enforcement of lobbying disclosure be put under the folks in the Justice Department who do FARA—the Foreign Agents Registration Act. We think they know something about compliance.

Leech: Could you describe what ALL is doing to try to get these changes to the Lobbying Disclosure Act, and why you are doing what you're doing?

Marlowe: We decided reform of the Lobbying Disclosure Act is needed because we've always been on the defensive. We thought that if we're considered part of the problem, then we have to become a part of the solution.

Leech: To do that, to become a part of the solution, what action is ALL taking?

Marlowe: In coming up with the proposals to reform the act, we felt that we were showing members of Congress, the media, and the public that we were serious. You've seen all the news coverage. We got headlines that said "Lobbyists want to regulate themselves!"

It's not just public relations, though. I was up on the Hill yesterday for two appointments. I'm up on the Hill regularly and we have a couple of other board members who are spending time up on the Hill. We're serious about this. It's not just the PR thing. It's a struggle nevertheless to get members of Congress interested. I was at the Senate Ethics Committee meeting yesterday because we have a proposal to require ethics/compliance training for lobbyists. The senators on the committee were delighted with the idea of having ALL conduct that training, so that they don't have to arrange it.

So, people in Washington believe that ALL is serious about this reform. A particular member of Congress or a congressional staffer may question details like the ten percent cutoff: "Why ten percent and not some other number?" But they know we're serious. That's true also of the public interest folks. I met with some of them as we were developing our proposals: Sunlight

Foundation, Center for Responsive Politics, Project On Government Oversight, Citizens for Responsibility and Ethics in Washington, Public Citizen—all of those folks. We made progress because they realize that we're serious about what we wanted to do and it was not just a papering over.

Leech: ALL and the good-government groups both are working on lobbying disclosure reform, but don't some of those groups have pretty different ideas about what that reform should entail?

Marlowe: There are some differences. Our difference with Sunlight, for example, is the question of what counts as a lobbying contact and what triggers the registration. On the other hand, we're in a better position to move the boat than they are. We are the professional association. We have a better ability to go in a bipartisan way, and therefore we have some leverage. But we remain in discussions with those public interest groups.

Our proposals don't have legislative language and I'm not in a rush to get to legislative language. That was done for a reason. It gives us a chance to talk with people. There are a lot of details: Should a "lobbying contact" include any phone call or letter or visit by anyone, even the company CEO? How do we decide which activities count as being preparation for lobbying and counting toward the ten percent trigger? We wanted to allow flexibility. I'm not particularly rushing right now at this time of the year to put together a bill or to get somebody to sponsor a bill because it's not going anywhere at this time.

Leech: Right before the election.

Marlowe: Instead, ALL is trying to get a congressional oversight hearing to draw more attention to the issue. If I can get that, I would be delighted right now. We're working particularly with the House Judiciary Committee but we'll move over to Senate Homeland Security and Governmental Affairs. The House Judiciary Committee so far seems to have an appetite for an oversight hearing. There is some worry, however, about whether House leadership can control their own members. And as the election gets closer, there is always a worry that a hearing on lobbying reform could become politicized.

Leech: Then why would you even want the hearing before the election?

Marlowe: Because I'm afraid I won't get it afterward. But if committee leadership tells me that they can't control other members of the committee, then I'm stuck. I'll wait till after election in hopes we can get it in then. To me, as long as it gets done this year. We've got to press for it now.

Leech: So, as you're reaching out and meeting with people on the Hill, how do you decide whom to meet with?

Marlowe: Primarily, we target the committees of jurisdiction and we're looking at committee staff. We're also looking at some of the rank-and-file members of those committees who we think might be interested. That's basically it.

Leech: And can you describe what would happen in one of those meetings?

Marlowe: Sure. I would sit down and talk to you and say, "Beth, here are our proposals. Here is why we did them and what we spent fifteen months coming up with. We're serious about them." Of course, we would have sent the proposal to the office in advance and, if I am lucky, the staff person would have read the proposal in advance. I complimented one guy who had read the proposal and had questions. In any case, I'd run through what our proposals are and then I would say, "Okay, here's what we're looking for. We're looking for an oversight hearing of Judiciary."

We are trying to find somebody who will pick at least a piece of this and say, "Oh, yeah. My boss is interested and we'll run with this. What are the downsides of it?" It's a lobbying job just like anything else. I say, "Here are the facts, here are the reasons to do it, and here are the reasons you might not want to do it. I think it's a win-win, but maybe you are concerned that if you get into this, you're going to pay a price because somebody's going to attack you." And as I look for members of Congress to become involved in this issue, I've got to make sure that it is bipartisan. I can't have it any other way.

Leech: And why is it so important to have bipartisanship?

Marlowe: Because, otherwise, it will die, particularly in this partisan environment. The League of Lobbyists was responsible for starting the effort for the original Lobbying Disclosure Act in 1995. It was a different environment back then. We started out with an oversight hearing before the Senate Government Affairs Committee at which the League testified, and then we sat down with the staff and started working on what needed to be done. It took a few years. I was president of the League when it started. It took about five or six years to get it done, but it was done bipartisan and that was very helpful. It shouldn't be a Republican or a Democratic issue.

I don't know whether you saw this, but in a recent Gallup poll, the public ratings of lobbyists were about equal with those of Congress.

Leech: I missed that story.

Marlowe: Only seven percent of the public thought lobbyists deserved a "high" rating on ethics and honesty, and Congress got the same score. We both are in the toilet together. If we're going to get ourselves out of it, reforming the Lobbying Disclosure Act is one of the things that members of Congress can do to help their image and say, "Yeah, we put these lobbyists under control. Now all the bad actors have to report." Whatever bad they want to say about lobbyists is fine. The important thing is that the system gets accountability and transparency.

Leech: You mentioned the bad public opinion of lobbyists, and outside the Beltway, people certainly have that attitude. If I mention that I study lobbyists, people react by saying, "Oh, those are terrible people!" The general public equates lobbying with campaign contributions, graft, and Jack Abramoff.

But if that impression is misguided, and if lobbying is not just about the money, why do you think members of Congress and their staff listen to you?

Marlowe: I meet with staff members all the time. They listen to me for our clients at Marlowe & Company. They listen because I'm an expert in water resources. I spent a lot of years becoming an expert in that. I've got facts behind me and we can get into a dialogue about it. They know that I'm an expert and that they can ask me questions—and I'm likely to have the answer. If I don't have the answer, I will get it. So I have credibility and I could help them craft policies.

We had a client in town yesterday, the City of Flagler Beach in Florida, and staff people from our office were up on the Hill with a group of people from Flagler Beach. Since the House ban on earmarks, members of Congress can't do very much directly for our clients, but we were on the Hill seeking congressional assistance to help our clients get through the bureaucracy. Flagler Beach has a typical FEMA [Federal Emergency Management Agency] problem. FEMA agreed a few years ago to reimburse the city for some damage. The program and the rules and regulations changed after FEMA agreed to it. So now, the local FEMA people say, "No, we're not going to reimburse the city for doing this, even though we agreed to it before the rule was a changed." So we're trying to help. Most people don't realize how much of lobbying is grunt work.

Leech: So you're trying to help those municipalities get through that bureaucratic process and figure out how they could get that reimbursement.

Marlowe: Sure. In this case, we are dealing with the members of Congress who represent Flagler Beach, asking them what they can do to help. This particular client has another ongoing issue with the Army Corps of Engineers. Normally, we would bring them over to the Corps and talk about it, but it wasn't quite ripe at the moment. Next time they are in town, we'll go over there. The folks at Corps headquarters know us, but just because they know us, they don't necessarily just agree with us. And we can't give money there. It doesn't make any difference.

Leech: Right. The staff at FEMA and the Army Corps of Engineers are civil servants and are not elected.

Marlowe: So when we talk to them, we are operating on just the facts. Now let's go back to the issue of money in politics. ALL's working group on lobbying and campaign finance punted on campaign finance, with the exception of a very strong statement of concern about the new tendency to mix legislative policy and political funding. The reason is that most of us in the working group are experienced lobbyists and have been around the block a few times.

Suppose there were a fundraiser in this office—which there hasn't been—but suppose there were, and Congresswoman Mary Jones was up at the head of the table. Fifteen years ago, Miss Jones would have said, "I'm having a difficult race. I only won by sixty-five percent last time. I've got a real rough race this time. I really need your support." Today, it would be Miss Jones saying, "I'm helping you out. What's *your* issue?" She would go around the room and ask each lobbyist who paid to come to the fundraiser what they want.

Leech: Why do you think that changed?

Marlowe: Some of it is the Honest Leadership and Open Government Act [HLOGA] of 2008 and its gift ban. I don't have a full answer to your question, but I blame HLOGA to some extent. Demands on members' time and staff members' time are enormous, even in the do-nothing Congress. Between the e-mails, and the tweets, and the video conferences with the district, it is hard to get their attention in the office. So if I could get them out to the cafeteria, or to the Monocle or something like that for lunch, it would be absolutely great. But instead, because of HLOGA's gift ban, I can see that legislative person only at the campaign fundraiser, and members of Congress take advantage of that. I will not use those fundraisers as a way to advance policy because I was brought up in another tradition. The younger lobbyists don't know anything different. If you tell them it used to be different, their eyes go wide and they say, "It was?" It's sad. I don't know that we can turn back the clock on that.

The other reason why policy issues have become so prominent at campaign fundraisers is the profusion of money that is required to get elected or reelected. We don't give very much money here, but I guarantee you by the end of the day, there will be a dozen e-mailed invitations to fundraisers, and half of them will be repeats of ones from last week. There's one guy I already saw today who seems to have one fundraiser every other week.

Leech: Marlowe & Company doesn't give very much. In the last election cycle, the company's PAC donated only about $1,800 to candidates.

Marlowe: It pains me to even think of $1,800 because it comes out of my pocket, since we represent primarily local governments and nonprofits, and they can't give. When I do give, to me what it means is, "Here. This is a token of appreciation."

I can't come up with $1,000 for one of these fundraisers, although sometimes we'll do $500. And the members and their staff usually understand that, because of the type of clients that we have, we're not going to be big givers. But even if I were a big giver, and gave the legal limit, it doesn't mean anything in today's environment. For it to mean something, I would have to put together one fundraiser after another. Some lobbyists lobby by fundraising only. Those lobbyists then get to regularly see Congresswoman Jones and all the other people that they're raising money for in the fundraising environment. They get to know the members of Congress at the fundraisers. They get to talk all the time.

Leech: And, in your efforts for reform, you've currently dropped campaign finance reform because it's too complicated?

Marlowe: There was concern in the working group that campaign finance would distract attention away from lobbying disclosure reform and that we as lobbyists weren't likely to be able to solve the campaign finance problem—that's got to be done by members of Congress. Well, that's true to a large extent. Members of Congress don't view campaign finance as a problem right now, and until and unless they do, it's hard to get any traction with them on campaign finance reform. One of the things that I think will start to get their attention is the super PACs moving into the congressional districts. Congressman Silvestre Reyes' primary bid got knocked out by a super PAC coming into his district.

But campaign finance issues worry me a lot. I was on C-SPAN a couple of weeks ago, on their *Washington Journal* program.

Leech: I saw the link on your web site.

Marlowe: The anger that you were talking about, the belief that we lobbyists are buying members of Congress, was all people called in about. It was constant. I was trying to get a couple of folks from the League of Lobbyists to call in. They were on the phone but they couldn't get through.

Most folks are very angry at us, not because of the words that come out of our mouths, but because of the money out of our pockets that they believe is buying members of Congress. So, if we're buying, then they're bought, and I think we have an equal problem together.

I personally don't think in any way that we're buying. If we are, then you know the member of Congress is going to be caught—she is going to wind up in jail and, hopefully, the lobbyist will be caught also. I don't think that's what is happening. And the issue academically to take a look at is what is being bought with the campaign contribution. Access, definitely, I already mentioned that, but that's not all of it.

Leech: Is it attention? Is it time? That's related to access.

Marlowe: It is and that certainly is part of it. But there are things short of a vote that you can get a member of Congress to do. A lobbyist might use money to say, "Look, would you introduce this amendment for me or will you make this speech or this argument?" Is it illegal? No, not at all, but again it needs to be looked at more. I think we need to learn what, if anything, lobbyists are buying.

My shorthand version of it in the past was: everybody who is contributing wants to be one of that Congress member's two hundred and seventy best friends. I was in a meeting yesterday. Lobbyists were dropping names all over the place—and names not only of members but key staff members. And most of the lobbyists who are around the table there undoubtedly were giving large amounts of money. There could be public interest groups that were there also, and dropping names, too. It's a typical Washington thing. Lobbyists want to show that they know important people. It makes you a member of the club. But name-dropping and ally-building is not what the public thinks is happening and I'd like to know more about what is happening. I don't hear theories about campaign contributions from our member lobbyists. I don't know that they know or that they ever sit around the table and say in a thoughtful way, "Here. This is what I've been able to get this member of Congress to do since I raised $20,000 for him last year." Do they connect that dot? I don't know. It's not as easy to deal with this as people think.

Leech: There's a theory within political science that it has to do with subsidizing your friends. So, that it's not a matter of buying the vote—the votes are already yours or the activity is already yours—but the lobbyist is making it easier for the legislator to act in the way that they both prefer. Does that resonate with your experience?

Marlowe: Members of Congress, by and large, are not going to do anything that is not in the interest of getting reelected, not in the interest of their constituents, or that would get them into trouble. I can see that lobbyists may subsidize what a member of Congress is already inclined to do anyway, but may not necessarily be thinking about. So, there are times that you have to do a lot of persuading, even if it's a known constituent interest. You have to convince them that some nutso group in the district is not going to come after them for that particular issue.

Leech: Most of the issues that Marlowe & Company would work on for its clients—the cities, and townships, and other governmental entities—would not be large, highly publicized bills, right?

Marlowe: It would be programmatic, connected to a particular program within a particular appropriations bill. Despite the current ban on earmarked funds to benefit one particular location, there are things that Congress can do. Let's take my area, which is primarily Corps of Engineers and the Energy and Water Bill. Congress can and has "plussed-up" the president's budget request, adding money for particular programs. The programs benefit our clients at the same time that they benefit other people, so we're trying to make sure that the programs our clients care about get plussed-up.

And then we do a lot of grants work here, helping educate our clients and others about how to get federal grants. And anything related to water policy or transportation policy is likely to be an issue for us. There is language in both the House and Senate Surface Transportation bills that is important to a client of ours, so we are monitoring that as well.

Leech: I'd like to ask you about your background, your training. You have a bachelor's degree in economics and a law degree. To what extent is it necessary to have—or important to have–a law degree to be a lobbyist?

Marlowe: It's not.

Leech: But a lot of lobbyists have law degrees.

Marlowe: These young people who are here at Marlowe & Company as interns believe, and I understand why they do, that they need to have some graduate degree in order to work on the Hill or be an effective lobbyist. You don't. My background has those degrees but I was also a high school teacher. I came down here, in essence, by accident, then worked on the Hill for four years in Senator Vance Hartke of Indiana's office. I had no connection with Indiana. So a lot of things were accidents in my life, but it worked out very well for me.

What a lobbyist really needs is a love of the political process or public policy process, and a political perceptiveness about who is important for a given issue. Part of that is learned. Besides that, a lobbyist needs the ability to write.

Leech: And why is writing important for lobbyists?

Marlowe: We write one- or two-page fact sheets about our issues. We write letters for our clients to send to government officials. We write letters for members of Congress to send to their colleagues, or agencies, or whatever. We serve as extra staff to our clients and to members of Congress. If we can't write well, then we can't communicate well for them.

What we do is like advocacy journalism. It's being able to write well, and make your point, and make it succinct. That will start to teach you, if you don't already know, how you'd have to make that argument orally because you know you only have limited time. I can't remember the number of times that elected officials have told me I have three minutes to make my argument.

Leech: Wow.

Marlowe: I can do it. Once I waited for two or three hours for a senator, who, when I got into his office, told me I had five minutes. I left a couple of hours later, but I did my initial pitch in five minutes.

Leech: So, you gave the five-minute pitch and after he heard it, he said, "Okay, I'll listen to more."?

Marlowe: Yes. Another senator, defeated not long ago, used to have his staff person interrupt at precisely seven minutes into it. Now, unless you've been there a few times, you didn't realize it was going to happen. So, one time that I went in, I told the staff person, "You don't need to interrupt. I will tell the senator that I will get done within seven minutes." Now, that staff person got into trouble for not interrupting, but I did finish in my seven minutes. And, of course, there were times before that when we were interrupted at the seven-minute mark, the senator said, "Oh, I don't have to worry about this next appointment. I will be late and we can keep talking."

It's kind of fun to learn these personalities and how you deal with them, but it's not as much fun in this environment because the members dislike each other so much. We've got all these members of Congress up there who came to change the system and haven't done anything except to throw monkey wrenches into that system and to make it Republicans fighting Republicans, Democrats fighting Republicans. If I step back, it's very discouraging. So I try not to step back too much.

Leech: A lobbyist lives in the moment.

Marlowe: You have to. You have to serve your clients. If we can't do anything for them, we're going to tell them we can't. In essence, we fire our own clients. Sometimes at Marlowe & Company, we have to say to a client, "Hey, we want to help you, but unless you change what you're asking us to do, we won't be able to get what you're looking for."

Leech: It's honest.

Marlowe: I love their money, but on the other hand, I don't want the company to be mad at us for not getting what they want. I don't like when people are mad at us.

Leech: Can you walk me through what an average day would look like for you? What do you end up spending your time on?

Marlowe: I'm a ten-thirty to eight-thirty person. The average day is spent mostly on phone calls and e-mails to the Hill, and managing the office. For instance, yesterday, the chief administrative officer here says, "We need to buy two computers. This is what we've chosen. You've got to sign off on this and sign this paperwork for the League of Lobbyists. I need you to sign a check."

Yesterday, I also got a chance to go up to the Hill. A reporter from *Businessweek* was shadowing me. The article is coming out next week and I'm scared to death. If you shadowed me, you would find it's not as interesting as I would like you to think it is. She shadowed me for the trip to the Hill, but when we got back here for a League of Lobbyists education committee meeting, she left. Wasn't interesting.

Leech: So, ten thirty to eight thirty. You're the second person who's told me that. Is there a reason for that sort of staggered day, or is that just how you like it? Is there a Washington-based reason for that day?

Marlowe: No, there isn't any Washington reason. Marlowe & Company is open nine to six. I guess I get my thinking stuff done in the evening. I'm trying lately to get home a bit earlier for domestic relations, but it won't be too much earlier probably.

Leech: That leads to my next question. Is lobbying life conducive to family life?

Marlowe: It's not easy. Particularly if you're going on the fundraising circuit every evening, but for a lot of folks, it's becoming easier. You have lobbyists leaving during the day because Junior has to go to the soccer game, or whatever it may be. They work that in pretty well. I don't know how they do it, I couldn't.

Leech: Do you have kids?

Marlowe: They're all grown, so it's easy for me. But I've got staff members here with kids. And if the kids get sick, then family comes first. And there are some days that they go home earlier than others for domestic relations. They want to make sure they spend some time with the kids before they go to bed. But it is a bit difficult to fit in.

Leech: What sort of person are you looking for and what sort of skills are you looking for when you hire a lobbyist for your company?

Marlowe: Somebody who has good political instincts. Judgment is a lot of it. I rely particularly on one of my lobbyists for that kind of judgment. He provides me with a second opinion. He has not been lobbying for that many years, but he was on the Hill for several years and it was sort of built into him, I think, when he was born.

Besides good political instincts, a person's writing example is probably the most crucial thing that we're looking at. If the candidate fails in the writing example, that candidate will get tossed right away.

Leech: What's an example of the kind of thing you might ask advice about?

Marlowe: It would be: "Well, who would you think I should meet with? Do you think I should approach the issue this way or that way? Do you think I should call so-and-so and ask him to do this?" I mean, those were the examples from yesterday.

Leech: What advice do you have for people who might be thinking about lobbying as a career?

Marlowe: I think it's a great profession. I used to shun the usual advice to get experience on the Hill. I don't shun it anymore because spending time on the Hill is part of network building. It might be drinking beer at night or just playing on Hill softball teams, but it helps create a network. Lobbyists who have that network can use that to call somebody on the Hill to get information that may not be as easy to get for someone without that experience.

Having said that, it's hard to get that position on the Hill, and student interns are unpaid, just like they are at Marlowe & Company. Also, Congress is not doing much these days, so it's hard to get useful experience with the legislative process by working up there. Students who intern here benefit from the experience that Marlowe & Company has in going up on the Hill. But those interns are also writing policy papers and sometimes screwing up, but they're learning. You don't learn by always being right, you've got to learn by making mistakes.

CHAPTER

2

Robert Walker

Executive Chairman

Wexler & Walker Public Policy Associates

***The Honorable Robert S. Walker**, known on Capitol Hill as Bob Walker, is a former member of Congress who represented Pennsylvania's 16th District for 20 years. When he left the US House of Representatives in 1997, he joined the lobbying firm the Wexler Group, which then became Wexler & Walker Public Policy Associates. The firm reported billings of more than $10 million in 2011, representing a wide range of clients in aviation, communication, finance, automotive, health, and technology sectors. It gave $131,000 in campaign contributions during the 2012 election cycle.*

Former members of Congress make up only one percent of all lobbyists in Washington, according to research conducted by Timothy La Pira of James Madison University, and most of them work for lobbying firms such as Wexler & Walker. The prestige of former members, along with their insider status and knowledge of the system, make them sought-after advocates, hired primarily by major corporations (although Wexler & Walker also has some nonprofit and governmental clients). Walker himself has been cited as one of Washington's top lobbyists by several national publications.

While in Congress, Walker was chairman of the House Committee on Science, Space and Technology (then called the Science Committee) and rose to become chief deputy minority whip. As part of that leadership position, he was responsible for counting votes and mobilizing support for legislation among the Republicans in the House. After leaving Congress, he served as chairman of the Commission on the Future of the United States Aerospace Industry, and as a member of the Presidential Commission on the Implementation of the United States Space Exploration Policy and the President's Commission on the United States Postal Service. He serves on the boards of the Aerospace Corporation and Space Adventures, and as a director emeritus of the Space Foundation. He was chairman of the US Department of Energy's Hydrogen and Fuel Cell Technical Advisory Committee.

Walker received a bachelor's degree in education from Millersville University in 1964, and taught high school for three years before earning a master's degree in political science from the University of Delaware in 1968. He then served on the staff of Rep. Edwin Eshleman of Pennsylvania for 10 years; when Eshleman retired, Walker ran for and was elected to his seat.

Beth Leech: I know that you spent twenty years in Congress before you came to this firm. Why did you choose to come here over any other place you could have gone?

Bob Walker: Well, this organization impressed me for a number of reasons. Coming off the Hill, I was interested in finding someplace where the culture would be somewhat similar to what I was used to. As I did my interview, it was clear that the teamwork approach and the bipartisan approach that was taken by this firm was similar to the kind of atmosphere that I grew up with on the Hill. My own orientation toward this was to be able to extend my public service career, but do so in a venue that gave me a little more latitude than what I had in Congress, both in terms of schedule and in the issues.

Leech: Who, in general, are the clients that you tend to deal with? I understand that your areas of expertise come from your time on the Hill, right?

Walker: Yes, a lot of it. I deal primarily in science, space, technology, and energy issues because those were things that I was deeply involved in as part of my work on the Science Committee when I was in Congress. I was also a parliamentary tactician when I was on the Hill, so a lot of what I do here is strategizing based upon what's possible inside of the operational process of the Congress. But my role in the firm is such that I get involved in broad, general issues, most of which are familiar to me because of my years in leadership in Congress, where we had to deal with a little bit of everything.

Since coming here, I've expanded my range of issues because of some of my corporate board work and so on in the areas of intelligence and defense, but it largely builds off of some of the things that I was doing when I was in Congress.

Leech: And how did you happen to get interested in those areas when you were in Congress?

Walker: I got assigned to it. I went to Congress with the intention of ultimately getting on the Rules Committee. As a member of a minority party, that was not going to happen in my early career, so I asked to be assigned to a generalist committee. I asked for what was then called Government Operations because of its broad, general jurisdiction, not so much legislatively but in oversight. My representative on the Committee on Committees called me to say, "Well, I can get you Government Operations if you're willing to take Science, Space and

Technology as a second assignment." I said, "Sure, why not?" And about three science professors flipped over in their graves.

Leech: That was not your subject in your early years?

Walker: No, it was not. Although I must admit that as a kid, the space program really fascinated me, and so when I realized that this was one of the areas I was going to get a chance to deal in, I found that exciting. I got there and figured out that I didn't have to know theorems in order to do science policy. What I was getting a chance to do was look over the science and technology horizon ten or fifteen years to see if I could figure out what those technologies were going to do to impact culture, and culture to impact politics. And so I ended up specializing in it because I found it fascinating. When I became the chief deputy whip for the Republicans, I had to give up a committee. I gave up the Government Operations Committee in order to stay on the Science Committee. Later, just a few months after that, I was offered a chance to go to the Rules Committee, but I turned it down in order to stay on the Science Committee.

Leech: Oh, that's interesting. Your ideal committee assignment changed as science policy drew you in.

Walker: Yes, and I've remained close to it—and not just because of work here, but I've done a lot of special projects for NASA on a pro bono basis. I served on two presidential commissions that worked with NASA, defense aerospace issues, and commercial aerospace issues. I'm on the board of Aerospace Corporation, which is a major, federally funded research and development center. So I've stayed involved even beyond the work that I do here.

Leech: Could you give the reader an idea of what life is like when you're you? Could you walk me through an average day at work?

Walker: Yesterday, I played in the congressional golf tournament on behalf of the Wounded Warriors Project, and so I spent my day on the golf course with some of my former colleagues and some of the present members of Congress. We were golfing with a group of just outstanding people who were wounded in either Iraq or Afghanistan and are in the process of recuperating.

Leech: Was it a fundraiser?

Walker: Yes. We raised about $300,000 for the Wounded Warriors organization.

Leech: And when you're at an event like this, do people talk shop, talk about politics—or is that considered sort a faux pas?

Walker: No, it's minimal. Usually, it's just kind of reminiscing about time on the Hill, but, for example, I had a conversation with the chairman of the Armed Services Committee about sequestration before we teed off. One of the fellows who was playing with me was playing for the Democratic team, but we rode together and talked a little bit of shop—but not much in the course of the day. So that's not a faux pas, but it just usually doesn't fit. Most of what you talk about is how bad your golf game is.

Leech: So the golf tournament yesterday—and I know last week you were out of town part of the week. Is there another day that would be closer to typical?

Walker: Well, today is semi-typical. I started the day by meeting with a client in a large group meeting. We have a coalition of lobby organizations around town that work for a client, and so I had a meeting this morning where we were discussing strategy with them. I came back down here and worked for a while on just catching up with news and events, and so on, because I'd been out of town. I went up to the Hill and had lunch with a former colleague who is a current member of Congress, but she is leaving Congress and wanted to talk to me about what life would be like on the outside and discuss some of her options about that.

Then I came back here and, again, worked on answering e-mails and so on. I'm chairman of the Australian American Leadership Dialogue. I just got off the phone with the president of that group. We just did our big event last week, which is the reason why I wasn't in the office. So we were doing an after-event analysis of what had gone on. And I just got off the phone with a scientist who wants to come in and talk to me about some research that she's doing, so we're making arrangements on that. Now I'm doing an interview with you. I do press interviews on a lot of days. Later on today, I have another client meeting that I have to do. And then—I lose track myself—it seems to me I have something this evening as well.

Leech: How often will you have something going on in the evening that's work-related?

Walker: Fairly often. It's certainly not every night, but fairly often there will be fundraising events or something of that kind. Oh, yeah, and I have another meeting here in about a half an hour with somebody who's doing a job search. I meet with a lot of foreign groups. I'm involved with the US Association of Former Members of Congress, and through that, I have worked to build communications between countries. I have worked on issues relating to China and some on Europe.

I sometimes do seminars in the evenings. I do a lot of speaking to federal employee groups that come into town.

Leech: And when you do these seminars or you're speaking to visiting groups, what are the topics that you speak on?

Walker: It's usually the legislative process of one kind or another. Brookings Institution has me talk fairly often and it's usually on how science policy is developed inside the Congress.

Leech: You were talking about the different meetings you're having with clients. How do clients come to you? How does one get clients?

Walker: A lot of it is what we call "over the transom." It's just people who know the reputation of the firm and have an issue that they think would fit, and they come to us. Many of our clients here have been here for a long, long time. We have a couple clients here that have been here ever since the firm opened back in 1981. So we've got some traditional clients, and then there is special project work, and usually those projects come to us based on reputation. It may be the reputation of the firm. It may be the reputation of individual members of the firm. New clients also come from the outreach we do. All these things I'm wandering around doing are ways of getting to know people who then get some impression of your capabilities.

Leech: Things like the Australian American Leadership Dialogue?

Walker: Well, we haven't actually gotten very much business out of that. We served as the secretary for that group for a long time. It was a joy of my former and late colleague, Anne Wexler. She was one of the founding members, but it hasn't been something that's generated an awful lot of business. Of course, I have made contacts with other people inside the group that sometimes are business possibilities.

Leech: What does a lobbyist do when someone comes to him and says, "Can you help me?"

Walker: Well, a large portion of what we do is educate our clients. Often, when they come in, they think that there's some magical button that can be pushed or some string that can be pulled that automatically gets them what they want. And they think that what they're hiring you to do is to talk with people who can then magically make what they want happen. A lot of what we have to do is to educate clients that it doesn't work that way. In fact, it often takes a considerable period of time to educate people within government about what the client is doing, what it is they want, and why it would be good for the country, not just for a particular group or individual.

You have to convince the client that they've got to be in this for the long haul—this isn't something that's probably going to happen in weeks or months. The legislative process or even the business of working inside the agencies is a very long-term type of thing. So, the first thing is to educate the client, and then give them a strategy—begin to give them some idea of what we'd have to do in order to be successful.

Once a strategy is put together, we decide here what the team would be that would be necessary to carry out that strategy. Then, depending upon where the client's needs can be met, we begin to work. Usually people come here and say, "Just give me a piece of legislation passed." Well, that's one of the toughest things to do, so what you have to say is, "It probably doesn't take a piece of legislation. It probably takes language in a committee report, or it takes an amendment to an authorization bill." We try to give them ideas about routes that they can go. Sometimes, it just involves a member of Congress writing a letter to the agency involved and pointing out what the advantages of some action would be. That gets the agency interested in it and then begins the conversation. Then it is a process of getting all the people on board that have to be on board in order to accomplish the end result.

Leech: When you're presented with a problem, how do you figure out what to do?

Walker: You rely upon the expertise of the people that you've gathered in the firm. We usually start with the premise that we want to do the thing that is likely to be the most successful to get the project done and in the shortest amount of time. We want to treat the client fairly, and at the same time, recognize everything that we would have to go through. And so we rely upon our people to know whether there is any provision in law that would give us an ability to do what the client wants. If not, we might have to consider whether a piece of legislation is necessary to get it done.

We have a client right now for whom we would like to get a tax provision that would allow their work to be a tax deduction. There is no such provision in law at the present time. Maybe it's something that would be good policy because it would affect the entire industry, but we have one client who is paying us for it. So, in that case, we're going to have to get the law changed. We've looked at a lot of other avenues, but in the end, it's going to take that.

In other cases, it's clear that the law already authorizes whatever it is that the client is seeking, but that it simply has not been detailed. And so often what is necessary at that point is just a report from a congressional committee that says that, inside the provisions of law, this is an activity that we would like to see happen. But to do that, you've got to work to find somebody who's willing to put the needed language into the committee report and is willing to be the sponsor to do that. So then we have to figure out who might be the potential member of Congress to do what is needed, and whether they have a constituency interest in the issue. Do they have a personal interest in it? Do they have a committee interest in it? Then we locate that person and then try to figure out who here has relationships with that person or that person's staff so that we can begin to educate them about the need.

So everything we do is customized to the precise nature of the issue or problem that we've been presented.

Leech: How would working on an issue that's primarily regulatory be different, or do you not handle things like that very often?

Walker: Well, the regulatory stuff is really more in the range of legal rather than legislative policy. So we do some of that, but it's usually an informational campaign. It is not really lobbying, because it's very difficult to lobby independent commissioners of regulatory agencies. But there are times when what we at least try to do is provide them with information off the shelf as it were, and we usually team with regulatory lawyers if we're deeply involved in some matter that takes regulatory approval.

Leech: And do you have those regulatory lawyers on staff, or do you go outside?

Walker: No. We go outside.

Leech: How big a firm is Wexler & Walker?

Walker: We're twenty-two professionals and then some support staff on top of that, and we keep it right in that range. We're usually anywhere from twenty to twenty-five professionals.

Leech: You mentioned going to lots of fundraisers at night. To what extent is the firm involved in fundraising here?

Walker: We have a PAC. We have our own PAC that we utilize on behalf of our clients, and individual members of the firm do fundraising for individual members of Congress—usually members who they've worked with before or that they know from other venues. So we give individual contributions to candidates. We do individual fundraising. And we have our own PAC.

Leech: I'm sure you know the public view on all this, and that news stories pretty much portray PAC contributions as equaling bribery—that you're buying the vote. I would just like to hear your opinion about this public view of what PACs are doing.

Walker: It's a public view that's been largely formulated by the press because it's an easy story to write, but it looks ridiculous on the face of it. Most of my contributions are in the $250 to $500 range. This is to people who are raising hundreds of thousands of dollars, if not millions of dollars, for their campaigns. The dirty little secret of lobbying is that nobody can persuade anybody to do something that they wouldn't be in favor of doing anyhow.

Most of the money goes to your friends—to people who have supported you in the past and who have had a record of being supportive of your issues. So there's no sense that any of this is a pay-off for anything. Our PAC has a maximum contribution level of $1,000. Again, not enough money there to make a huge difference, but what it does is, it allows you to go to dinners or receptions and so on where at least the individual gets a chance to say hello to you and knows that you're being supportive of the work that they're doing. And that's about all you get out of it.

Every once in a while, if you have a direct issue and so on, you actually get a chance to say, "I'd like to come in and see you about such-and-such and so on," and the answer will usually be, "Sure, stop by and see me sometime." That's about as much work that gets done at any of these events.

Leech: And if you go and see somebody, how likely is it that they're going to respond in the way that you want them to?

Walker: You don't know. I mean, there's no quid pro quo in any of this. The idea that because they saw you at the fundraiser, they're immediately going to say, "Oh, yeah, absolutely! I've got to do this!" It just doesn't work that way. By the time you go and have the appointment, the chances are that they've forgotten the fact that you were in the room, so it's not as though all this is easily recognized as a part of a relationship. Most of this is—you've done it because you have an acquaintance with them, and you've contributed to them, and you go in to see them because you have an acquaintance.

I do know that there are places around town where the way in which they build those acquaintanceships is through fundraising. They become an instrument of raising a lot of money. It's not just the money they contribute, but they raise a lot of money for candidates from other people and become personally associated with members of Congress through that mechanism. But again, that often causes you more problems than it gets you results, because you do get in the public eye. You become one of these hated bundlers at this point who are seen as people who have undue influence inside the process.

Again, I've just never found that to be the case. Are there people who do something that looks like it's directly related to the money that they got? Well, yeah. The press can write that easy story. But the fact is, even without the money, the legislator probably would have made that decision anyway, because it's where they are philosophically, or it's where their district is. I mean, for a whole variety of reasons, they would be in that position.

Leech: So why do you think a legislator listens to you?

Walker: Because you have credibility with them. Because they know that you'll give them an honest viewpoint about the issues that you're discussing. You'll discuss both the pros and the cons. You have a long-term reputation for being substantive on issues. There are a variety of reasons why legislators would listen to us, and one reason is to get educated. The fact is that their staffs are not capable of keeping up with all the issues, and certainly not capable of dealing with them in depth.

Even committee staffs that tend to be far more specialized don't have an opportunity to deal with issues in the kind of depth that we do out in the lobbying community, because we've narrowed down the field into the universe of clients that we have. In the case of Wexler & Walker, we have probably between fifty and one hundred clients at any given time, and that means we can get very much in-depth on those issues, so that when we go in to talk to legislators or we go in to talk to staff, we give them detailed information that they don't have.

Now, somebody else might come in on the same subject and give them detailed information from the other side of the question, but that's how they learn. The most important thing that lobbyists do—and what gives them credibility—is that when asked the question, "What would the opposition say?", lobbyists tell clients in detail what the other side of it is, with full confidence that the lobbyist's point of view is going to carry the day.

Leech: How does having been a member of Congress help in all this? What does that experience bring to the table?

Walker: Well, you simply understand the kinds of things that Congress members are interested in knowing and hearing. You tend not to deal with some of the superfluous issues that people who have never been a part of the process tend to get into. People who are subject-matter experts tend to get into too much detail about the subject matter and not enough about what the policy would be. If you've been in Congress, you understand there's a difference between the practitioner and the policymaker.

On the science committee, I wasn't a bench scientist, but I learned the policy well enough to understand when I was being told something that just didn't make any sense. So what I bring to the table as a lobbyist is an ability to speak to people about the policy options, and that's what gets appreciated. I think that the reason why former members have a great deal of value inside the process is simply because we've been there. We've been a part of the club. We maintained some ties to the club. That gives us some credibility, unless we destroy that credibility by doing something stupid. We do have ways of telling members, "Let's get to the bottom line—this is the reason why this is important and why it's probably important that you be involved." We intuitively understand that better than people who haven't been inside that kind of a maelstrom.

Leech: And how does having been a member of Congress differ from someone who, say, was a long-time congressional staffer?

Walker: I was a staffer and then I became a member, and it's entirely different to be a member than to be a staffer. There are some staffers who believe that they're members, but the fact is that a member has a very different role than a staffer has. A staffer never has to do the thing that is ultimately the chief role of a legislator, which is cast the vote. It's fine to stand on the sides and talk about the issues, and be an expert on the issues, and so on, but when you actually have to say yes or no, that's a very, very different role. When you actually have to put your name on a ballot and have people make a determination about whether or not you've done a good job or whether you haven't, that's a very different role. It was the thing that I found most intimidating about moving out of the staff role. All of a sudden, it was my name on the ballot, and the voters weren't making a judgment about the issues—they were making a judgment about me. Staffers don't have to face that reality in politics.

The communication among people who have been there, done that, is at a different level of communication than people who have performed in a staff role. And I'm not disparaging the staff people. There are people who bring a lot of expertise and who have been inside the committee process and know how it works. We've got several of them around here who are just absolutely tremendous assets for this firm. But there is something special about members talking to members.

Leech: That shared experience?

Walker: Yeah.

Leech: I know you said you have a meeting coming up, so we'll try to get this wrapped up relatively soon. I want to shift gears a little bit and talk about what's it like to be a lobbyist in terms of personal life. Do you think being a lobbyist is conducive to family life? Is it fun?

Walker: Number one—you have much more control of your schedule than you do in Congress. In the House of Representatives, you have four hundred thirty-four other people whose lives are impacting yours, and you have seven hundred thousand people in the congressional district who have no hesitancy to call you at midnight to discuss their Social Security problem with you. So outside of Congress, you have much more control of your schedule. We operate pretty family-friendly around this firm, so I usually have most weekends available to me, whereas in Congress, I was doing ten meetings on weekends and all kinds of other things. Yeah, I think it's significantly more family-friendly to be in the lobbying community than to be in Congress.

Leech: What do you like about your job? What's your favorite thing about your job?

Walker: I've always been a person who's been involved in public policy. I remain involved with public policy. I still believe that the work we do contributes significantly to molding public policies that are good for the country and ultimately good for the world. So I find a sense of excitement in doing that. I'm far more free to do things that I enjoy doing: the work on corporate boards, the work on the commissions, and the broader reach that I now have to use the knowledge that I've built during the time I was on Capitol Hill.

Leech: What are some policies that you're proud of that you've worked on as a lobbyist?

Walker: I think some of the work that we've done toward moving ahead with the concept of commercial space. We're getting to the point where it's really beginning to sink in. We helped a company called DigitalGlobe from their earliest days. They now have become one of the prime companies providing the government with digital photography from outer space.

Leech: And what had to be changed for them to be able to do that?

Walker: The attitude of government needed to change. The intelligence communities needed to understand that they could get much of what they needed by buying it from a commercial firm rather than flying the satellites themselves. That involved a cultural change inside the government and to a large extent on Capitol Hill.

I'm proud of the work that we did for a number of years in trying to build the idea of utilizing hydrogen more broadly in the economy, ultimately to be used for automobile power. We did a lot of work with that over the years, and it's something that I had a personal interest in and helped influence the Bush Administration to develop as part of their chief energy initiatives. Sadly, the Obama Administration didn't follow through, but nevertheless, the whole world effort, largely inspired by what Bush did, is now moving forward at a very rapid pace, and we're very close to having commercially produced, viable fuel for automobiles, and we were instrumental in that. As a matter of fact, many people give me credit for having convinced President Bush to put the line in the State of the Union message that highlighted what they were doing with the hydrogen program.

Leech: That is a level of access that not very many lobbyists can claim to have, being able to convince the president of something.

Walker: I didn't talk to him verbally about it. We worked through the Energy Department to do that.

Leech: All right. Well, you are just a stone's throw away from the White House in this office.

Walker: Yes, and we did have relationships. Jack Howard, who works with us here at the firm, was a very close aide to President Bush for a number of years. So we do have people that we're in direct communication with. A lot of the folks from that administration are close friends.

Leech: Two more questions, if you have time?

Walker: Sure.

Leech: What's your least favorite thing about your job?

Walker: Oh, geez, I have a hard time coming up with those because I like what I do. I guess if I had to pick out one thing, it is the role of fundraising. It's the idea that people do see that as being a sign that lobbying is kind of a dirty profession and that it's buying access. It's just not the case, and so you sometimes chafe at the idea that people's perception of what you do is so totally misconstrued. So if I had to pick something, it would probably be that.

Leech: When you're hiring a new lobbyist or a new associate here at the firm, what are you looking for? What are you looking for in someone who's going into this line of work?

Walker: Well, first of all, their background. We like to hire people who have in-depth experience either in the executive branch or in the legislative branch, because we want them to understand the rhythm of government here. If you just bring in somebody off the street, you can train them on the issues but you can't train them in what the rhythm is that operates on Capitol Hill or inside an agency. So we look for that kind of experience.

We also look to try to make certain that they're enthusiastic about doing what we do. There is a tendency these days of going to the Hill or going downtown and trying to get your ticket stamped so that you can come out and make real money. Well, we are very well-compensated in these firms, but to have somebody who's here just collecting a check and is not enthusiastic about the work usually ends up badly. So part of what we look for is whether or not this is somebody who really, really wants to do what we do and can really contribute to the overall cause.

Leech: Do you have any advice—not necessarily for people who are coming here—but just for people who might be interested in pursuing lobbying as a career? What would you say to a young person who said, "Oh, that sounds interesting"?

Walker: Well, get some background that allows you to be conversant on the way in which Congress operates or the way in which the government operates, and then also make certain that it's what you really want to do. Do you want to be an advocate? For some people that's very tough to do, and so you better have some of the same qualities that draw people into the business of being a lawyer, because in the end, what you are is an advocate for your clients.

CHAPTER

3

Nick Allard

Dean, Brooklyn Law School

Partner, Patton Boggs

***Nicholas Allard** became the dean of Brooklyn Law School in July 2012 and remains a senior partner at Patton Boggs, the largest firm in the country. The firm reported lobbying billings of $48 million in 2011 and gave more than $480,000 in campaign contributions during the 2012 campaign cycle (evenly split between Republicans and Democrats). Patton Boggs's clients come from almost every area of policy, from oil and finance, to cities and universities, to health and transportation.*

Allard, who came to Patton Boggs in 2005, has repeatedly been named one of Washington's top lobbyists. He is cheerfully self-deprecating, full of names and stories and jokes, but throughout it is a fierce advocate for his profession. He has published numerous articles on lobbying, including one entitled "Lobbying Is an Honorable Profession," in the Stanford Law and Policy Review, *and a column in* Newsweek *in which he argued that "We Need More Lobbyists."*

Before becoming a lobbyist, he spent time on Capitol Hill as administrative assistant and chief of staff to Sen. Daniel Patrick Moynihan (D-NY) and as minority staff counsel to the Senate Committee on the Judiciary for Sen. Edward Kennedy (D-MA). He also worked at the law firms Kaye Scholer and Latham & Watkins, and he worked full-time on Vice President Al Gore's election campaign.

Allard has an elite educational pedigree. His bachelor's degree in public policy is from Princeton University's Woodrow Wilson School, and hismaster's degree is from Oxford University, where he was a Rhodes Scholar in 1976. After receiving his law degree from Yale University, he served as law clerk for Chief US District Judge Robert F. Peckham in San Francisco and for US Circuit Judge Patricia M. Wald in Washington, DC.

Beth Leech: Let's start with where you began your career in Washington. I know that you went to Princeton, were a Rhodes Scholar at Oxford, went to Yale Law School, clerked for a couple of judges, and then ended up in Washington. Was working for the Senate Judiciary Committee your first position in Washington?

Nick Allard: No. First I was in private practice. When I finished the second clerkship, my father-in-law said, "It's time for you to get a real job." I imagined the job opportunity at the law firm as the big fork in the road. I always wanted to be a lawyer.

Leech: And that comes out of your family experience?

Allard: No, it just comes out of an aversion to blood. Otherwise, I probably would have been a very good doctor.

A person could look at my résumé and think that I've jumped around, but in reality, from high school through college, studying overseas, law school, all of my jobs, there are two constant threads. One is that what I've done has always been connected to law, policy, and politics. Second, while I may have had many different positions and opportunities, there has been a consistent theme in terms of the people. Whether the people come with me or I'm joining people, I've had relationships where there's a lot consistency. People sometimes say to me, "You have a big network." In reality, I think that there are only about six hundred people in anybody's world, and central casting just moves them around. I keep running into the same people over and over again.

Leech: So why don't you walk me through some of those experiences?

Allard: I began in high school, walking precincts to get out the vote. Then in college I was at the Woodrow Wilson School of Public and International Affairs. I've always had this combination of academically pursuing policy and politics. I was an urban affairs concentrator. My thesis was on NIMBY-type [Not In My Back Yard] issues and residential treatment centers for juvenile offenders.

Leech: Oh, very impressive.

Allard: Dave McNally and Jim Doig were my advisors. Jim Doig had one of the great comments of all time on my thesis. He wrote up three single-space pages of detailed comments about my thesis. I was a pretty good student, but I was also pretty busy. I was senior class president, honor committee chairman, blah, blah, blah. I worked a gazillion hours in the dining halls. Played rugby. My senior year I had two severely dislocated shoulders, and my arms were in slings. I had to get my classmates, twenty of them at one time, to simultaneously type, because we had this new technology at the computer center involving a mainframe computer and key punch. I was rushing around right up to the last minute, getting it typeset and getting it bound and rushing, and rushing, and rushing. Doig's comment was something like, "Page 217 is upside down." Or, "Mr. Allard, knowing your work, I suspect that page 217 is the only page that's correct and that all the other pages are upside down."

At Oxford I studied PPE, which is politics, philosophy, and economics. That was the major for most of the American Rhodes Scholars who were heading into law or government for their careers. Then Yale Law School was the classic policy approach to law. The federal clerkships were also instrumental. The first judge I had, Judge Robert Peckham, was a wonderful man who loved politics. He was a chief judge in the Northern District of California, in San Francisco. I was there in 1979, a year full of fascinating issues. The first day I showed up I had to write, with the judge, an injunction in their ongoing monitoring of the San Francisco police and firefighters—in terms of which policemen and firefighters were going to be promoted to sergeant and which ones were going to be eligible for promotion.

Leech: I remember this case.

Allard: Then I came to DC and clerked for Judge Patricia Wald. The DC Circuit Court is a very special court because it hears all the appeals on regulatory proceedings. I worked on everything from oil drilling on the outer continental shelf, to environmental standards for clean air, to patent cases involving the birth of the computer in the digital era. I helped the judge write what is still the longest appellate opinion ever. You're going to think that was my fault because I talk so much, but it wasn't.

Leech: I see the connection and interest in policy coming in.

Allard: Then Reagan was elected president, so that foreclosed another opportunity, because I'm a hardwired Democrat. Otherwise, I might have gone right into the government, working for the Justice Department or something, but I wasn't going to do that with a Republican in the White House.

So I went into private practice, working for a small Washington office of a New York firm, Kaye Scholer. I wanted to maintain my political and family ties in New York. My wife and I are both from New York. But by this time, we were already in Washington and my wife had this great job on the Hill, and we had twins. I had gone to Washington for one year for the clerkship and I ended up staying for thirty, which often happens.

Kaye Scholer was a very traditional commercial antitrust firm based in New York and it was opening a brand-new Washington office. I got a phone call from Ken Feinberg—whom you've probably heard of. He's the "value of life" expert who designed the compensation systems for victims of 9-11, the BP Gulf of Mexico oil spill, and the Virginia Tech shootings. Ken had been Senator Edward Kennedy's chief of staff. He was opening the new law office and in that office was Senator Abraham Ribicoff—who had just retired, Allan Fox—Senator Jacob Javits's former chief of staff, Alan Bennett—former counsel of the Food and Drug Administration, and Tom Madden—who had been the head of the LEAA, the Law Enforcement Assistance Administration of the Justice Department. That was it: five partners. I was the one associate. I joined the firm and hitched my wagon to Ribicoff. He was such a great mentor. He taught me so much about the Senate and Congress, and about being a boss. I traveled all over the world with him and learned politics. He was a remarkable man.

Leech: What type of work was the firm doing in Washington?

Allard: Soup to nuts. It was very political but it was also law. Since none of those five new partners at this really traditional, hard-biting law firm had ever practiced with a law firm before, when something new came around, I was like the utility infielder. I got to experience many different things. First of all, they made me head of recruiting for the whole firm. I talked them into it.

They called me the managing associate. In the first year, we hired five appellate clerks, including Thurgood Marshall Jr. Ribicoff brought in Bob Cassidy as a partner. He had been the US trade representative's counsel. Ribicoff's assignment, because he had been the former chairman of the Trade Subcommittee, was to plant the Kaye Scholer flag all throughout the Pacific Rim. So I would travel with him. It was a great opportunity.

Leech: How long were you with the firm?

Allard: Three years. Let me tell you a funny story that shows one reason that the Washington offices of New York firms often fail. It's because the New York guys never let go. One of Kaye Scholer's huge clients had to oppose a temporary restraining order in a labor case. They had a hearing before Judge Barrington Parker in Washington, and lawyers from our New York office were going to fly in to handle the case. Judge Barrington Parker had the reputation of being unbelievably tough and refusing to tolerate fools. He was a terror to appear before.

Sure enough, there was a thunderstorm the morning when these New Yorkers were supposed to fly in on the shuttle. They were due in the hearing at ten o'clock a.m. They could not make it. So I get into the office at nine o'clock and they want somebody to go cover the hearing, and there was no one else in the office besides me who even knew where the courthouse was.

I had at least worked in the courthouse for a year. I knew what the process was because I had worked with federal district judge and chief judge. I knew what a TRO [temporary restraining order] was. But I knew nothing about this case—nothing. And the file was enormous.

Allard: So I'm in the cab on the way to the courthouse, papers flying every which way. I get there and I'm standing there and my knees are knocking together. The plaintiff—the labor union guy—gets up. I'm trying to power-read through what the case is about. I am not absorbing it. Barrington Parker is crucifying the labor union guy. I say to myself, "Oh no, I'm next." So the labor union guy sits down, and I stand up and I say, "May it please the court, Nick Allard."

He says, "Young man, let me get this straight. If I understand your position correctly, you are arguing A, B, C and so on. The relief you want is 'T'."

I don't know where this came from, like some little angel on my shoulder. I said, "So moved."

He says, "Granted." And I never actually had to say anything about the case myself.

Leech: That is hilarious. You've been lucky in your life as well.

Allard: Most of the time.

Leech: You know how to take that luck when you see it.

Allard: So here's fast-forward. Toward the end of my three years with the firm, Ribicoff calls me in. Feinberg's sitting there, and they say, "Senator Kennedy called us and they need somebody to fill in on the Judiciary Committee staff. And so we told them we would send you." There's an important message in there—that's one I'm telling law students. First of all, that's why I had gone to this law firm.

Leech: To get into government?

Allard: Well, I knew it would give me those relationships, but it also gave me the experience that prepared me for going immediately into a senior position with Senator Kennedy. You also have to have the ability to feel confident and to plan, but when there's an opportunity, go through the door. To me the opportunity to work with Senator Kennedy on the Judiciary Committee was great. The other lesson is that to get those great Washington jobs, you have to be on the ground there. Jobs are filled before they're announced. That's the way things work.

Leech: So, your advice to students is to get out of Brooklyn and down to Washington?

Allard: And once they get there, be present, work their network, get some experience, and don't be afraid to fail. Don't be afraid to seize an opportunity. If it doesn't work out, do something else. There's a lot of serendipity, but you've got to be in a position to make the luck. It's not a formal bureaucratic process.

So I worked with Senator Kennedy. He was the most demanding, hardworking boss I've ever had. His staff was an assemblage of the brightest people I've ever worked with. I've got a great story about the job interview with Kennedy. If you get invited in to see the senator, you know that the staff has recommended that he hire you. So if you go in, you have to be prepared. If he likes you and he makes you an offer, you've got to accept, right?

At this point in my life, I had been around. I'd been a Rhodes Scholar, I'd worked campaigns, and I'd worked for the firm. I go in to meet with Senator Kennedy, and he and his legislative director Carey Parker are sitting in this big room that has, it seems like, twelve huge, dark oak doors. While I'm having this interview, staff are running in and out, doors are opening and closing, opening and closing. They put a document in front of him and he signs it, they put a photo in front of him and he signs it, and all the while he's talking to me. That's the scene. I have this out-of-body experience: he is larger than life. I'm looking at this enormous head and behind him is John F. Kennedy's PT-109 medal, pictures of the three Kennedy brothers together, and he's saying, blah, blah… He's talking and at some point I realize he's saying something about the line-item veto, or Roe v. Wade, blah, blah, blah. I'm looking at him, and I'm thinking to myself, "Mom. Not bad, huh? I'm doing pretty good here."

Leech: Could be why you're not processing.

Allard: I'm not processing. Suddenly he says, "So Nick, when can you start?" I blurt out something totally ridiculous. I said, "Well, my family and I are going to be on *Family Feud* and we have to tape that show in ten days." Why would I say something so stupid, even though it was true?

Leech: It was true? This sounds apocryphal.

Allard: It was true. We were scheduled to be on *Family Feud* with Richard Dawson in California. The senator looked at me as if I had just suddenly and inexplicably started speaking French. He said, "Okay, when you get here, I want to see you the first day. I've got something I want to talk to you about."

I stand up. I said, "Thank you very much. I'm really looking forward to becoming part of your team."

He said, "Carey, would you show Nick out?"

I tried to regain some of my dignity. "I'll find my way out. Thank you. I'm sure you guys have stuff to do." I turn around and open one of the twelve doors, walk in, and I'm in the janitor's closet. I open the door and I look out and the two of them are looking at me like, "We just hired this idiot?"

Fortunately, it was downhill from there.

That was my Kennedy story.

Leech: Your funny Kennedy story. So you worked for Kennedy, you were a counsel for the Judiciary Committee, and then…

Allard: Senator Moynihan's chief of staff.

Leech: How did you end up there?

Allard: I was very happy with Senator Kennedy, and it's very unusual in Washington to go from one senator to the other. But I walked around the corner of the office building one day and ran into Joe Gale, who was a classmate of mine at Princeton. Joe was Senator Moynihan's legislative aide for tax policy. Joe looks at me and says, "Aren't you from New York?"

I said, "Yeah."

He says, "We're going to be in touch with you. Moynihan's looking for a chief of staff."

Now, the reason he asked that question was that Moynihan went through chiefs of staff like toilet paper.

Moynihan was looking for somebody who had scholarly distinction. He was looking for somebody who had Senate experience. He was looking for somebody who was New Yorker, but not tied to Koch or Cuomo. There are plenty of people within those categories who had more distinction than I did. But there are very few people who match on all three requirements. So, that's why that opportunity presented itself. For me, it was an incredible break to work for this distinguished senator from my home state, to be chief of staff at the age of thirty-two.

I had that job for a year and a half. I lined up the campaign, raised money for the campaign, ran it, and got through the Tax Reform Act. I often say that Moynihan got a decade of work out of me in a year. Then a new opportunity presented itself and the timing was good. My twins were eight and my youngest was three. A small boutique law firm focusing on health policy was starting up, and I was offered a partnership in the firm. It was the same people, minus Feinberg, who had been at Kaye Scholer's office when I was there. It was a great opportunity, having really only been an associate for three years, to become a partner at a very promising, big-time boutique.

I was there for five years. I worked on health regulatory and health legislation at the state and federal level. And I started to get involved in this very big communications practice with some of my friends at Latham & Watkins, including Reed Hundt, who later became the FCC chairman. But I knew Reed before either of us knew much about communications. He was a top antitrust lawyer. He was also my next-door neighbor and our kids grew up together.

Latham was a firm that had offices in these big cities that are known for certain businesses, but it was never a part of that business. It just did its own traditional corporate work and litigation. So in Los Angeles, Latham was not a part of Hollywood. In Washington, it stood apart from lobbying and much of the government work.

Leech: How interesting.

Allard: That since has changed. But back then, Latham was representing lots of clients that had legislative and regulatory problems. And Latham would refer them to me, and more and more were related to communications. I became a one-man army of communications, doing all of the government relations and legislative work that Latham referred to me. Two things happened simultaneously. I outgrew the boutique and Latham said, "This is ridiculous. We should just have Nick come in with us." So, I moved to Latham and they asked me to not only handle the government relations work, but to build up their government relations practice, which I did for twelve years.

Then in 2004, I was recruited by Patton Boggs, which is the number-one public policy lobbying firm in the world. And since nobody has this level of lobbying except the United States, you could also say it's the largest in the galaxy.

I had many friends at Patton Boggs, and frankly, I had this image of them being sort of cowboys, more roll-around, warrior-type lobbyists. They approached me and I was very impressed with a couple of things. One is that they were in the process of moving into the next century and becoming a much stronger firm. Also, the opportunity was almost irresistible. They realized they needed reenergizing. They wanted me to come in and help lead the practice. So I did it. I went over there and I had eight really successful, tremendous years.

Leech: So you remain a partner in both the New York and Washington, DC, offices of the firm, but when you were at Patton Boggs full time, what types of clients did you primarily represent?

Allard: The variety of the clients is very large. Many of them are Fortune 100 companies in communications, online services, health, and energy.

Leech: Are those the fields that you, in particular, tended to focus on?

Allard: I'm accused of being an expert in health, communications, and Internet law. That's because I've written and published and do more and more work in those areas. They are areas of enormous change, and when there's enormous change, the relevance of existing laws and rules is challenged. So, the question of what should the law be becomes very relevant. It's not surprising that I've developed a lot of experience in those areas. In some ways, what I do is generic, like a litigator. I know how to argue a case. But it's very important to have some sort of expertise.

I've worked across the board: on international projects, the appeal of a regulation, acting as arbitrator in a telecom dispute, or arbitrations overseas. I worked on the Telecom Act of 1996, then the one hundred and eighty-eight regulations to implement that act, and all the issues since then. I also have worked for nonprofits, represented major universities, and had some very significant pro bono projects. One of those cases was advocacy related to the Dream Act.

Leech: Who was the client in that case?

Allard: I had one client whose name was Dan-el Padilla Peralta, who was a salutatorian for Princeton University. He was brought here as an infant from the Dominican Republic. His father left and his mother was a drug-addicted street person. He and his brother bounced around from foster home to foster home. He ended up with a couple who were acting as his foster parents when he was a young teenager. He became fascinated with the stories in the books that they had about the Romans and the Greeks. He became one of the leading classic scholars at the age of twenty or twenty-one. He graduated and won a scholarship to study in Britain, at Oxford. The Department of Homeland Security, in its wisdom, said, "Well, congratulations. You can leave, but you can't come back."

Leech: In your advocacy on this, and in your advocacy for him, what sorts of activities did you do? How would you approach an issue like this?

Allard: You organize students—some from conservative Christian colleges in the Midwest, people like him who had these incredible stories. By the way, he had no idea that he was an undocumented illegal alien until he applied for a summer job to help pay for college.

Leech: Oh, no.

Allard: Right. There's no concept of fault, since they were brought here as infants. Plus they are success stories. These are the kind of people that we don't want to push away. We should want these people to stay with us. To advocate for these young people, we took them around to congressional offices representing the districts where they were from or where their universities were. We made the case. We tried to work out the politics, the very tricky immigration politics. A lot of advocates, if quoted, would deny this, but there are advocates of immigration reform who don't want the Dream Act to be passed freestanding because there is more support for the Dream Act than for other aspects of immigration reform.

The immigration advocates are saying, "We don't want to do this piece. We want to do our comprehensive package." We tried to negotiate those differences. Then we were involved in drafting and negotiating, trying to hear what people's concerns are, and then addressing that. For instance, saying: "Since there is a problem in terms of what's the path toward citizenship, what if we extended the waiting period before citizenship another six to eight years?" We would work out the conflicts, listen to all of the competing but legitimate interests. That was one of my recent cases with very compelling stories. We were not able to get the Dream Act passed at that time, but we were still able to help those particular individuals, including Dan-el. They were allowed to stay. That was fulfilling.

Leech: That's great.

Allard: I also represented an Air Force Academy cadet in a pro bono case. It was a good case for me because I have a lot of honor committee experience because of my work for Princeton. This cadet was number two academically in her class and eight days short of graduation when she was kicked out on trumped-up honor committee charges. One of the members of the honor committee was also the fellow she formally accused of sexual harassment. She had been subject to a sexual attack.

We had statements from faculty saying that there could not be an honor code violation because it was a take-home group exercise. What the Air Force eventually got her on was not the honor code violation. The Committee kept her in a room for an unreasonably long period of time, questioning her until she was exhausted, and because her statements were inconsistent, she was said to be lying, which also violates the code of conduct.

She was told she wasn't going to graduate, that she had to pay back her full four years of tuition to the government within the next three months, and she now had to serve as an enlisted Air Force person. All she ever wanted to do was fly. Even though no honor committee case had ever been overturned, the merits of her case and the sheer weakness of the counter case gave us great confidence that we could overturn the decision.

The family was adamant that her case was part of a larger problem. They wanted to take on the whole Air Force Academy. I kept saying, "That's a much heavier lift and you don't understand that you can win on your case—just you. You don't have to turn the entire Air Force Academy and the Air Force upside down." But when we got into her case, we found such an organized system of abuse, protection of perpetrators, and punishment of the victims that we had no choice. Her case helped to precipitate a much broader scrutiny of the academy, and I'm sure you're familiar with it from media reports.

Leech: That was the thread that pulled everything else apart.

Allard: And she graduated. She didn't have to pay. In the history of the Air Force Academy, no honor committee case had ever been overturned—that's what we did. Unfortunately, even though she would have been eligible, she had missed flight training with her cycle and it would have been very difficult for her to go back. She also was frightened and believed her career in the Air Force was finished. So, she never actually got her chance to get her wings. But the Air Force Academy has become a much better place because of her.

Leech: As a lobbyist, how do you begin your work on a tough case like this?

Allard: We pursued and exhausted the academy process and the military process until we hit a dead end. We went around congressionally. Then we started generating letters to the secretary of defense and the secretary of the Air Force. I started a press and media campaign. Eventually, other cadets started coming out with their stories. It kind of snowballed. Her case was one of the first public cases.

What a lobbyist does is problem solving. For the best lobbyists, it's not necessarily any one set of actions. A good lobbyist looks at the problem or challenge, or whatever it is that a client wants to accomplish, and the lobbyist analyzes it and comes up with a solution. It's not as if all lobbyists have a Chinese menu of things that they do, and that a lobbyist just applies those, picking randomly from that bag. A good lobbyist has to think creatively think about how to accomplish what needs to be accomplished.

Leech: How do you do that? Can you walk me through how you analyze a situation?

Allard: A good lobbyist has to try to become an expert about every aspect of each project. A good lobbyist has to learn their business or learn their situation, or learn their facts and understand them. A lot of times it helps to have the collective wisdom of other people, it's a collaborative process in different perspectives. And here I am not talking about all lobbyists but people who are working as lawyer-lobbyists at the level that involves problem solving.

I tell you what good lobbying isn't. There are a lot of times that lobbyists are marketing their relationships, so it doesn't matter if you're an Air Force Academy cadet or you're somebody with their arm missing. They're going to say: "Because I worked with Senator so-and-so, let's have a meeting with Senator so-and-so or let's have a meeting with these three other people I know." Or the lobbyist does one thing—public relations, for example—and applies that to every problem. Really good lobbying is figuring out what needs to be done to solve the problem and then accomplishing that.

Leech: Could you break down your process for doing that?

Allard: I've broken it down this way, and I'm going to give this to you, free of charge.

Leech: Free of charge.

Allard: I had planned to send this out as an op-ed to say as I'm about to go to the academy, "Here's a teaching moment."

[Clears throat.] The Seven Deadly Virtues of Lobbying:

There are three hundred fifty million experts in the United States, more or less, about our government. Most of those people have a very negative view about what lobbyists do. For example, they may believe that lobbyists buy results or that lobbyists are corrupt. But in reality, that is not the case. First of all, it can be shown that money does not buy results. As for corruption, professional lobbyists comply with the rules because that's essential for them to have a career and a business.

What do lobbyists do? The first thing lobbyists do—and this is the best understood function—is provide information to the government. That gets all the attention, but I think it is the least important thing lobbyists do. Now sure, it helps to have a professional advocate. We have a saying: "Anybody who represents themselves in court has a fool for a lawyer and an idiot for a client." The same applies even more in the political arena. There are a million compelling stories and needs and wants competing for the attention of lawmakers and regulators. Just to be heard over the noise takes professional advocacy. But members of Congress and other government officials have many sources of information. They don't just have to rely on lobbyists. They have the Congressional Research Service, they have staff, and they have public domain. If there were no lobbyists, they would still be getting information.

Second, and even more important, is that lobbyists provide information to their clients. They provide information, for example, in the intake discussion. When a client presents an issue, good lawyer-lobbyists will be able to tell the client whether it's doable or not. They will explain to the client that maybe if you try to get something slightly different, you could accomplish something close to what you wanted.

I'm talking about the good lobbyists, not Jack Abramoff. It makes me bridle when people call him a super-lobbyist. Because he wasn't a lobbyist. He was a crook. He was getting paid for things he couldn't deliver. The good lobbyists will not take credit for the sun coming up, and they will also say when they can't do something. They will say, "That tax change has no chance of getting enacted this year." And, "By the way, what is the public policy argument for what you want done?" Because unless there is a compelling policy argument, members of Congress aren't going to do it because it's not sustainable.

Number three: lobbyists provide information about the other side. There's competition. It's an adversarial process. They keep the system honest by making everybody check their math. This assumes transparency. It assumes that you know what's going on. Sunlight is one of the great disinfectants. Professional lobbyists who play by the rules don't fear transparency. They want it because they want to have the opportunity, like a lawyer in court has the opportunity, to challenge the other side. This is why one of the most effective techniques of being a lobbyist is to say to a decision maker: "Here's our case and this is why we like it. And this is what the other side is going to say, and this is why you should discount that." The lobbyists for each side hold each other accountable. That's number three.

Number four: lobbyists hold the government accountable. This may be the most important thing. This derives from the right to petition in the First Amendment. Lobbyists sometimes mistakenly say, "The rules of lobbying violate my First Amendment rights." The lobbyists don't have any First Amendment rights. The First Amendment rights are of their clients. But every court that has addressed the issue throughout history has said that the right to petition includes the right to do it well. That means the right to hire somebody, because lobbyists can help. Holding the government accountable is not convenient to the government.

Number five is something that, once I say it, will be obvious. But it's actually not what's in people's minds. Professional lobbyists comply with the rules. The reason for that is if you don't comply with the rules, not only does that give your opposition a cheap argument, but it will embarrass you and your client and you won't get work. Ironically, the bigger the company, the more the company is interested in compliance. A related point is that the rules for lobbying—including things like the "toothpick rule" for what food a lobbyist can serve to members and staff—are so complicated that a layperson could not be expected to comply. The rules are not common sense. So clients need professional lobbyists to make sure that when they're making their case, they're doing it in a way that's appropriate and complies with the rules.

The sixth thing that lobbyists do is make sure the other guy is complying with the rules—playing fair and honest. Now, one of the standard playbooks of being a lobbyist in an adversarial situation is to check the lobbying registration of the adversary and start making noise if they're violating the rules. You think that Jack Abramoff or any case of scandal was discovered by the Justice Department? Heck, no. It was the other side that ratted them out. Professional lobbyists keep the system honest.

The seventh thing is that good lobbyists provide a much-needed sense of stability, accommodation, and mediation that leads to solutions. When there are uncivil partisan quarrels in Congress and in the government, lobbyists can be back-channel messengers, come up with solutions, talk to people, reduce the temperature, and figure out how overcome the impasse. That's what professional lobbyists do. You can accuse lobbyists of many things, but I can't think of a single lobbyist who is rude or makes uncivil comments. Those are the seven things lobbyist do, and here's a case that shows that.

Clients approach a lobbying firm because they want to accomplish something. As a lobbyist, you have to listen, then adjust the clients' expectations of what they want and figure out how to actually get it. So, say, hypothetically, that a major pharmaceutical company has a life-saving drug that it holds exclusively and it's not ready to lose its exclusive license and let the drug go generic. The company will lose hundreds of millions of dollars when that happens, so every moment that the company can keep its exclusivity will enable them to continue to charge higher prices and make more money. So the people at the company want you, the lobbyist, to get Congress to extend the license.

Once you, the hypothetical lobbyist, start having a conversation with the research team, the first thing to say say is: "Put yourself in the shoes of any member of Congress. Why would any member of Congress or any secretary of Health and Human Services [HHS] want to make it possible for you to charge sick people higher prices?" First of all, you have to get the client ed to realize that they are not sympathetic. By the way, sometimes that's not the easiest thing to do.

Leech: I bet.

Allard: Then you start to learn about the public policy merits of the case for extending the license. You talk with them and talk with them and talk until you understand the product and the science of it and everything else. Until you realize, "Wait a minute. This is interesting. This product is the leading product in its field in the world. However, it has unfulfilled potential. The benefits now are actually a fraction of what the benefits to the entire population could be if more research were done." You also learn that this product is so devastating in its present formulation that some people die from it. If there were more research, other formulations could be developed that would allow more people to take it with lower risks.

Why won't that research get done? Well, if the drug goes generic, there would be no incentive to do the research. In addition, no company would be willing to go through the laborious, time-consuming, and very expensive process of getting the United States Food and Drug Administration [FDA] to agree that any new formulation is safe and effective. The financial incentive would be gone.

Once you have an idea, you check it out with some scientists. Then you explore the patient population and talk with their representatives. You ask, "What do you think about this?" They reply, "We think it actually makes some sense." Then you float the idea with Health and Human Services and the White House, and you inform members of Congress about the plan so they know you, genuinely—that is a key word—are trying to help. Then you have another conversation with the company and say, "This is what we are going to propose, and everybody supports this. You get an extension of your license for this many years, but you are going to commit each year X millions of dollars on research." Then you might say, "Oh, and by the way, client. You don't get to choose what research is done, so that no one can say that you're just picking what's commercially most valuable. You're going to commit that money to a National Institute, and it will decide where the money goes." Guess what? Saying this to a corporate executive is like breaking wind in a board meeting.

You also tell them, "By the way, you're going to agree to reduce your prices. It's not going to be the huge reduction that you would face if the drug went generic, but the price will drop a little the first year, then a little more the next year, and so on." And lots of more complicated details—but that's the gist of it. Then you say to them, "The White House, HHS, the members of Congress—everybody seems to agree with us. But we're going to put this proposal in the Federal Register to give public notice and invite comments—not just have it announced." The reason for that is we don't anybody who's been waiting out there for the drug to go generic to have a case that they were denied due process. Let them come in and make their arguments. Otherwise, there will be companies tying this up in litigation on procedural issues even though the merits are compelling and advance the public health.

So, that's what good lawyer-lobbyists do. The result is that it's announced in the Federal Register. There are ferocious comments by other companies. But patients think it's great, medical researchers think it's great, the government thinks it's great, and members of Congress decided that it's great. Not one lawsuit is filed against it because it was all open, solid, based on good science and health policy, and fair. Not quite the silver bullet, simple phone call, political fix image of lobbying. Rather, an arduous, detail-driven, long-haul, nuanced, law-based endeavor. Now here I should emphasize my hypothetical is dramatized to convey my point. Its compiled based on experiences and situations I've known about, but any resemblance to an actual project and real people is purely coincidental.

Leech: Problem solving.

Allard: And I oversimplified. Actually, extensions of this kind can happen in bites over several years, and one might be an executive order and another required passing some legislation. It's multiyear. It's multiarena. It's not simply because a lobbyist knows the secretary of HHS or the FDA commissioner and picks up the phone to persuade them. People have the impression that there are these silver bullets. That is rarely the case. One of the reasons for that is well known in Washington: anything that is done can be undone. If somebody pulls a fast one, persuades a member of Congress to slip something into a bill late at night—like an extension for exclusive license—it gets in the press the next day, as soon as somebody realizes this is what's going on. People are embarrassed and it gets the client nowhere.

Leech: When we were talking earlier, you mentioned the influence peddling and the idea that the public has that Washington is for sale. What do you say to those people? What's your explanation for why an organization like Patton Boggs gives something close to half a million dollars in campaign contributions in an election cycle?

Allard: I don't have a great explanation for that. I have always been engaged in politics, so part of the answer is that we are people who enjoy politics and want to help. I only give to people I sincerely believe in, and mostly I only give to Democrats. The only Republican I can remember giving to is my college roommate Bill Frist, who was Senate majority leader. I knew him when he was a Democrat. He'd be really mad if he knew I said that.

That's only part of the answer—that we're involved in politics and that we like it and support it. There's not a really satisfying answer. That is a very fair point. Still, I really don't believe that you get anything for your campaign contributions.

What I do think is that the reason the public feels that the whole system is corrupt and that money buys results is because there's so much money and so much campaign financing. Not that it really corrupts the system.

Leech: So you see it as more of a problem of perception.

Allard: The real scam is that the members of Congress and the president have to spend so much time raising money that it interferes with their ability to function. That's the big scam. It's a big scandal that when observers walk into the gallery of the Senate, overlooking the world's greatest deliberating body, there will only be two or three senators most of the time. What's really shocking is the senators are all someplace else, dialing for dollars around the clock. That's the real scandal.

The problem members of Congress always have is that they really believe they need the money to campaign. So they feel that they have to convey to contributors that they get something for those contributions when, in reality, no member of Congress who's going to serve and be there long is going to make a decision based on a campaign contribution.

I'll clean this story up for you. I've been politically incorrect so many times—I'm still going to clean this up. You know that Jessie Unruh quote?

Leech: I don't think so.

Allard: He actually stole the line. Unruh was a legendary state senator in California. He said about lobbyists: "If you can't take their money, drink their booze"—and here's where I'm cleaning it up—"and dance with their women, and still vote against them the next day. You don't deserve to be and you won't be in the legislature for very long."

Here's the other perverse thing about campaign contributors: I saw it happen often with people who are very close to me. Presidential candidates or even senatorial candidates encourage people to keep doing this fundraising stuff. These people who fundraise often do it because they're successful in life—they're really great, talented people. They work their rear ends off to raise money because they believe in a candidate, a cause. Then they become marginalized afterward because now they are just the money people. They thought they would be ambassador or secretary of commerce or be able to serve in government, but now they are marginalized.

Leech: Is that because politically it would look bad to be too close to the fundraisers?

Allard: If I suggested to three quarters of my partners, "Let's unilaterally stop making campaign contributions"—they would not agree to do it. People do not agree with me on this. They would say, "How would we operate? We've got to be players." I'm just highly skeptical about the value of the contribution.

The way a lobbyist prevails in a case is by being the best-prepared, smartest person in the room, and having the most compelling case.

The other thing that helps support my point is that I only give to Democrats, I only vote Democratic, and I volunteer my time only to Democrats. I have never had a problem working with the Republican administration or a Republican member of Congress. Well, with two exceptions: you can guess who they were. I just got somebody else to do the meeting. My party didn't matter. Now maybe things have been changing in that direction.

Leech: Your firm also donated to both parties.

Allard: Yeah, of course, but nobody asked me about my partisanship. Nobody asked me that. It's not about me, it's about who is it that I'm representing and why a government official should be interested in them.

Leech: Before we end, could you walk me through what your day was like when you were still at Patton Boggs in DC?

Allard: This is my day. And the funny thing is, it's the same at the law school. I get up at the crack of dawn to do writing. It's the only time of the day I can do it. Part of what I write is the list of things I absolutely have to do that day. Then I hit the office, after going to the gym.

I then spend the whole day doing triage on whatever has come over the transom. I'm reviewing exciting opportunities, dealing with crises, trying somehow to get back to the five critical things that had to be done that day. The whole day is dealing with the unexpected and performing triage on the unexpected, so that I can get done what really needs to be done. That's what my days are like. There is no normal or typical day. Really, there is none. I would say—and I'm making this number up—seventy-three percent of all statistics are made up on the spot. But I would say eighty percent of lobbying is preparation—through conversations, research, writing, and brainstorming—and twenty percent is actual advocacy. If I'm off, I've erred in saying that the advocacy part is as big as twenty percent. It might be nine to one.

When people think of what a lobbyist does, they forget about the preparation. Maybe I'm doing my colleagues a disservice by making the job seem less sexy than they think it is. But there's a lot of hard work in preparation and research. Don't let that secret out—it may damage our reputation forever—but that's the case. People have this sort of image of the bag-carrying, bourbon-swilling, philandering, duck-hunting magician that can make Washington dance on a string like a puppet and gets by with a phone call or a single meeting. That caricature never really existed. But to the extent that it did exist, it's now in the La Brea Tar Pits with the other extinct mammals. It may have been the case in the sixties or early seventies when there were few decision makers and so there were few people that you had to know to get anything done. But there's been such a dispersion of power and there have been so many good-government types of rules enacted that it's much harder to get things done. Today it requires more work and a more professional lobbyist.

Leech: Very interesting. I cannot tell you how much I appreciate your taking the time to talk about this. It's going to be a great chapter.

Allard: It's a novel, right?

Leech: It is a novel. The novel of Nick Allard. And as we near the end of the chapter, I should ask you about your new job as dean of Brooklyn Law School.

Allard: I've always had a foot in higher education, as an author, teacher, member of boards, member of search committees, or trustee. I was finding increasingly that the things that interested me the most were related to higher education. I also had already done what I needed to in those eight years at the firm. I already had eight successful years—number one every year. During my time there, the firm made a lot of changes through the compensation structure, more teamwork, more structure to the department, and fantastic hires. The firm continued to do that and make a lot of money. I was looking for an opportunity to put something back and to make a contribution to something exciting. Brooklyn was irresistible because, as *GQ* just said, "It's the coolest city in the world."

Leech: *Très Brooklyn* is French for being hip.

Allard: And our law school is in a very exciting position. So it was irresistible to come on board and be part of the only law school in the most exciting place on earth. The Above the Law website recently listed Brooklyn Law School [BLS] as one of the top five law schools in the country that deserve more attention. We have a huge potential to build on. There are challenges for law schools and new lawyers today, thanks to a soft job market and high student debt, and our school is responding. BLS has one of the most rigorous clinical and externship programs in the country. We've created a "business boot camp" and expanded a program on running your own law firm, so that students learn the skills they will need once they graduate. But more importantly, we are working to train students to be creative problem solvers. My lobbyist-lawyer skills have always been about problem solving: being curious and figuring out how things fit together and building consensus, and that fits our approach at Brooklyn Law School.

And remember what I told you earlier about central casting? Ken Feinberg, whom I worked with at the start of my career, will be the speaker at my first commencement at BLS. The continuous loop holds.

Leech: The jobs you've had throughout your career really do all fit together.

Allard: Do you speak or read Chinese?

Leech: What's up with China?

Allard: Here's a copy of *China GQ*.

Leech: Oh, hilarious. You're in the magazine.

Allard: The latest issue is about interacting with the government.

Leech: That is great.

Allard: Everybody says, "You want to get this translated?" I said, "Hell no. I want to tell everybody what it says. It says that I'm the most persuasive, attractive, irresistible...."

I was actually really irritated. I called the editor up and I said, "You used the worst picture. I look like a fat slob."

And they said, "Hey listen, in China appearing well-fed and prosperous is a very impressive and good thing. People are very respectful of that."

I said, "Now you're making me feel even worse because you're not denying it."

Leech: You know, I think the picture doesn't look that much like you.

Allard: Thank you. You'd make a great lobbyist!

CHAPTER

4

Julie Stewart

President

Families Against Mandatory Minimums

***Julie Stewart** is founder and president of Families Against Mandatory Minimums (FAMM), a nonpartisan nonprofit that advocates against mandatory sentencing laws. Stewart started FAMM in 1991 after her brother was sentenced to five years in prison for growing marijuana. FAMM's advocacy has led to reduced sentences for an estimated 170,000 drug defendants nationwide and has opened debate regarding the problems caused by mandatory sentencing policies. FAMM spends less than $20,000 a year on lobbying and does not give campaign contributions.*

Stewart has testified before Congress and the US Sentencing Commission about mandatory sentences and prison overcrowding, and has been interviewed on many national television shows and in local media throughout the country. She is the recipient of the Thomas Szasz Award for Outstanding Contributions to the Cause of Civil Liberties, the Champion of Justice Award from the National Association of Criminal Defense Attorneys, the Leadership for a Changing World Award from the Ford Foundation, and the Citizen Activist Award from the Gleitsman Foundation.

Before starting FAMM, Stewart worked as director of public affairs at the Cato Institute, a libertarian think tank in Washington. She graduated from Mills College in Oakland, California, with a degree in international relations.

Beth Leech: The name of this book is *Lobbyists at Work*—but do you even consider yourself a lobbyist?

Julie Stewart: Well, technically, I'm not. I have not registered as a lobbyist, although our government affairs counsel has. When I started FAMM, I knew nothing about lobbying. I just knew that what I needed to do was introduce members of Congress to the kinds of people who were going to prison under the laws that they passed. I hoped that by meeting with members of Congress and introducing them to the families of prisoners sentenced under their laws, they would say, "Oh, gee, I'm sorry—we didn't mean to do that. We'll change the laws." So, my strategy was to make them face—in concrete terms—the human cost of the sentences that they had enacted. I don't think I realized that was "lobbying," but I suppose it was.

Leech: You're not a lobbyist in the legal sense, but you are a lobbyist in the practical sense that you're a policy advocate.

Stewart: Yes, I'm a lobbyist in the sense that I try to persuade legislators to adopt my perspective. I certainly intended to do that from the beginning and still do, but I don't spend enough time directly lobbying to meet the threshold needed to register.

Leech: What is the perspective you advocate? How would you describe FAMM's mission?

Stewart: FAMM's mission is to ensure that the punishment fits the crime and the offender's role in the crime. Mandatory sentencing has removed the judge's ability to look at the individual as an individual, see what the crime was and his or her role in the crime, and then determine what the sentence should be given all of that information. So we're lobbying for individualized sentencing.

We're lobbying to restore a basic tenet of American justice that most Americans still believe in: if you come before a judge, are found guilty, and are facing sentencing, the judge ought to take into account everything he knows about you, your case, your role, your culpability, your remorse, and your likelihood of rehabilitation, and then fashion a proportionate and fitting sentence.

Leech: That's not what...

Stewart: That's not what happens! Right! That's not what happens when the crime carries a mandatory sentence—when the sentence is based solely on the fact that you've committed the crime. Drug crimes commonly carry mandatory minimum sentences. Let's say you're convicted of being party to a drug transaction involving fifty grams of crack cocaine. The type of drug and its weight automatically trigger your sentence: you're going to prison for five years. Prior to changes in the law that FAMM succeeded in effecting a couple of years ago, the sentence for 50 grams of crack cocaine was ten years.

Leech: That's under federal sentencing?

Stewart: Exactly. The judge would not have been able to say, "But really you were just the girlfriend of the guy who was selling the drugs. You were in the car when the drug transaction happened but you weren't an active participant. Therefore, I'm just going to give you a year." The judge would have no choice but to sentence the person to five years—or whatever the mandatory minimum was.

Leech: Did FAMM get involved at all with the issue of unfairness between powder cocaine and crack cocaine?

Stewart: Yes. I started FAMM in 1991. In 1993, we sent a survey to our prisoner members to ask them whether they were serving time for powder cocaine or crack cocaine and, if so, what the quantity and sentence were. From that informal survey we created a chart showing how disparate the sentences were among our members for crack and powder cocaine. So, from very early on, we were concerned about the 100:1 disparity between the two drugs. For years, we have fought to make crack cocaine sentences fairer and ideally, to bring them into sentencing parity with powder cocaine, so that for sentencing purposes, cocaine is cocaine is cocaine.

What happened, though, is that as more groups got involved in this, we talked more about the inequity of the one hundred–to-one ratio than we did about the unjust severity of the mandatory crack cocaine sentences, leaving open the possibility that the ratio could be lowered simply by making powder sentences stiffer. Someone on the Hill said to me: "Be careful what you ask for. If you're complaining about the one hundred–to-one ratio between crack and powder, Congress can say, 'Fine. We'll leave crack where it is and we'll just make the powder penalty worse.'"

Leech: Which was not what you wanted.

Stewart: Not at all. No one had ever complained that powder sentences were too light. So we learned early on that when you lobby, you have to be very careful how you ask for what you want.

Leech: How did FAMM get started? Can you tell me that story?

Stewart: Yes. It's one I know well. I was working at the Cato Institute in Washington, DC, as a director of public affairs, when I got a call from my brother. He was calling me from a jail in Spokane, Washington, about eighty miles from where we grew up. He told me that he'd been arrested for growing marijuana and he was in jail. My first thought was, "How stupid of you to be doing this." My second thought was, "Well, at least it's *only* marijuana. It won't be such a stiff penalty."

As things unfolded, I learned that, in fact, there is a stiff penalty associated with *even* marijuana. This was back in 1990 and there wasn't a lot of information out there about mandatory sentences. There was no Internet that made it easy to find out what mandatory minimums were or what quantity it took to trigger a five- or ten-year sentence. So it took a lot of legwork to figure it all out—including phone calls to a few lawyers who helped me piece it together.

Leech: What quantity are we talking about?

Stewart: He was growing about three hundred sixty-five plants that were about six inches tall when he was arrested. The plants were growing in a house my brother owned but didn't live in. Two other semi-friends of my brother's lived there and they had filled the garage with as many of the little plastic plant containers as would fit in that space, which happened to be about three hundred sixty-five. One of the guys who lived there opened the garage door to show the neighbor what they were doing, and the neighbor turned them in.

When the police arrived, the two men who were living at the house said, "Oh, this isn't ours. It's Jeff Stewart's," even though they were all equally involved in growing the marijuana. One guy was an electrician so he had hung the lights. Anyway, they turned Jeff in and in exchange for their cooperation, they both got probation, even though one of them had a prior felony conviction for a drug offense.

That's how Jeff got arrested. He was guilty of growing marijuana with the other two men, so he pled guilty. He could have reduced his sentence if he had informed on someone else who was involved in illegal drug activity. He knew somebody who was growing marijuana but he chose not to inform on him because he didn't want to destroy that man's life. The guy was a father and married with several children, so Jeff just decided to be what they call in prison a "stand up guy," and not inform. As a result he had nothing to give the prosecutor for a shorter sentence and he served his full five years in prison. Five years is a very long time behind bars. I feel that one of the things that has been lost in the twenty-one years that I have been running FAMM is that people have become inured to what a five-year prison sentence actually is.

Leech: It's a long time.

Stewart: It is a long time, but today people think it's no big deal. The judge understood how long it was, though. At the sentencing he said, "I don't want to give you this much time, but my hands are tied by these mandatory sentencing laws that Congress passed in 1986."

Leech: Why did it become a federal issue?

Stewart: Why *did* small time drug cases become federal cases? Such an excellent question. In the old days, federal cases required some federal nexus–crossing state lines, for instance. In the late eighties and early nineties, it became more a matter of jurisdiction shopping. When the police arrested a person, they took him into the local county jail. Then the state and the federal prosecutors would get together and decide: "Let's see, who wants this case? Who should take this one?" Almost always, the defendant would get more time if the case went into the federal system rather than the state system. It's totally unclear to me why Jeff's case went federal. There was certainly no federal nexus.

I have seen thousands of cases like Jeff's over the years that are basically local offenses that could have been handled locally, yet they've gone federal for no apparent reason other than the defendant would get more time. My brother's sentencing judge was a senior district judge who had been on the bench for twenty-five years. He voiced his frustration that the prosecutor, basically fresh out of law school, was telling him what sentence to give my brother based on the fact that my brother's plant count had triggered the automatic five-year prison sentence.

The judge's comments at sentencing and my own observations of what my brother went through led me to see that the justice system did not work as I had been taught in school or imagined. I came away with the belief that "Something is terribly wrong and somebody needs to let members of Congress know about it."

Leech: So you decided to become that person.

Stewart: [Laughs.] Well, it was foisted on me a little, but I was a willing victim, I guess. I started talking to lawyers I met here in Washington who knew something about this—one of them worked with the National Association of Criminal Defense Lawyers [NACDL]—and everyone was in agreement that the system was wrong and completely counter to what most Americans believe our justice system is or should be like. So we decided to try to reach out to other families who had been affected by mandatory sentencing laws.

In the spring of 1991, the lawyer who worked for NACDL sent a letter to member lawyers asking them to let their clients in prison know that we would be holding a meeting in Washington, DC, and that their families were invited to attend.

About thirty families from as far north as Maine and as far south as Florida attended. We sat in a room in the Rayburn House Office Building and went around the table: "I am here because I have a son serving seventeen years on his first offense for a drug offense." "I am here because my husband is doing ten years for a drug offense." "I am here because my brother is doing …"

It was really powerful and very motivating to meet other people who were in the same boat, but who were so much worse off in many ways than I was. First, it was my brother—not my husband or my son. Second, as much as I hate to say it, my brother's five years paled in comparison to a lot of the other sentences I was hearing described around the table that day. The collective feeling was almost palpable: "This can't stand. Somebody needs to do something."

Because I was in DC, because I had been affected, and because I had a small network of lawyers who were already beginning to help me, everyone looked at me and said, "Well, we'll back you. So let's start something."

Leech: So in the beginning, staff-wise, it was just you, right?

Stewart: Yes.

Leech: Did you even get paid?

Stewart: No, for two years I worked for free. Because I was married, I could afford to do that, even though my husband worked in another nonprofit so we weren't exactly rich! After six months, I hired an assistant to help answer the phone and deal with mail, because we were getting a lot of it.

I left the Cato Institute and started FAMM on September 1, 1991. Shortly after, I was on the *Phil Donahue Show.* I helped them put together a whole show on sentencing. I introduced them to a husband and wife who were about to go to prison for a heroin conviction, leaving their kids behind, alone with no parents. And I suggested they invite a lawyer on the show who was an expert on drug cases. It was my first experience with a national TV talk show, and I probably wasn't as prepared as I should have been. But they put FAMM's address and phone number up on the screen several times, and we were inundated after that. The people who had someone in prison all of a sudden felt, "Wow, this is the place to go. There is someone who cares, someone who gets it, someone who is trying to do something." So that became the foundation of FAMM: the families who joined right away and the prisoners who heard about us and started mailing us letters and building our cases.

Leech: At that point, were you working out of your home?

Stewart: No, I never did. I had good advice from someone who actually became a board member. He said I should never work out of my home, because when you work from your home it doesn't have the necessary legitimacy that working in an office does. Also, it is easy to get sidetracked with household duties. So he gave me free space in his office for a couple of months. Then I found a sublet from another organization for $500 a month. So I was able to sublet space for five years at a really reasonable price in a beautiful building in downtown DC.

Leech: At that point, where did the funding come from?

Stewart: Funding came mostly from families. But the biggest chunk of change I got right away, $25,000, came from a man named Richard Dennis. When I left Cato, the president, Ed Crane, gave me his mailing list of people who supported Cato's work on drug policy reform and said I could contact them. So I mailed letters to them, telling them what I was doing and why, and I got a number of nice responses as well as $1,000 here or $50 there—but I got a $25,000 check from Richard Dennis, who really felt that what I was trying to do was incredibly important.

Rich has a special place in my heart forever, because here he was giving $25,000 to a woman who had an idea of what should be done and hoped she knew how to do it but had no track record! It was a great leap of faith on his part, but I think it was not misplaced. It worked out very well. Rich helped a lot: $25,000 went a long way twenty years ago with no salary and practically no staff, and we made it last a long time.

Leech: Today, how much of your budget ends up coming from donations like that and how much is families' bits and pieces?

Stewart: Today about half our budget comes from foundations. Next comes individual major donors, like Richard Dennis, who account for forty percent of our budget. We get $100,000 from three or four individuals, and contributions in the $25,000 to $50,000 range from a larger pool of individuals. The final ten percent comes from small donors—meaning prisoners and their wives and families.

Leech: How big is your office today?

Stewart: It's not huge. We have twelve staff—eight in DC and four around the country. Our budget is about $1.4 million right now. It was higher at one point, when the market was booming and Bernie Madoff hadn't crashed yet. There was one foundation that was solely funded by Bernie Madoff investments and it gave us $250,000 a year. When he went under, they went under and we lost that money. So we get by. We could do much more if we had more, but sentencing is a difficult issue to get people to focus on unless it has happened to them, or they are particularly libertarian, or they have a social justice conscience that is fine-tuned.

Leech: With a staff of twelve, you obviously can't get involved with every single case or every single issue that is out there. How do you decide whether you are going to become involved in something?

Stewart: In some ways, we're at an advantage to be so narrowly focused on sentencing reform. It keeps us focused laser-like on sentencing and not getting drawn into the related areas that could easily lead to mission-creep: drug policy reform, prison conditions, juvenile justice, etc. While all of those issues are important, we can't afford to diffuse our limited resources and energy in too many directions. It would limit our effectiveness.

As to how we pick and choose which sentencing issues to get involved in, it's partly by opportunity. We're doing a lot of work on clemency right now. "Clemency" involves both presidential pardons and commutations of sentences. A pardon is issued once a prisoner has done her time and gotten out. The president pardons her so that she can, for example, vote again. What FAMM is concerned about are commutations of sentence for the people who are serving outrageously long mandatory sentences and have no other recourse for shortening their sentences. For instance, President Clinton granted a commutation to a woman who had an eighty-five-year sentence for a drug crime she committed when she was twenty-four. She would have died in prison, but for that commutation.

So we get involved when an opportunity presents itself, as it did with Clinton. I knew that he had commuted two people in July 1999, and I expected in his lame duck months that he would commute more. So we put together a list of twenty-one people serving time for nonviolent drug offenses and sent them to the White House, and lobbied every way we could to persuade the president to grant commutations. He granted seventeen of them.

Leech: So when you have an issue like that, and you are trying to lobby the president and the White House, what in particular do you do?

Stewart: The Office of the Pardon Attorney [OPA] told us to go to the White House with our cases, so we sent them to the White House Counsel's office. We enlisted donors of ours and anybody else who knew the president or might be able to influence him to try to talk to him about these cases. We also recruited members of Congress to support some of the petitions. Senator [Orrin] Hatch, for instance, supported one.

Leech: More recently, FAMM staged an event at the National Press Club that attracted a lot of media attention.

Stewart: Yes. In May 2012, ProPublica did a really great exposé on misconduct at the Office of the Pardon Attorney that was detrimental to applications for sentence commutations. FAMM leveraged that exposé into a briefing and panel discussion that we held at the National Press Club to call for a Senate Judiciary Committee investigation of OPA practices. In addition to the ProPublica reporter and a former staff attorney at the OPA, we had speakers on the panel who put a human face on this issue: a woman whose commutation petitions were denied three times and the mother of a prisoner who was the focus of the ProPublica exposé.

What FAMM does is unique: we bring individuals and their stories to the members of Congress so they can see how their laws impact real people's lives. Over the course of FAMM's life, there have been times when we've gotten into doing more formal reports and studies, but in the last few years, it's been clear to me that what we do uniquely well is put the human face on sentencing laws. We tell the stories well and the prisoners and their families tell them well. Their narratives drive our arguments and make them compelling. For example, we arranged congressional meetings for the woman whose commutation petitions were denied three times and the mother of the prisoner who was the focus of the ProPublica report. We accompanied them on visits to meet with staffers from Senators [Jefferson] Sessions and [Richard] Durbin's offices, and Representatives Bobby Scott and John Conyers.

Leech: How do you choose which members of Congress these people should meet with?

Stewart: The mother of Clarence Aaron, the man who was featured in the ProPublica exposé, lives in Alabama. Senator Sessions is her senator, and he's on Judiciary and he's a former US attorney from that state. So he knows this issue and it was important for her to meet with him because she is his constituent. Senator Durbin is very interested in clemency and we want him to hold a hearing, so that's why we visited his office. So there's always a strategic reason. In the House, Bobby Scott has been our champion on these issues forever. He is very interested in all of this and wants to know more and wants to meet the people affected by our sentencing laws. And John Conyers is the chair of the House Subcommittee on Crime.

Leech: What was your goal with these meetings? What did you hope to have come out in the end?

Stewart: With Sessions, we want him to write a letter to the president on behalf of Clarence Aaron, his constituent's son. With Durbin, we want him to hold a hearing on clemency. Also, the more you introduce them to the people who are affected by mandatory sentences, the more they picture those people when the issue comes up.

Leech: There are both constituency representation issues and also appeals to their prior knowledge and concerns?

Stewart: Yes—and trying to persuade them to do certain things. In this case, we were lobbying Durbin to hold a hearing.

Leech: Now, it's interesting to me because the popular view of lobbying is that the biggest donation is the be-all and end-all of who wins and who loses.

Stewart: Well, I'll tell you, since we have no money, that's never been an issue for us. Instead of cash, we use people. We don't have cash to give to anybody, but we have stories. We have people's stories, and we have the people, and we bring them to Washington to meet with certain members of Congress who can, in fact, help—whether by introducing a bill, holding a hearing, writing a letter to the president, or whatever the goal is of the particular meeting.

Several years ago, there was a hearing in the Senate on crack cocaine. One of the people who testified was the brother of a woman who was in prison serving a long mandatory sentence for a drug crime. We knew the woman, we'd met the brother, and we suggested to the Senate Judiciary Committee that they invite him to speak, and they did. He came and brought pictures of his sister and pictures of himself with his child, his sister's niece. Senator Durbin was so taken with this man's testimony—and the photographs—that he became deeply engaged in helping this woman get a commutation. She was released in 2011. She's the only person whose sentence President Obama has commuted. If Senator Durbin had not met her brother, she would probably still be in prison.

Leech: So this is his first commutation. How many requests for commutations come across every year?

Stewart: There have been seven thousand commutation requests since Obama took office—and one was granted. That has less to do with his selectivity than it does with the dysfunction of the Office of the Pardon Attorney.

Leech: That's what you were exposing with the panel discussion.

Stewart: Exactly. But back to the other ways we choose to get involved: we work in certain states with bad sentencing laws. We were involved in Michigan for years after I first started FAMM, because they had a life-without-parole bill for nonviolent drug offenses.

Leech: Were you successful in Michigan?

Stewart: Yes. I couldn't believe that sentence. First offenders were serving life without parole for being involved with 650 grams of cocaine or heroin. Even possession alone triggered that sentence. Within a four-year period in the mid-1990s, FAMM led a coalition to reform the law so that all the two hundred forty people who were serving life without parole became eligible for parole after fifteen to twenty years, depending on the circumstances of their cases. At this point, I think all of those prisoners have been paroled.

Leech: So that's why you chose to work in Michigan. And other states?

Stewart: New York also had terrible sentencing laws known as the Rockefeller Drug Laws, but there were so many other groups already working on their reform that FAMM's added value wasn't great enough to spend the time and money there, so we played a very peripheral role.

Florida has terrible mandatory drug sentencing laws, as well as mandatory gun-sentencing laws. The sentences for prescription drug violations are particularly appalling. For instance, if you have your mother's prescription of Vicodin and you're caught with it, and she didn't give it to you, you can go to prison for fifteen to twenty-five years. So our original intent in Florida was to address those sentencing laws, which we are doing.

But we have also jumped on other opportunities in Florida. In the wake of the Trayvon Martin shooting, we learned about other cases in Florida in which people have tried to use the "stand your ground" defense and lost. The prosecutor decides whether or not to grant that defense. When defendants are denied that motion, many have gone to trial because they maintain that they're innocent. If the jury doesn't agree and finds the defendant technically guilty of the crime, they are subjected to a mandatory twenty-year sentence under Florida's 10-20-Life gun law.

For example, a woman named Marissa Alexander shot a gun in her house to defend herself against her abusive husband who had put her in the hospital a couple times. She had every right to be fearful, but he reported her to the police for shooting her gun at him, which she did not actually do. She shot into the wall of the house to scare him away. They arrested her and charged her with aggravated assault. She said, "Wait. I was standing my ground. I was protecting myself here." They replied, "Nope. We are not going to accept that motion of yours." So she took her case to trial feeling she was innocent. The jury found her guilty of the technical violation of the law and she was sentenced to a mandatory minimum of twenty years in prison.

Leech: What do you do to address that case?

Stewart: We have a fantastic project director in Florida who is one of our four staff outside of this office, and he jumped all over it. He called Marissa's lawyer. He called the family. He got involved. It helped that he's a lawyer himself. He gathered as much information as he could about the case, including the transcripts. He got everything he needed to understand what happened because we do not want to jump all over a case without knowing the facts. We are really careful about that.

Then we got involved in organizing a rally for Marissa and getting media coverage for her sentencing. We wanted it covered so people could better understand the effect of the mandatory gun-sentencing law in Florida. Lots of people in Florida don't ever think about it. Marissa had a legally registered firearm that she used it to protect herself, and now she is in prison for twenty years. So the mandatory nature of the 10-20-Life gun sentence is what we were objecting to.

As a result, Greg, our director in Florida, has become the go-to guy for the media on the 10-20-Life gun law. He is receiving calls and emails from individuals and their families about other cases similar to Marissa's. As we build our file of evidence that the law is over the top, Greg will use those cases to help persuade state legislators to introduce a bill to reform Florida's 10-20-Life gun laws.

Leech: So these are the sorts of issues you spend time on at FAMM. How else do you spend your time at FAMM?

Stewart: Fundraising!

Leech: What percent of your day or what percent of your week would you say ends up being spent on fundraising?

Stewart: Oh, not enough. We are still small enough that I do a lot of brainstorming and strategizing on the various issues that we are dealing with. I probably should be out of the office fundraising much more than I am. Because there are only eight of us here in DC, a lot of what we do is done in meetings where many of us are involved. Just before this conversation, we were talking about a briefing that we want to hold in a few months with people who Clinton granted commutations to in 2001 before he left office.

Leech: This would be a briefing for the media?

Stewart: For the media and for the Hill. That was actually part of our group discussion just now. What is the purpose of the briefing? Just to influence the media? Or are we also trying to influence staff members of members of Congress when we say: "Sentences are too long. This person should never have been in prison for so long, and here is another one, and here is another one—and they're just the lucky few who actually got a commutation!"? So we think we should bring them to Washington to do a fundraiser and a briefing on the Hill. We are also asking the people whose sentences were commuted by President Clinton to write letters to President Obama urging him to reform the Office of the Pardon Attorney.

Leech: Could you walk me through your average day—if there is such a thing?

Stewart: No, there is not.

Leech: Well, why don't you talk about what is happening today, and as you do, point to things that are unusual or usual. When does the day start? How early does the day start?

Stewart: I usually get in around ten—which is kind of lazy of me, but it often takes that long after I get my kids off to school. I first focus on what e-mails have come in and what is on my desk that needs to be taken care of immediately. There are checks to be signed and thank-yous to be signed, things like that. Then today I had a meeting at eleven with our finance and administrative person, and our vice president on our financial situation. We meet once a month to make sure that we are on track financially and to determine where we are in comparison to last year. It always gets me fired up to go out and fundraise! Then, right after our financials meeting, I had an internal meeting following up on our clemency briefing last week: whether we did what we said we were going to do after the briefing—and if not, why not and let's get going!

And now this interview with you. Next, I might grab some lunch and then I have a meeting at three o'clock with an internal person. One of the reviews I have undertaken in the last couple of months is taking a look at how FAMM is operating. Are we doing what we should be doing? Are we doing it as efficiently as we should? Are some people in the wrong role here? Are there people who have strengths that are not being realized because they are not in a position that allows them to utilize them? Are we asking some people to do things that are just not a natural fit and maybe they could be shifted to a different place?

I've learned over the years that you may hire somebody to do one particular job, but as time goes on, it may not be the right fit for them, or maybe it wasn't even the right fit from the get-go. So, rather than just fire somebody in that situation, if they are committed to our issue, like what we do, are smart, strategic, can write well—whatever the qualities are that I look for—maybe there's another way to use them. So I have a meeting at three o'clock with a person on our staff to talk about her role. I am sure that will last longer than it should, but let's say it goes till at least four o'clock.

Then I will probably come back to my desk to try to do the things that I said all day long that I would be doing, such as calling the White House Counsel's office to find out what they think about clemency. And contacting some of our donors whom I haven't talked to for a while—including one who promised us $100,000 that hasn't materialized yet. We have a package of articles and a cover letter that I need to finish that's going out to our biggest donors—hopefully today and, if not, tomorrow.

Leech: When does the day usually end?

Stewart: Around five thirty.

Leech: Do you have many evening events, or does it stay pretty constrained to the day?

Stewart: It's mostly during the day. My kids are nine and twelve now. Since I've had kids, I've definitely been more restricted in my after-work freedom. They are old enough that they don't need me every minute but my husband is out of town this week, so it's a little trickier.

Leech: Do you think jobs like yours or policy advocacy positions in general are conducive to family life?

Stewart: I do. I mean, Washington is a crazy workaholic town. But that is probably true of lots of towns.

Leech: No. Washington is special.

Stewart: Everybody in this town thinks that what they do is incredibly important. I think what I do is important, too, but I do realize that if I don't do it for a day, or a week, or an evening, new mandatory sentences aren't going to be put in place while I'm off-duty. Something terrible isn't going to happen. In any event, now I have this great staff and when I am on vacation or out of town, there are other people here who can deal with whatever comes up. So I think we shouldn't take ourselves so seriously that we have to obsess that if we are not at our desks, some bad policy is going to pass. I don't know—I just feel that Washington takes itself too seriously. So is it conducive to having kids? Sure, but you've got to put your priorities in order.

Leech: Did FAMM develop in the way that you expected going into it?

Stewart: If I had known when I started FAMM how hard it would be to do what I do, I wouldn't have done it. So there is some truth to the aphorism that "ignorance is bliss." I was naïve enough to think that if legislators could see who they were putting to prison for so long that they would say,

"Oh, my God, that is not what we meant. We meant to put away just the drug kingpins!" And they'd change the laws. In fact, I wasn't that misguided, because I started FAMM in 1991, and in 1994, three years later, Congress passed a "safety valve" provision that allows judges in drug cases to ignore the federal mandatory minimum if the defendant meets certain criteria, including being a first offender and nonviolent.

Leech: So that was a big step.

Stewart: It was huge. So I wasn't totally naïve, because it was true that when we started putting the human faces of their laws in front of members of Congress, they started responding—maybe not out loud, but tacitly recognizing that their laws were incarcerating a lot of people for far longer than they had meant to happen. Instead of just repealing the mandatory minimum laws, they said, "We'll give the judges a little bit of discretion in certain cases." But it was a big step. In fact, it applies in about a quarter of the federal drug cases that are sentenced each year. Of the twenty to twenty-five thousand people who are sentenced each year for federal drug crimes, roughly five thousand of them benefit from the 1994 safety valve.

Leech: What in your education, or training, or background has best prepared you for what you do today?

Stewart: The quality I bring to this job that is probably the most useful is that I am a layperson and not a lawyer.

Leech: How so?

Stewart: I came to the sentencing issue with no knowledge of it. That is how most people come to it, unless you've learned about it in law school or you've somehow been involved in the criminal justice system before. To be able to help other people understand why it's an important issue, I remind myself how I once knew nothing about this. What was it that made me care? Initially, of course, it was what happened to my brother. But subsequently and more generally, it's the stories I read or hear from the affected families. The plain language and raw hurt get right to the heart of what's wrong with the sentencing laws we have.

After twenty-one years I am not, I suppose, a layperson any more. But I continually remind myself what it was like to know nothing about this, and I draw on that memory to help me convince people who know nothing about sentencing why it should matter to them.

Leech: Does your public relations background help you at all? That is what you did for Cato, right?

Stewart: Yes, I did. It does help. It's funny that it's actually so much easier here than it was at Cato, at least back when I was there. Cato's so much bigger now and has a fantastic PR department, but back then it was really hard to get the media to pay attention to the issues that Cato dealt with. They were a little esoteric then. I remember during the one hundredth anniversary of the Sherman Antitrust Act in 1990, I was trying to drum up coverage, and the reaction was like: "Yeah, right. Who cares?"

But I found out about a man who owned a paint store and for some reason he was going to be shut down because of something to do with the Sherman Antitrust Act. So I put together a one-page pitch using that person's story and sent it to the television reporter John Stossel, and within a day he called me.

What that told me is what I've already said to you: the human story is the best tack to take. Telling how a law affects an individual person is so compelling. If I hadn't included that person's story in the Sherman Antitrust Act pitch to John Stossel, he probably would have just tossed it. But when you show how a law affects individuals, how it effects human being, it begins to make good media sense to a reporter, and especially a TV reporter.

Within the first month of starting FAMM, I got a call from ABC News and they wanted to do a two-minute segment on sentencing for a feature at the end of the news called "The American Agenda." They came and interviewed me, and we put the whole story together. We gave them the expert, and the family, and everything they needed. I thought, "Wow, it is so easy!" They came to me. I didn't have to kick the door down to get them to care about issues, which I felt I had to do at Cato. Certainly my experience as a PR person there has been instructive and helpful.

Leech: When you are looking for someone to hire to work at FAMM, what sorts of qualities or what sort of background and experience are you looking for? Let's say you were hiring a new lobbyist.

Stewart: We actually are. We're hiring one.

Leech: Okay, there you go.

Stewart: Our lobbyist just left. One of the main requirements is that he or she should be a good writer. I came to value great writing when I worked at Cato. They are excellent writers and editors and I became a much better writer by working there. Sadly, writing well is a skill that way too few people have these days.

Leech: Why are lobbyists important?

Stewart: We did not have an official lobbyist until four years ago. Up until then, I was doing it—not full-time by any stretch of the imagination—but, between myself and our vice president, we would read and stay on top of all the sentencing bills in Congress. What I'm looking for now—which may not have been what I was looking for four years ago—is somebody who has worked on the Hill.

Leech: For a member of Congress?

Stewart: Yes. Again, if I'm painting my ideal picture, it would be someone who worked for a Republican member of Congress.

Leech: Why?

Stewart: Although I don't think either party is very good on our issue, I think Republicans have the Nixon-goes-to-China magic. If they support sentencing reforms, Democrats are more likely to go along with it. If Democrats support sentencing reforms, Republicans just say, "You're soft on crime." So if we can find somebody who at least has some conservative credentials, it would be really helpful. Ideally, they can also read legislation. It's not as easy as it sounds to analyze a bill.

Leech: How do you judge whether they're able to do that or not?

Stewart: Well, if they've worked on the Hill, they've probably analyzed bills. It's not rocket science but it requires a lot of attention to detail and cross referencing. In addition, I'm looking for someone who is strategic and outside-the-box in her thinking. It's one thing to wait for a bill to come along and then either support it or oppose it. It's another thing to create the motion around our issue, get a good bill introduced, and line up bipartisan support for it before it's even introduced.

So it's not just, "Okay, we want a bill. Let's see who among our friends can introduce it." Right now if Democrats in the House introduce a bill without bipartisan support, it will never get a hearing because the Republicans control the House. You've got to think beyond what's possible at the moment and think about what might be possible if you pushed for it. How do you get around a chairman of the House Judiciary Committee who doesn't like sentencing reform? Do you try to find somebody who knows him who can talk to him personally about our issues? Do you try to figure out some other way to circumvent him? What is our strategy around that obstacle? I want somebody who can think creatively.

Leech: Right. You mentioned the writing and I was wondering if you could explain why the writing is important.

Stewart: It's important because we write a lot of pieces that go to the Hill. We write testimony for all kinds of people, whether it's for me or for someone at FAMM, or someone who's not at FAMM. When the brother of the woman in prison testified before Senator Durbin, we wrote his testimony for him. We've written testimony for a lot of different people. So that would fall on this person's plate.

Leech: You're writing testimonies for them because...?

Stewart: Because if the committee chairs aren't going to invite me or someone else from FAMM to testify, we will suggest other people we think would be good. We call the person and say, "Look, we're happy to draft your testimony for you. You can use it or not but, if you want us to, we'll do the first draft." I know from my own experience when I need to prepare testimony, it's much easier if somebody does a draft that I can then edit and turn into my own, rather than stare at a blank piece of paper wondering what to write.

Leech: And this allows them to have the technicalities down there in front of them. They don't have to look up the details and facts and figures themselves.

Stewart: Exactly. But of course, we don't make it more complicated than the person would naturally know. No one expects a prisoner family member to know all the details of legislation or the number of people in prison or whatever. You write it for the individual.

We also write sign-on letters for our coalitions to show their support on various issues, and we analyze bills and do side-by-side comparisons. If there are a couple of bills out there that are doing more or less the same thing, we dumb them down to make them easy to understand and we share those with staff on the Hill. We do one-pagers on different issues so congressional staffers understand them in the most basic way, because a lot of staff know very little about sentencing. Even Judiciary staffers don't always understand sentencing. The more accessible we can make the information, the better.

Leech: How about the interpersonal profile of this person you're looking to hire? Are there specific things you would want the person you're hiring to have in terms of interpersonal skills? How important are they?

Stewart: Very important! I'm looking for somebody who is … *aggressive* is too strong of a word … *confident* enough to be comfortable going up to a member of Congress or staffer and saying, "Hi. I'm so-and-so from FAMM and we really want you to take a look at our bill (or whatever)" and then speaking to the issue with fluency, ease, and knowledge.

Leech: My final question. What advice do you have for someone who wants to be a policy advocate or a lobbyist?

Stewart: My advice is to prepare for the long haul: policy reform is painfully slow. Even with the best advocacy around it, it's going to be hard going if it's at all controversial—and even if it's not controversial, it's hard to make progress nowadays when Congress has become so partisan and divided. Even if you've got a sponsor from one party, it's really hard to find a sponsor from the other party, and then even harder for both of them to bring along enough people to get the bill passed. Bottom line: don't expect quick results.

Leech: Okay. Good advice.

Stewart: In contrast to that advice is something I tell prisoners and their families a lot: nothing is set in stone. Everything changes in the long run. I have families whose loved ones are in prison for twenty-five to forty years. I say to them, "Don't give up, because things do change." In the twenty-one years that I've been doing this, I have seen reforms. We have pushed them. We have worked for them. And we have helped make them happen. Things do, in fact, change if you keep pushing long and hard enough. So don't give up.

CHAPTER

5

Laura Murphy

Director, Washington Legislative Office, American Civil Liberties Union

Laura Murphy *is the director of the American Civil Liberties Union's Washington, DC, office—a position she held from 1993 to 2005 and again since 2010. Before returning to the ACLU, she ran her own lobbying firm, Laura Murphy & Associates, LLC, representing both corporate and nonprofit clients.*

*Murphy has been named one of the 50 most influential lobbyists by two insider newspapers on Capitol Hill—*Roll Call *and* The Hill*—and has twice been honored by the Congressional Black Caucus for her work on civil rights and civil liberties. A 2012 analysis by* The Washington Post *showed that she was one of the most frequent lobbyist visitors to the Obama White House. In 2007, she received the President's Award for Outstanding Service from the Leadership Council on Civil Rights. She has testified more than a dozen times before Congress and is a frequently quoted source in the national news media.*

Before joining the ACLU, Murphy served as chief of staff to a California Assembly speaker, as a cabinet member for the mayor of the District of Columbia, and as a legislative assistant for two members of Congress. She is a graduate of Wellesley College with a bachelor's degree in history.

Beth Leech: Did you grow up wanting to be a lobbyist? What brought you to lobbying as a career?

Laura Murphy: There were fourteen runs for public office in my immediate family. I grew up in Baltimore, and my mother put a picture of me in the newspaper at eleven, saying, "I'm too young to vote but please vote for my mother for city council." She used my picture without my permission, and I found out from my classmates. I was upset that she would use my photo without my permission.

Anyway, I grew up giving out campaign literature. One of the things was that my parents and my two older brothers lost a lot of elections. I felt like, "There has got to be a better infrastructure here. They're great people. They have a great platform. What is wrong?" I decided I never wanted to be a candidate, but I wanted to understand why candidates won and why candidates lost. I wanted to work in the back of the house, because I didn't like the violation of privacy that came with holding a public office. As a kid growing up, I saw my parents trot us out all the time. We had to be on good behavior. We couldn't ever get into any trouble. We were under a microscope. I did not want to subject myself or my family to that.

At fifteen, I organized a group called The Strike Force. We went door to door supporting a ticket of candidates who were running in Baltimore citywide. My father was on the ticket and so was a guy named Parren Mitchell, who was the first black congressman from Baltimore. He ran in '68 and lost, and he ran again in '70 and won. My father was running for citywide judgeship, and he won. As a result, I now knew this member of Congress, so during my junior year of college, I called his office like a dozen times, saying, "I really want to be an intern... I really want to be an intern... I really want to be an intern." They gave me an internship and then they invited me to come back and become a legislative assistant when I had graduated from Wellesley College. So I did.

I worked there for a while, and then I found out that my dear congressman did not believe in paying women the same salary as men for the same job. He said, "Laura, men are breadwinners. One day, you will get married and some man will take care of you." Then I had a friend who worked for Representative Shirley Chisholm, who came from Brooklyn, New York, and was the first black congresswoman. There were about a dozen women on the staff. Mrs. Chisholm just empowered the women and she was really great. Then a friend of my friend who worked for the Congressional Black Caucus said to me that the ACLU was looking for a civil rights and women's rights lobbyist.

Leech: Perfect for you.

Murphy: So this friend recommended me, and the ACLU called me for an interview. I got the job and worked there from 1979 to 1982, when I got married and moved to Los Angeles, where I continued to work in politics. But I had loved being an ACLU lobbyist and missed it. I had worked on the passage of the Voting Rights Act extension of 1982. My boss told me, "Look, this bill is not going to pass. Here, I'm going to give this bill to you, but it's not going anywhere because Ronald Reagan is in the White House and he's never going to sign it." I remember saying in my head, "We'll see about that." I left on a really big high, since we succeeded in getting Ronald Reagan to sign a major civil rights bill.

Leech: Never say never.

Murphy: Right! I have always loved advocacy on behalf of people who cannot speak up for themselves. I think it is a part of my religious upbringing. My mother was a Sunday school teacher, and I grew up believing that we have to care for the less fortunate. We have this foundational document promising liberty—the Constitution and Bill of Rights—yet left and right, the government is violating our liberty. Somebody needs to speak up, and I really believe one person can make a huge difference. One dedicated individual can make a tremendous difference.

Leech: And how did that conviction lead you to lobbying?

Murphy: It was something I could do without going to law school. I was under tremendous family pressure to go to law school and I had already demonstrated that I could be a good lobbyist to the ACLU. I just continued to get jobs in politics, working for elected officials or working for the ACLU. I had a variety of different jobs in Los Angeles from 1982 to 1987 and in Chicago from 1987 to 1992. Then I got a call from Sharon Pratt Kelly, the mayor of Washington, DC. She wanted me to be her director of tourism, but the problem was that there was no office of tourism.

Leech: So what did you do?

Murphy: Sharon said to me, "Look, I know I told you I want you to be my director of tourism, but I cannot use my political capital with the city council to create another agency."

I said, "Okay, that's fine. Can I? If you don't have to do any heavy lifting, can I? Can I work the council?" I worked the council and got them to create an office of tourism, so then I became a cabinet official. I had to make my own agency.

Leech: That was very entrepreneurial!

Murphy: Then Ira Glasser, who was head of the ACLU, called me and said, "We would like you to come back to the ACLU as director of the Washington Legislative Office." That was in 1993. I left the district government and I came back to the ACLU, this time as director of the office where I was once a lobbyist.

Leech: You were in that position a long time.

Murphy: Twelve years. In 2003, a lot of illness and death descended on my family. My father died in 2003. My husband was diagnosed with a brain tumor. My son's father died in 2003. My brother-in-law was diagnosed with stage IV lung cancer. My brother was dying of complications arising from multiple sclerosis. By 2005, I just needed to take time off. My husband was supportive, so I took two years off and I was able to spend time with my mother and my brother. They passed away, and I said, "They wouldn't want me sitting around."

I started my own lobbying firm out of my house. Within two years, I had eight clients. I had two corporate clients and six nonprofit clients.

Leech: You were lobbying on a number of issues that were very similar to issues that you had lobbied on for the ACLU, right?

Murphy: Yes, and some different issues as well. I was lobbying for the National Urban League. I was lobbying on employment training and housing counseling. I was lobbying for a corporate coalition on tax issues. I was lobbying for a nonprofit on energy, Citizens for Affordable Energy.

Leech: You also lobbied on human rights.

Murphy: That was for a coalition that was created right after Obama was elected, to push the human rights agenda in front of Congress and the Obama administration.

Leech: You did this for about two years. What made you decide it was time to come back to the ACLU?

Murphy: A lot of my former colleagues were still there, and so I knew it was a good team, and the boss who was there when I left in 2005 was still there. I knew my relationship with him, and I was at the point in my business where I would have to take most of my profit and invest it in the business because I was getting too big to be a one-lobbyist shop. I would have either had to commit to building the business, or I would take a job somewhere.

I wasn't looking to quit my business. I was making all the plans to invest, but Anthony Romero, the executive director of the ACLU, caught me just at that critical juncture where I hadn't really hired permanent staff and rented space. I was still working out of my house. I still had part-time employees. He said, "Hey, I can give you great benefits, signing bonus, this, that. You can start when you want." But a lot of the staff had been laid off because after Obama was elected, membership contributions to the ACLU went way down and the ACLU lost a major donor who gave us about $20 million a year. So when I returned, I spent a lot of time rebuilding morale and making people feel empowered in their jobs.

Leech: The public thought their civil liberties problems were solved as a result of Obama's election?

Murphy: Obama ran as a civil libertarian, so people thought, "We don't need the ACLU as much." They'd felt they really needed us during the Bush administration to offset torture, Guantanamo, and the Patriot Act—but not so much with Barack Obama. Many believed in each and every one of his campaign pledges on civil liberties issues.

Leech: So you came back when times were hard at the ACLU?

Murphy: Between losing a major donor and the membership dues doing down, the dollars were not available for lobbying. Anthony said, "Here, look. We'll ask you back, but you are going to have a smaller shop. Eventually, we will be able to grow it back. If you can live with these conditions, the job is yours." I never lost passion for the issues, so I returned.

Leech: Let's talk a little bit more about the ACLU itself. How would you describe the ACLU's mission and what you are trying to accomplish for it as a lobbyist?

Murphy: The ACLU is more than ninety years old. It's an organization devoted to making real the promise of the Bill of Rights. The Washington office is sixty years old. Our job is to press the agenda of the ACLU in the policy realm in Congress and in the administration. Our litigation projects are primarily based in New York. Our lobbying is out of Washington. Our job here in Washington is not just to change policy one lawsuit at a time, but to try to reach thousands and millions of people by affecting the policy of the administration and the legislation of Congress. That means blocking bad bills and supporting bills that expand civil liberties. It means pressing the administration to issue directives to make immigration policy more humane, to cover contraception under the Affordable Care Act, or to repeal Don't Ask, Don't Tell. It's a lot of work.

Leech: Back in 2000, when we first met, we talked about criminal justice reform for another book that I was working on. That issue didn't go very far in the four years that my colleagues and I studied it, just because it was not even formally on the agenda yet. It was in the building stage.

Murphy: I am pleased to report, however, the groundwork we laid ten years ago led to guidance out of the Bush Justice Department on the use of race in federal law enforcement. That came out of our collective efforts to make racial profiling a bigger issue, and the ACLU's report, called "Driving While Black." In the 2000 elections, we took out ads in certain senatorial districts. One of those ads was in the state of Missouri, where John Ashcroft was running for reelection. We targeted him because Missouri has a large black population and Ashcroft was on the Senate Judiciary Committee and he was a holdout on co-sponsorship of a bill that would end racial profiling.

The black population in Missouri became agitated, seeing these ads on cable television. We also took out newspaper ads. They started organizing and asking him at town hall meetings what is he going to do about the problem of racial profiling. He lost his election and he was appointed to be attorney general by George Bush. Early in his tenure, he said, "We've got to do something about this racial profiling problem." In 2003, he issued guidance on the use of race in federal law enforcement. That guidance has, unfortunately, not been updated by the Obama administration.

Leech: How interesting. Is that something you're continuing to work on?

Murphy: Yes, we are continuing to work on that. We're doing Capitol Hill teach-ins on racial profiling and why Congress should pass The End Racial Profiling Act. We did a press conference around the introduction of that bill recently. Last year, we streamed a popular event from our conference room called "The Three Phases of Racial Profiling." We compared and contrasted racial profiling of African Americans in relation to traditional crime control, of Hispanics in relation to immigration control, and of Muslims and South Asians in relation to perceived national security risks.

The problem we face in raising consciousness and pushing reform on racial profiling has been that a majority of the public sees racial profiling as a positive in the national security context. While the public may not approve of blacks being pulled over disproportionately for traffic offenses or being targeted under Mayor Bloomberg's stop-and-frisk policy in New York, people are more likely to condone heightened scrutiny of Arabs, Muslims, and South Asians by border control and domestic law enforcement.

We also have had a major success in one area related to racial profiling. We helped get a law passed and signed by President Obama to reduce the sentencing disparity between crack and powder cocaine.

Leech: This is the Fair Sentencing Act of 2010.

Murphy: Yes. We were in a big coalition in which we played a leading role. One of the unique assets that the ACLU brought to the coalition table was a Republican lobbyist we hired to target Republicans to vote for the measure. At the time, prior to the midterm elections, Democrats held both the House and the Senate. But the Democratic leadership in the House said, "We can't deliver all the Democrats. We can't promise that the Blue Dog Democrats will vote yes on this." The Blue Dogs, who came predominantly from states that McCain had carried in 2008, looked for guidance to what the Republicans were doing, since they had to worry about how to cater to their split electorates.

Leech: An electorate that might easily go Republican if the member of Congress seemed too liberal.

Murphy: Exactly. So we hired a Republican lobbyist to pitch the issue to Republicans and do a Republican vote count. Then we went to the Democratic leadership and said, "Look, we can guarantee that these Republicans are going to vote for the bill."

They said, "You're kidding me."

We said, "No, we are not kidding you." They finally agreed to schedule the bill because it had passed the Senate, but we could not get it through the House because the House leadership did not want to be embarrassed for scheduling a bill for a vote that they thought wouldn't pass.

Leech: How often does the ACLU hire outside lobbyists?

Murphy: I do it all the time. When something is really getting ready to get going on the House or Senate floor, I want to have everything lined up. I don't want any surprises. When I started working for the speaker of the California Assembly, Willie Brown, the first thing he asked me was, "Can you count?"

I said, "Yes, Mr. Speaker, I can count."

He says, "Good, because I need to know where my votes are at all times."

To be effective in passing legislation on the Hill, you not only have to bring real people to Washington to tell their personal stories, you not only need to forge your coalition of interest groups, but you really need to know, once the bill is formulated, who is prepared to commit. What the Democratic leadership didn't know was that the Republicans on the House Judiciary Committee were not supporting their ranking member, Lamar Smith. Representative Smith was opposed to this bill, but a lot of the Republicans on the committee were not standing behind their ranking member because a lot of them didn't like him. Didn't like the way he was running the committee. They didn't like his rhetoric. They went to the floor of the House then, and they spoke in favor of the Fair Sentencing Act. Representative Smith was the only voice in opposition. It was really fascinating.

Leech: So that vote was within Congress. What sorts of things would you be doing within the administration?

Murphy: Meeting with them, encouraging them to file lawsuits, encouraging them to issue regulations, clarifying policies.

Leech: Which agencies were involved?

Murphy: We worked with the Department of Education to get data on the racial element involved in school push-outs, where schools discipline their students by suspending or expelling them. It was astonishing how disproportionately push-outs are children of color.

We also worked with the Department of Education and the Department of Justice on making sure that school districts understood they are obligated by law to educate undocumented children, who have as much right to a public education as US citizen children. We did an event that featured the head of the DOJ's Civil Rights Division, Tom Perez, and the head of the Department of Education's Office for Civil Rights, Russlynn Ali, on the anniversary of *Plyler v. Doe*: the Supreme Court decision that decided immigrant children have a right to public education. It was really interesting, because we were able to affirm that the Administration had issued these great regulations to school districts. We were able to praise them at this event.

We do a lot of work with the Department of Homeland Security, because they do immigration enforcement, and they also do screening at the airports. Many passengers object to invasive pat downs and going through these machines that give you kind of a naked image.

Leech: Homeland Security is an interesting one, because most people assume, "How could you ever influence them? Why would they ever listen to someone? They seem to have all this power." How, as the ACLU, do you try and approach a department like Homeland Security?

Murphy: We've met with them more times than I can count. We tell them that people in various communities around the country are complaining that US citizens are being detained by US Immigration and Customs Enforcement and that women and children are being sexually assaulted in detention facilities custody. We tell them that people are complaining about Border Patrol and Customs officials engaging in racial profiling, and that they have no mechanism for handling those complaints or sanctioning officers who are abusing their authority.

Sometimes we go in individually. Sometimes we go in with coalition partners. Sometimes we bring affected individuals. The ACLU is partly responsible for the president's decision to help stop the deportation of young people who are in school. It's an issue that we endorsed about two years ago. Once we endorsed it, we did a lot of lobbying on the Dream Act but we also did a lot of lobbying with Homeland Security, saying, "These are kids who are doing something right. They are either in school or they are in the military. They're defending our country. Many of them came here too young to know that they did not have the proper documentation. They are providing the intellectual capital we need, or they're protecting and defending our country, and you are deporting them? Come on, what does that serve?"

Leech: For these people within the agencies, especially these agencies that have power over immigration and homeland security, when they do listen to you, why do you think that is? Students who come into my class, as well people I talk to at cocktail parties, when they find out I study lobbyists, often say: "Lobbying is just people paying money and getting what they want, right?" They see it as contributions equaling outcomes, quid pro quo.

Murphy: We have no political action committee, which means we don't engage in any partisan political activity. We have no money to give to elected officials, only our policy positions and strategic advice.

Leech: So the ACLU does not give campaign contributions. Explain, then, why someone in government would listen to you. What do you think is the mechanism?

Murphy: We appeal to their enlightened self interest. Staffers want to get their boss reelected. Their boss is the president or a member of Congress. If they understand that there is real unrest among key populations, they will do something. For example, one of the things that really helped get the repeal of

Don't Ask, Don't Tell moving was Lieutenant Dan Choi's chaining himself to the White House fence. What people do not know is that that was a public relations stunt. He was also very personally upset, but there was a PR person who called reporters and said, "This guy is about to chain himself to the White House fence."

Leech: Alerting the reporters that they should get right over there.

Murphy: Another person went to a fundraiser for Senator Barbara Boxer when the president was there and heckled the president about Don't Ask, Don't Tell. The president was like, "What the heck is going on?" to his staff.

So we use media stunts, but we also use public policy papers. People in the White House complimented us greatly on the transition plan we prepared for President Obama's first term, which said, "In the first one hundred days, you should do this, you should do that."

One of those action items was, "You've got to close Guantanamo." The president said he would try to close it within a year. It didn't happen, but he tried. Another one of those action items was, "Denounce and end the use of torture." And the president did that on his first day.

We use a variety of tools, such as polling data. We'll have briefings and say, "X percent of Americans believe Y about Z issue." That can be persuasive. We meet with the attorney general. I remember one very, very critical meeting last year. We said to Attorney General Holder: "Look, we've met with every level of your department and they are not getting it. These photo ID laws that the states are passing are ways to suppress certain populations from voting. What are those populations? African Americans, the elderly, the disabled, students." You could just almost see the lightbulb go off in his head.

His staff had told him about it, but not with the passion and intensity that was in that room of twenty leaders sitting around a long conference table. We said, "You've got to use the Voting Rights Act to say no to those states that are trying to pass these suppressive laws." Personal engagement is a huge factor in getting people's attention and giving them a narrative, but you've got to go in and you've got to know what you are talking about. You've got to know about the affected populations, and you've got to be strategic about the use of media.

That conversation we had with the attorney general was not something we talked to the press about. There was no press commentary whatsoever, but we did ask him to give a public speech. He went down to the Lyndon Baines Johnson library in Texas and gave a speech about all of these voter suppression tactics and what had happened.

Leech: And so you allow him to come out on the good side than rather than embarrassing him.

Murphy: He comes out on the good side. We all fly down there to support him and we issue our press releases lauding the attorney general's speech. He uses his press operation to generate coverage, and we use our press operations to generate coverage. Then he gives another speech in South Carolina, the same day as the South Carolina Republican presidential primary. He begins to build up confidence in his message. He gives a speech to Al Sharpton's group, and then he gives a speech to a Latino group, and he begins to be on a roll. We all try to show up whenever he speaks to say, "Yay, Attorney General! That's right! Tell 'em!" I tell people lobbying is like dating.

Leech: How so?

Murphy: You've got to attract people's attention. You've got to persuade the other person why they should trust you, and why this is a good fit: "I care about your message. You care about my message." In dating, it's like, "I like baseball, too." Then, once you trust each other a good boyfriend or good girlfriend will protect and defend your interests, because you've entered into a relationship.

The same elements that go into any relationship have got to be in the lobbying relationship. People have got to trust you, and they have got to be attracted to you for some reason. Why do they meet with the ACLU? The ACLU has built up a reputation for knowing what it is talking about—coming prepared with the facts. That makes us an attractive group to work with. And if they say something is off the record, the ACLU will keep it off the record.

Leech: What if it is someone who you don't agree with?

Murphy: If someone says to us in public, "I am going to fight your position," the ACLU will not only fight back to get their measure voted down, we will probably also file a lawsuit against their regulations or against a bill that they passed if we believe the law is unconstitutional.

We have firepower, and that is respected. Not many groups both lobby and litigate. I will give you an old example. In 1996, Congress passed the Communications Decency Act to regulate offensive content on the Internet, and President Bill Clinton signed it. We were outraged. We sued and won the case *ACLU v. Reno*, which struck down that provision of law.

Leech: If a bad bill becomes a law, the ACLU has an answer.

Murphy: Right. It's not like we go away with our tail between our legs. We believe in what we say, so when we come a-calling, people say, "Uh-oh, here comes the ACLU. What are they going to do? Are they going to denounce our proposal? Are they going to issue a release attacking our legislation?" People know we'll always take the fight to another venue.

Leech: Can you walk me through your average day? What does a day for Laura Murphy look like?

Murphy: I would say an average day has at least three or four meetings.

Leech: With people internally, or outside in government, or mixed?

Murphy: Mixed. There are two external meetings today, and one internal meeting and conference calls with colleagues in New York.

Leech: What time would you wake and come in? Then how would the day go from there?

Murphy: I am not a morning person, so I will come in between nine thirty and ten o'clock most days. I probably won't have a meeting before nine thirty, under any circumstances. I force myself to leave the office at five thirty by having this fitness training, which I have just started.

Leech: I am so impressed that you are fitting this into your busy schedule. You're my inspiration.

Murphy: Now, that is not common. That is not common. The level of stress is really high. It's not unusual for me to leave at eight o'clock or nine o'clock at night, because after six o'clock is when the phone stops ringing. If I've got to read a speech or if I have got to write a letter, that is really my quiet time. I don't have the same responsibilities I had during my first twelve years here. My son just graduated from Haverford. He can feed himself. My husband can feed himself. I started as a single mom in this job, when my son was three. I don't know how I did it.

Leech: It's hard for single moms.

Murphy: What I would end up doing is taking care of him, picking him up from after-school care, feeding him, supervising the homework, and then going back on the computer.

Even today, I don't really think I ever turn off the BlackBerry. Even on vacation, I am checking it. I can't turn on the news without working, because if there is breaking news I am thinking, "Okay, what is the ACLU response going to be?" If the Supreme Court upholds the Affordable Care Act, what are we going to say? If the Supreme Court strikes down portions of it, or upholds portions of Arizona's anti-immigrant law, SB 1070, what are we going to say? What are we going to do? What are our next steps?

Leech: When you see something like that in the news, what are your next steps? What will you do?

Murphy: I fire off an e-mail to my senior lobbyist, saying, "Did you see this?" I fire off something to our communications colleagues and say, "I think we ought to issue a quick quote. I think Anthony needs to respond to this."

Leech: You're always thinking about the media response as well as the internal government response: the public as well as the policymakers.

Murphy: You can have all the best policy arguments you want, but if you can't get it picked up in the media or in popular culture, it's like a tree falling in the forest. No one ever hears it. People just do not read newspapers the way they used to. They have their computers, and smartphones, and tablets set so that they open to Google, or *Sports Illustrated*, or *E! News*, or whatever. They're not plowing through a print newspaper once a day. We've got to use social media. We've got to use all tools at our disposal to push out a perspective on the events of the day. Fortunately, I am not responsible for daily output, but a lot of our lobbyists and their assistants blog.

There was a front-page article on Monday in *The New York Times* about the number of cell phone records that are intercepted by the government. One of my lobbyists was quoted on that front-page story. Later that day, he issued a blog post. We thought that my boss in New York and a congressperson were going to co-author an op-ed piece. But the traditional newspaper cycle is so slow that an op-ed would sit in some editor's box for maybe five days before they would push it out. We wanted to make sure we put our spin out there, and so that is why we try to keep our web site fresh, so that people keep clicking through. We'll send out an e-mail saying, "Look at Chris's blog."

I consider this part of the ACLU in Washington the emergency room for civil liberties. I consider litigation elective surgery. We can't control what Congress will do, we can't control what the Obama administration does. My job is to have a well-run emergency room, to expect crises, to have the infrastructure to deal with it, to make sure my staff is not totally burned out all the time, to affirm them, to empower them, and to get them training so that they can be some of the best lobbyists in Washington. I think we've got one of the best lobbying shops in Washington. If you include my chief of staff and me, we've got eighteen lobbyists. How many nonprofits do you know that have eighteen lobbyists and policy counsels? Very few.

Leech: Yes, that is impressive.

Murphy: When I started in 1979, there were three of us.

Leech: I have to ask you because I have wondered this ever since I first met you. How did you learn to speak so clearly and interestingly on issues, or did you always have that skill? Lots of people have interesting things to say, but often their speech is scattered. Your narrative is so clear and focused. Where does that come from? Did you train? Did you work at it? Did you learn it as a child?

Murphy: Yes, I worked at it. I was the youngest of five. My four siblings would say, "Shut up, Laura. You're boring." Around the dinner table, they made fun when I tried to tell jokes, because my jokes didn't make any sense. I kept trying until I could finally tell a joke like they could. I wanted to be funny like they were. When I first started getting on TV, my family would say, "You are so boring. You looked really nice, but you were really boring."

Why am I the way I am? It is because I have experienced a great deal of rejection and I have adjusted and worked at it. I like elementary school children. If I can't explain something to the children at my family gathering or the elderly people at my family gathering, I need to work at it some more. I have always liked the company of people and I have always liked the engagement of people. I have always liked the feeling that my parents could generate or the elected officials that I like could generate in a room, where the people were focused and excited and they clapped. I want that. You need that buy-in, that excitement—it has got to appeal to you.

There are certain lobbyists I will never be able to put on television. Some of them just cannot help themselves. With all of the media training in the world, they just can't do it. So I get them to do other things. They are leaders in other areas. You do not have to do everything well.

Leech: Washington has a reputation of being an old boys' club. How open is Washington to women and people of color?

Murphy: I think politics is still very male-dominated, and I strongly feel that women can excel in politics. We need more female elected officials. That doesn't mean that every woman that you elect is going to be pro-ACLU. But Michelle Bachman and Sarah Palin, although I probably disagree with many of their positions, still bring something different to the conversation than men do.

The fact of the matter is that women get paid seventy cents on the dollar of what men get paid. That will only change when we change certain laws to require employers to be nondiscriminatory in their policies. I just can't believe that contraception is controversial. If women aren't allowed to control their reproductive functions, they can't work or go to school—it is just that simple. If we get more women in elected office, we will not have to reargue these issues over, and over, and over, and over again. I work in what is predominately a man's world.

Leech: How do you cope with that reality?

Murphy: I have given events for women. I have hired a number of women in jobs and in issue areas that were traditionally male-oriented. A couple of women lobbyists approached me when I returned to the ACLU, saying that they felt like they were out of the circle. I said, "We're going to fix that," so I sent some women to leadership training to empower them. I counseled others. I do not want to leave this field and be the first woman and the first African American and not pave the way for other women and people of color. I just cannot do that. What am I here for?

It's not about me. It's about changing the dynamic in our culture that allows people in positions of power to continue to oppress people. That is where we started out in this interview. We can't change the condition of people until we change the thinking or the population of the decision makers.

It is a long-term game. It's not going to change overnight, and there are certain of us who just have to burrow in and say, "Okay, we are just going to stand our ground, and guess what: we are going to build reinforcements. We are going to build up momentum. We are going to build the grass roots. We will take the issue to Washington, but if we get rejected in Washington, we will take it back to the states. It is an endurance test, a marathon—not a sprint."

One of the challenges women have is that we have to go in and out of the workplace to care for our relatives, because that still largely falls to women. Even though we go to law school or medical school, when mom gets sick, who goes home? The daughters. Or when dad gets sick or when the children are staying out of school, who leaves work? More than likely, it is the mother not the husband.

We've got a lot of work to do in terms of gender equity, not just on the receiving end but in the leadership roles. The people who are making the decisions, who actually understand what it is like not to have birth control or childcare—those have got to be people in positions of authority too. Because if it is just left to men, it's never going to be as exciting as guns and wars.

Leech: How has the ACLU been involved in these gender equality issues?

Murphy: We are fighting for pay equity legislation. We are very big in the battle to retain contraception coverage in the Affordable Care Act. We are trying to get the United States to sign an international treaty eliminating all forms of discrimination against women—the Convention on the Elimination of All Forms of Discrimination Against Women [CEDAW]. We are one of the few countries that are not a party to it.

We are so on top of these women's issues. We are challenging advocates of sex-segregated education models that would not give girls the same math and science programs that boys are given. That is happening in some public schools in the United States. We are doing a lot of work around those issues, but we are not involved in the election of women.

Leech: Right. The ACLU, because of its tax status, cannot get involved in election campaigns.

Murphy: We also are not backing any particular cabinet secretary. We did not take a position on Hillary Clinton vs. Barack Obama for president. We are not involved in electoral politics, but we are involved in reproductive-health gender equity in the workplace. From the workplace to the hospitals to the prison systems to immigration systems, we are fighting gender equity issues or gender-based discrimination.

I look around and I think about all the legislation that I have influenced and all the people I have hired over my thirty-six-year career, yet I am still not part of the club. At some level, it still feels like guerilla warfare for a woman leader in this field.

Leech: Do you think it would be different if there were a man in this position, even though it's the ACLU?

Murphy: Oh yes, absolutely! The hanging out, the socializing, the going out for drinks, the mentoring: none of that is happening for me. But I am not upset with where I am. I am not a disgruntled leader. I was lucky that I had two male bosses who hired me and the second male boss hired me back. But I am going to make sure on my watch that for the women I hire it is not as challenging to be in the conversation as it was for me.

Leech: What advice do you have for someone who is in school, interested in becoming a lobbyist or policy advocate in Washington? What would you advise them to do? What experience would you advise them to get?

Murphy: My son wants to be a lobbyist too, because he just graduated from Haverford. He was driving me into work this week, and I asked him, "Do you want me to send your résumé out?" He said, "Yeah, but I also want to talk to this guy I met who's a lobbyist." I said, "Bert, I really think you would be much more attractive to a lobbying operation if you had Hill experience, because you would know the guts of the operation." He said, "Okay, can you help me get a job on the Hill?" I said, "Yeah, but you've got to want it and you've got to be able to say in thirty seconds what your assets are."

I would say that you should start now, working in the area that really fuels your passion. I do not think you should just be a lobbyist for the sake of being a lobbyist. You should be a lobbyist on an issue that really excites you, and develop a subject matter expertise in that issue area. If you can get a job on Capitol Hill, great! If you can't, try your state legislature.

Because how politics works—what goes on, how people are influenced—is the same wherever you are. Either you are with a very strong nonprofit or you are with a wealthy corporate or union interest. If you are going to play the influence game, figure out which organizations have the juice. For a lot of people, if you are concerned about immigrants' rights or prisoners' rights, your organization may not have the same power as the oil companies. If you are willing to work on it over a period of time, then you can build influence. I think it's important to really study something that you care about in school. My son majored in anthropology, but his thesis was on the culture of congressional offices.

Leech: Oh, very interesting.

Murphy: It's a great field. I don't think that what you major in is as important as your ability to read, write, and speak well.

Leech: What are you looking for when you hire an intern or a junior lobbyist?

Murphy: I want to know that they have done something on their own initiative. They have joined a group, and they have tried to achieve a leadership position in a group. I want to see some evidence of independent and strategic thinking. You could be in the marching band, but if you are able to tell me a story about how you took the marching band from ten volunteers to fifty volunteers, I am interested in you. I am more interested in that person than I am in the poli-sci major who has a 4.0 grade point average and did not do any extracurricular activities.

I want to see some action on your part, because this is not the place to learn how to take action—this is the place where activists take issues to another level. You've got to have the heart of a fighter, and I have got to see some evidence of that. You have to be personable, you have to have a sense of humor, and you cannot talk all the time. You have to listen. You have to be able to follow through. People who do not follow through really fail at being a lobbyist.

Leech: What do you mean by "follow through"?

Murphy: Let's say that you write a great letter explaining why a piece of legislation is bad for gay students, and you send it to Capitol Hill, but you do not make any phone calls to make sure that the legislative assistants in the Congressional office got it. Did they read it? Do they have time to meet about it? Would they like to meet with the delegation from your state? Can they insert something in the *Congressional Record*? Can they ask their boss to urge the Secretary of Education when he appears before the committee to do more about the problems of gay students being bullied in colleges and universities across the country?

You cannot just send it out there. You've got to make it happen, and your follow-through has to be measurable. How many phone calls did you make? Show me where it is in the *Congressional Record*. Who introduced the bill? Did you help? Why don't you write a bill, if you don't see the bill that the ACLU can support? Write a bill and then get somebody to introduce it. It's a whole bunch of skill sets. You have to have a high tolerance for rejection. You have to have great follow-through. You have to have good research skills. You have got to be personable. You cannot be a rain cloud.

CHAPTER

6

Lyle Dennis

Partner

CRD Associates

***Lyle Dennis** is a partner in the lobbying firm of Cavarocchi-Ruscio-Dennis Associates, where he specializes in representing medical and scientific organizations and public and private universities. CRD Associates is relatively small and focused in the world of lobbying firms—it had billings of nearly $4 million in 2011, about one-tenth the amount of the largest firms. The firm does not have a political action committee (PAC), but its three partners individually gave more than $108,000 in campaign contributions in the 2012 election cycle.*

Before coming to CRD Associates in 1994, Dennis directed the Washington office for the state of New Jersey. He came to Washington as chief of staff for Rep. Bernard Dwyer (D-NJ) after successfully managing Dwyer's congressional campaign. Dennis earlier held several top staff positions within the New Jersey state Senate.

Dennis is a member of the steering committee of the Ad Hoc Group for Medical Research, the leading advocacy organization for the National Institutes of Health, and he is co-editor of Health Care Advocacy: A Guide for Busy Clinicians *(Springer, 2011). He has bachelor's degree in political science from Rutgers University and a master's degree from the Eagleton Institute of Politics at Rutgers.*

Beth Leech: I understand that your first job as a lobbyist was working for the state of New Jersey.

Lyle Dennis: That is correct. I was the director of the state of New Jersey's Washington, DC, office. Most state governments have an office here in DC, most of them located just a few blocks from here in the Hall of the States.

Leech: Why do state governments need a lobbyist?

Dennis: The principal reason is because the interests of state government are not always the number-one thing on the minds of the congressional delegation from that state, and the interests of state government can be different than the interests of corporate constituents or individual constituents. There are very specific needs. For example, transportation aid is a huge issue for states. A congressional legislator from the state might not know exactly what the needs are in terms of construction or reconstruction of bridges throughout the entire state.

The member of Congress certainly knows what goes on in their district, but in terms of statewide issues, they may be less aware. For example, Medicaid is a joint federal-state program, and what happens at the federal level affects the state. A state's interests might also be related to law enforcement grants or just about anything where the federal government interacts with the state. The state governments' interests need to be represented to the delegation so that those members of Congress are aware of them going in to markups on legislation, negotiations, and conference committees—back in the days when there used to be conference committees and Congress used to pass legislation, which seems to happen so rarely these days.

When I represented the state of New Jersey, it was the last year of the Governor Jim Florio administration and the first year of the Clinton administration. But for twenty-six hundred votes, I would have had that job for five years instead of just one. At that point, directing the Washington office was considered a subcabinet position. It was essentially the same as being assistant commissioner, in terms of where it is on the hierarchy of state government.

Leech: Was the work primarily appropriations related, or were there other things as well?

Dennis: There are other, policy-related things as well. For example, there's a program under Medicaid referred to as Disproportionate Share Hospitals. These are hospitals that treat an inordinately large percentage of indigent patients. Exactly how that's defined can make a difference of tens of millions or even hundreds of millions of dollars of federal aid going to the state. We would work on issues like that.

The other thing that a lobbyist does in that position is serve as the governor's liaison to the administration, especially if the White House is of the same party and will talk to you, which was the case when I represented New Jersey. There's a political component to the job as well. Governor Florio was a high priority for President Clinton because that governorship was one of only two that were up in the off-year election.

Leech: Coming into that job, had you ever thought you would be a lobbyist? Did you want to be a lobbyist when you were back in graduate school?

Dennis: No. When I was in graduate school, my intention was to work in the state legislature, which I did for four and a half years. I came to Washington when the then-majority leader of the state Senate, Barney Dwyer, got elected to Congress and asked me to come along as his chief of staff. I was twenty-seven.

I had been with him about eight years when I started thinking, "You know, what am I going to do next? This guy I work for isn't getting any younger and neither am I. I have kids who are going to want to go to college. I started thinking that I would probably go into lobbying. I thought that I would probably be good at it or at least not bad at it.

Dwyer served twelve years before he retired. That was when I then went to work for New Jersey's Washington office.

Leech: And after that, when Governor Florio lost the election, you came to Cavarocchi-Ruscio-Dennis Associates, which was then Cavarocchi-Ruscio.

Dennis: Yes. I was interviewing around town and I had a job offer from a competitor firm. This is going to sound like I'm very clever and manipulative, but I'm actually not this smart. I called the people who are now my two partners and said, "Hey, I got this job offer from so-and-so down the street. Here's what he's offering me. What do you think? Should I take it? Should I negotiate more?" Because I knew Cavarocchi and Ruscio. They used to come in and lobby me when I was Dwyer's chief of staff. The response I got was, "We'll call you back." I thought that was an odd response.

The next day they called back and said, "Why don't you come in and see us? We'll beat that offer." That was how I ended up here and then five years later, became a partner, causing the renaming of the firm to the totally unpronounceable Cavarocchi-Ruscio-Dennis Associates.

Leech: Thus CRD?

Dennis: That's CRD in most people's minds.

Leech: What sorts of clients does the firm tend to represent? And what sorts of clients do you tend to represent, if that's different from the overall firm?

Dennis: I'm kind of a microcosm of the firm actually. We have forty-five or so clients. Earlier in their careers, my two partners were both appropriations subcommittee staffers for the Labor, Health, Human Services, and Education subcommittees—one of them on the House side, one on the Senate side. When the firm started, we had a very strong focus on appropriations issues, particularly in health and higher education. Over the years, we've expanded that fairly significantly, although it is still the majority of our client base.

For example, in the health area, we represent patient advocacy groups, physician organizations, and scientific research organizations, including the Society for Neuroscience, which is made up mostly of people with PhDs, and the American Association for the Study of Liver Diseases, which is mostly MD researchers with a few PhDs mixed in. We represent several universities, including the State University System of Florida, which is eleven universities and six medical schools.

There are a variety of other things as well. We are big on running coalitions. For seven years, I ran a coalition to support the Human Genome Project.

Leech: What was important about the Human Genome Project, in terms of advocacy?

Dennis: The Human Genome Project was a scientific project at the National Institutes of Health [NIH] that sequenced the entire genome, all three billion chemical base pairs that are inside of every cell in your DNA, and the whole project took ten years. It was $3 billon over that period. Congress doesn't appropriate multiyear, so it was an annual advocacy effort. What it ultimately led to is the stuff that you hear about all the time now on the news—that scientists have found the gene that causes a particular birth defect or scientists have now found the cause of a certain disease.

Leech: The coalition was there to help encourage funding?

Dennis: Yes, because there was also a private effort going on through a company called Celera. The difference between the public effort and the private effort was that all the public effort research was immediately put up online and was available freely to anyone within twenty-four hours of analysis. The private effort went into a for-profit company where the information was held internally. The societal benefit, of course, is to have the scientific information available for other researchers.

Leech: I hadn't realized this at the time. Was the private company trying to prevent the public effort from going forward?

Dennis: There were some pretty fierce rivalries, and some of this is just individual personalities and some of it is the for-profit motive versus the not-for-profit motive. While the company was not overtly trying to undercut the public effort, there was enough discussion that some members of Congress began to say, "Well now, wait a minute. Why do we have to put up taxpayer money if a private company is going to do to this?" There was an educational effort needed to explain what the differences were and why the public effort was so important, and then it ultimately got done. The two groups finished sequencing the genome at virtually the same time.

Leech: Without the coalition, it's very possible that the public side would not have succeeded.

Dennis: Yes. We once brought in three Nobel Prize winners to talk to key members of the Appropriations Committee to explain why this was so important. One of the Nobelists was James Watson of Watson & Crick fame, who discovered the structure of DNA. Three Nobel Prize winners and me—the guy who got a C in high school biology.

Leech: Each has their skills. What do you do when you're running a coalition like this?

Dennis: What we did in this case was we talked to some pharmaceutical companies, not Celera, but others that were interested in having this information publicly available so they could use it in their research. We talked to some patient advocacy groups that also were interested in having this project go forward and not have to buy access to the basic research from a company, and we put the coalition together.

Leech: Does the impetus for the coalition come from you guys or does someone approach you and say, "Would you do this for us?"

Dennis: It originally came from a discussion with some folks within government, but they, of course, can't lobby. Essentially what they said was, "Wouldn't it be nice if somebody did this?" It was really nothing more substantial than that. I was very new at lobbying at that point. I'd only been doing this for about a year, so I had the time. Coalitions are very time-intensive. First of all, there is an inverse relationship between the amount of work people expect from you and the amount that they're paying into the coalition.

Leech: The organization that's given $100….

Dennis: Has a question a day. And the organization that's giving $10,000, you never hear from. It's just the way it is.

Leech: They figure you'll handle it.

Dennis: What we try to do in this case was to balance the coalition with some industry folks, some big patient advocacy groups, things like the Cystic Fibrosis Foundation, and then some little mom-and-pop patient advocacy group for diseases that you've never heard of. Those small groups didn't pay anything because they couldn't. They were being run out of somebody's kitchen. It took a year or two, but we ended up putting together about one hundred and twenty-five different members. Then we were up on the Hill, presenting language to Appropriations to support the project.

The coalition sponsored an annual lecture at the National Academy of Sciences in Washington. One year Al Gore spoke. He was vice president at the time, so it was a pretty big deal. We were operating at a pretty high level, drawing a lot of attention to the project, hoping to fund an effort that ultimately is going to lead to cures for a lot of diseases.

Leech: Is it very common for lobbying firms to initiate coalitions as an entrepreneurial thing, a way of saying, "Hey, there's something you guys should be thinking about doing. We could represent you on that."

Dennis: Absolutely. And there is also the "Hey, wouldn't it be nice if we had a group that could do this because we can't lobby."

Leech: Is that coming from the legislative side or from the NIH side?

Dennis: It would be more NIH. There are groups that spring up around the institutes that are a combination of patient advocacy groups, physician groups, and sometimes corporate groups who are interested in the research that's being done there. At NIH, there are Friends of the National Institute of Child Health and Human Development, Friends of the National Institute on Aging, and Friends of the National Library of Medicine.

Those coalitions essentially are lobbying informally on behalf of a government agency to advocate for that agency's budget. There also are coalitions like this informally affiliated with the Department of Health and Human Services [HHS]. For example, one of the agencies under HHS, the Agency for Healthcare Research & Quality [AHRQ], does health services research and that sort of thing. One of the senior vice presidents here runs a coalition called the Friends of AHRQ.

Leech: You're on the steering committee of another ad hoc committee, right?

Dennis: I'm on the steering committee on the Ad Hoc Group for Medical Research, which is a pro-NIH advocacy group.

Leech: In these sorts of groups, are you participating because your clients are on them and you're representing them?

Dennis: For the most part, we're doing it because they are great sources of information for our clients and for ourselves to be able to impart to our clients. In some cases, it is directly because the client has asked us to do it.

Leech: In some cases, you would be paid directly and, in other cases, it's just good for business?

Dennis: It's just good for business, exactly. The steering committee for the Ad Hoc Group for Medical Research meets every year with all of the institute directors at NIH, which then gives me relationships there. If one of my clients says, "Hey, there's something going on in this institute where we've never been before," I can say, "Well gee, I just met with the director three weeks ago. I'll reach out there and see if we can't get a meeting."

There's also a general educational aspect to the groups in terms of keeping track. As tight as budgets are in the government right now, NIH still spends more than $30 billion a year. That's a lot of money. There's a lot of opportunity that can be missed if an organization is not at the table. That's what it's about—being at the table.

Leech: I took you off on a long tangent, which was very interesting, but let's back up because you were telling me about what your firm does.

Dennis: We also run something called the Coalition for Health Funding. There are seventy-five different organizations in the coalition and each of them pays dues to us to run it. It's very active and the agenda is broader than just the NIH. The agenda is the entire public health service, so that would include the Centers for Disease Control, the Health Resources and Services Administration, the Food and Drug Administration, and a lot of other health agencies. The coalition is looking at the bigger picture of funding for health. That has led to the creation of something called the NDD Coalition.

Leech: What is that?

Dennis: The Non-Defense Discretionary Spending Coalition. Under the Budget Control Act that passed last year as part of the debt-limit deal, there's a provision that says that if the Super Committee fails to make significant reductions in the deficit, there will be a process called sequestration that will take effect on January 2, 2013. That process will cut about eight percent from every discretionary program in the federal government—defense and nondefense.

The defense community—being wealthy, really well-organized, and all corporate—has started organizing to exempt defense from the sequestration. Because we're running this coalition for health funding and health is a big part of the federal budget, we got together with the Coalition for Education Funding and some housing, transportation, and justice groups—basically everything that's not defense—to create this NDD Coalition. We're actually not making any money from the coalition, but we're doing good work to ensure that defense and nondefense are all treated alike.

If you exempt defense from sequestration, you will double the cuts in nondefense spending. Now instead of losing eight percent of every program, nondefense programs would lose sixteen percent. That includes things like the FBI, the Immigration & Naturalization Service, border enforcement, and air traffic controllers. The cuts would occur a quarter of the way through the year, so they would effectively have a twenty percent cut through the rest of the fiscal year. So that is an important area to be involved.

I'll give you a couple of other examples of what the firm does. I have a senior vice president who is a master's-level genetic counselor. She worked in Francis Collins' lab when he was the head of the National Human Genome Research Institute. She represents companies that are doing cutting-edge genomics research. These companies are in California, a lot of them are venture-capital funded, and most of them have "gen" somewhere in their name.

Leech: Why do companies like that need to be represented?

Dennis: There are a lot of policy issues at the FDA in terms of the companies getting approval for the tests or treatments they're developing, and then there are payment issues with the Center for Medicare and Medicaid Services [CMS]. It doesn't do a company any good to get their new test approved by the FDA if CMS won't pay for it. If CMS won't pay for it, then private insurers won't pay for it. The whole system gets tied together.

We help the companies navigate that system, which is very complex, with a million people involved. There are aspects of it that we don't do because we're not a law firm. The "gen" companies will have an FDA counsel for the legal side and then a firm like ours to help them navigate the political side, including when to go in to meet with the key people at the FDA or who to see at CMS.

Leech: Very good. How about you personally?

Dennis: Most of my clients are on the health side. What I personally work on are a couple of patient advocacy groups for genetic-based diseases and a couple of physician groups, one being the Society for General Internal Medicine and one being the American Association for the Study of Liver Diseases.

Leech: How did you end up with this expertise? You just told me you got a C in biology.

Dennis: Part of it is because the congressman I worked for was on the subcommittee that funded NIH and funded all of these health programs, so I already had been conversing with those agencies when I came to CRD. Then part of it is the experience of just doing it. Now, let me say this: you don't want me touching your liver.

Leech: I'll remember that.

Dennis: That goes for everybody here. What we know is what we don't know, and at what point should we pick up the phone and say, "Dr. So-and-So, I need you to talk to this congressional office because they have a question on viral hepatitis that would have me practicing medicine without a license."

Do I know the difference between hepatitis B and hepatitis C? Yes, I do. Could I tell you with any great certainty whether your ALT scores should be 5.7 or 6.3? I have no idea. I don't even remember what the initials ALT stand for, other than the fact that it's something where the L is for liver. We go to the experts on that. Same thing in neuroscience: when we represent the Society for Neuroscience, we know when to stop and say, "Let us have someone get back to you with a definitive response on that."

Often in policy, you don't need to get into the real deep medical or scientific issues, but sometimes it happens. The Society for Neuroscience, a long-time client, asked us to work with a coalition that they wanted to develop called the American Brain Coalition. That coalition is comprised of the Society for Neuroscience, the American Academy of Neurology, and a bunch of patient advocacy groups for diseases like Parkinson's and Alzheimer's.

One of the things we do for this group is provide staff work to the Congressional Neuroscience Caucus, which is an unofficial congressional caucus of members and their staffs who are interested in neuroscience issues. It's now up to thirty or so members. We organize four briefings a year on Capitol Hill. We just did one a few weeks ago. It was about breakthroughs in neuroscience research. We brought in someone from Harvard and somebody from the University of California at San Diego. They were very prominent neuroscientists, who were able to talk in English as opposed to in neuroscience, and brief eighty Capitol Hill staffers on what's the latest and greatest in neuroscience.

Some of what they said related to brain imaging and some related to new medications, but it was all targeted at educating Congress through their staff on what's new in neuroscience, why it's important, and how it ultimately is going to save healthcare dollars and all of that.

Leech: Why would the staffers want to know this?

Dennis: The staffers would want to know because their bosses will be called upon to vote on funding for NIH and on policy issues related to neuroscience—for example, stem cell research or animal research. Members of Congress are under enormous pressure from groups like PETA [People for the Ethical Treatment of Animals] to not support the use of animals in research. Hearing the other side of it is important to keeping that research going.

There's always a reason why they need to know this. If there weren't, they wouldn't come to the briefing. The briefings have to be timely and pointed and they have to be an hour—maybe an hour and fifteen minutes. You can't go any longer than that because you'll lose them. It doesn't hurt if you have a little food there, although even that has changed from when I was on the Hill, when it would be a dinner. Now there are limitations under the new ethics rules. You can't buy a staffer dinner. It has to be hors d'oeuvres—food you eat with a toothpick.

We also are involved in a breakfast briefing next week. It's for a patient advocacy group for the Congressional Baby Caucus—something you also didn't know existed.

Leech: I did not.

Dennis: The group invited one of my clients to come in and testify about some newborn screening issues. We can get away with the small muffins and small bagels and that sort of thing, but we can't do bacon and eggs. This is the brave new world.

Leech: It sounds like a lot of what you do is related to appropriations.

Dennis: A lot of it is, but it's a decreasing percentage. If you'd asked me that question three or four years ago, I would have told you seventy percent. Now I would say it's less than fifty percent. The reason for that is that appropriations bills used to be must-pass legislation. It used to be no matter what else, Congress would do its twelve appropriations bills, and therefore they were a place where other policy issues could get added in as well.

Increasingly, Congress has resorted to using continuing resolutions to fund the government and not actually passing appropriations bills. Or if they do, they pass these mega bills, where they lump a bunch of appropriations bills together into one bill. Because of that, it's gotten harder for a lobbyist to get results in the appropriations process. We still do, but it's harder.

We have shifted some of our lobbying work from Congress to the agencies, and within Congress, we do more policy work. The big thing on policy work for us was healthcare reform, which obviously was an enormous piece of legislation in which individual people up and down the hallway in our office might have been interested in a particular twelve-page section. Everyone says, "Oh, the bill is twenty-seven hundred pages. How could you possibly deal with that?" But we might be interested in twelve pages for this client, and one section for another client, and getting a sentence added for a third client.

Leech: Can you give me an example of one of those small things?

Dennis: Sure. It was not a small thing to the client.

Leech: Indeed, but small in terms of pages.

Dennis: We worked on getting some language in the healthcare reform bill to provide a bonus payment to primary care docs. Primary care doctors historically are underpaid relative to specialists and they're underpaid for cognitive services. That is, they are underpaid for talking to a patient rather than for doing a medical procedure. If I have a basal cell carcinoma removed from my forehead, which takes three minutes, that dermatologist is going to get a lot more money than a primary care doctor who spends twenty minutes talking to an eighty-four-year-old patient with multiple illnesses, including diabetes, high blood pressure, high cholesterol, and the beginnings of dementia. Dealing with that patient for twenty minutes will be paid less than the three minutes of scraping a little thing off somebody's forehead.

What we were able to do, and it wasn't just us alone, was to get a bonus payment built into the Medicare part of the healthcare reform law that essentially pays doctors an additional ten percent on those cognitive types of services. It's not really enough. The problem we are trying to address is not, "Oh gee, these doctors make $180,000 and they ought to make $200,000." The problem is that, "I'm a patient and I need a primary care doctor. I can't find one because nobody's going into primary care because the pay is too low."

Leech: How do you go about changing language in a bill or getting something added in? When the general public thinks about lobbying, it's often focused on the outcome of the bill: "Were you for it or against it?"

Dennis: For it or against it is way down the road. With these additions or changes to bill language, we would go a member of the committee or the subcommittee that's writing the bill or writing that section of the bill. With healthcare reform, there were three committees in the House and two in the Senate that were involved. In this case, you would go to the Senate Finance and House Ways and Means committees. You would find a member who has a history of being supportive of primary care, and make your case to that member.

Leech: You go to speak to this person, and then if he or she agrees, is it done?

Dennis: No, but then the member of Congress essentially becomes the lobbyist on that issue. The member will go to the committee staff, which our office also meets with. The member also goes to the committee or subcommittee chairman or chairwoman and becomes an advocate for that provision. The member takes ownership of the issue.

Now, that's a good thing and a bad thing. It's a good thing in that ultimately only members of Congress can make these decisions and can do these things. The bad thing is once you turn it over to the member of Congress, you lose control of it. If somebody says, "Gee, why don't you do it this way?" and "this way" is a stupid idea, or an anathema to the client, it's very hard to turn it back around.

Leech: You're trying to stay in touch during this period, I'm imagining.

Dennis: Exactly. We're hopeful that we have a good enough relationship with the member or with the member's staff that if somebody comes up and says, "Gee, you ought to do it this way," that they'll come back to us and say, "What do you think about this approach? Would that be better or worse, or how would your groups look at this? How would the primary care docs regard doing the payment in nickels rather than in dollar bills or electronically?" Whatever the idea is.

We try to stay as involved in the process as we can, but ultimately lobbyists aren't really running the process. The staff has more influence than the lobbyists do, but ultimately the members really are the final bottom line. Now, having said that, are there things in bills that a staffer put there and no member really thought about it or paid attention to it—especially in a twenty-seven-hundred-page bill? Yes, of course, there are. But a lot of those are just routine wording changes, not major policy changes.

Leech: Why do you think members of Congress listen to you or to any lobbyist?

Dennis: There are a couple of reasons. First of all, I'm brilliant and charming.

Leech: Given.

Dennis: You can just erase that. There are a couple of reasons. First, you have to have a good argument. You have to have a case that matters. You have to have a case that fits in with their worldview.

You have to have something that doesn't conflict with the values in their district. If a member of Congress is from New Jersey and has seventeen pharmaceutical companies based in their district, and you suggest, "Let's do this to screw the pharmaceutical companies," it's going to be hard to get them to go along.

Leech: But what if the lobbyist is suggesting that the member of Congress should do something that supports the pharmaceutical industry? Why does a lobbyist need to say that? Why wouldn't the member just do it?

Dennis: Because the member may not know about it. No member of Congress can know all of the nuances of every issue that affects their district or their state. It's too much. There are too many variables. What the lobbyist is doing is providing information. Coming back to your question of why do they listen to you, let me answer it in the inverse: Why would they not listen to me?

If I provide them with bad information, if I provide them with heavily biased information, or if I provide them with information that doesn't take into account their world view, their party, their district, I will quickly lose them as an ally.

Leech: And you don't do that because you're in it for the long term?

Dennis: Yes. If I wanted to slash and burn and work with somebody once, then I wouldn't be able to go back to that person. They would say, "Geez, I did that thing for this guy and now I'm catching all this flack from this group or that group, and he never even told me they were against it."

Leech: Your firm used to be pretty involved in earmarks—line items that brought money to particular projects or particular regions—before the House decided to ban them.

Dennis: We were.

Leech: How was that different from the general appropriation process?

Dennis: First of all, I'm going to make the pro-earmark speech. The Constitution of the United States—you may be familiar with it—gives the power to legislate to Congress, not to a GS14 agency employee who lives in Vienna, Virginia, and commutes into DC every day. I have absolutely no problem with a member of Congress saying, "Of this $40 million going to rail projects, $1 million should be used to redo the Metuchen train station." I don't have any problem with that.

From a lobbying point of view, we never set out to become a big earmark firm, but because we did a lot of appropriations we ended up there. You have to understand that earmarks were very scarce, few and far between, until

Newt Gingrich became Speaker of the House. Part of Gingrich's philosophy, to help hold the majority and keep himself as Speaker, was to do earmarks out the wazoo because it's stuff you can bring home and talk about to your constituents. Ironically, ultimately it was the Republicans who eliminated them and turned them into, "Oh, this is all the Democrats' fault."

Leech: And the lobbyists' fault.

Dennis: And the lobbyists' fault, and part of that was the Democrats' fault because of various rascals. It's what happens when the lobbyist is too closely tied to the member of Congress. When there are fifty campaign contributions from employees of company XYZ on Tuesday and then an earmark for $3 million added to a bill on Thursday, that's bad stuff. The process got cleaned up after the Abramoff scandal. Unless a member was one hundred percent against earmarks, the member was portrayed politically as being for them. So that was the end of the earmarks, although as I said, we never set out to be an earmark firm.

Leech: Lots of universities were involved.

Dennis: Oh, tons of them. That was really Cassidy & Associates that began getting the earmarks for universities. By and large, they're justifiable if it's a good project. Our firm got the earmarks for the RUNet 2000 project, which wired the whole Rutgers University campus together and connected it to underprivileged high schools in New Brunswick, Newark, and Camden.

That was a good project. We got the university $10 million over a period of four years—a little over $10 million. They did good work with it. There were high school students in Newark who had completed all the math that was available to them in the Newark school system, and they could sit in their high school classroom and take a college-level math course.

Leech: That's a big deal.

Dennis: Yeah, it was a big deal and it was a good thing, but there was no competitive federal program to apply to for funding like that. The earmark ban completely wiped things like that out. In our case, we started seeing the writing on the wall. We started moving our clients into more policy-related issues and more broad appropriations issues. When earmarks went away, it barely made a dent in what we were doing because the clients were already doing other things. There are some firms in this town, and there are some individual lobbyists in this town whose business virtually got wiped out. Earmarks were all they did, and they were gone.

Leech: You mentioned campaign contributions. How important is that side of it to CRD?

Dennis: It's not huge, thank goodness, because we don't have a PAC. This is all out of our own individual pockets. It's not a huge factor. I think it's a factor. You're not certainly buying anybody's vote—certainly not at the level that we give. We're not buying anyone's vote any more than we're buying anything from the staff person if we bought him or her a cup of coffee, which we're no longer allowed to do.

Leech: I've looked at your filings with the Federal Election Commission, and the donations tend to be $500 here and $1000 there. Not across the board, by any means.

Dennis: Right, exactly. We tend to give to members of Congress who are helpful or who are supportive of our clients, but they are members who would probably be supportive regardless. I don't think that Representative Frank Pallone of New Jersey is more supportive of Rutgers because we hold a breakfast for him, and I give him $1,000, and one of my partners gives him $1,000, and he knows we get twenty other people in the room who give him $500 each or whatever. He's would be supportive of Rutgers regardless, because Rutgers is in his district.

Leech: So why do you do it?

Dennis: We do it because his people ask. We do it, I would say, just to deepen the relationship. It makes it easier to talk to him. It increases our recognition factor. I don't have to introduce myself to members of Congress for whom I've raised money. This morning, I went to a fundraiser because another lobbyist asked me to do it. It was for a congresswoman who is very influential because she's on the House Rules Committee, but I can't remember ever bringing an issue to the House Rules Committee. I don't need to know her better, but somebody asked me to do it. It was only $500, so I did it.

Leech: How often do you end up having to spend time either organizing or going to fundraisers like this?

Dennis: I just filed my semiannual report, and in the first half of the year, I made about nine contributions. That's about normal. I do roughly twenty campaign contributions a year. They range from $125 to $1000. The $125 was for an event that I didn't actually go to. I was trying to get somebody to stop bugging me, so I sent them $125.

My two partners probably do about the same. Our senior vice presidents tend to do a little less. Of course, they make less, and it all comes out of our own pockets.

Leech: I know at least some of your days—about twenty a year—are spent going to these fundraisers, but your average day, could you walk me through one of those?

Dennis: One of the things I like about what I do is that no two days are ever really alike, but there are certainly some generalizations I can give you. I usually am in the office by about seven fifteen a.m. I like that time between seven fifteen and nine o'clock because I can get organized, I can read all the newsletters, things like *CQ* [*Congressional Quarterly*] and those types of electronic newsletters that pop up onto our screens all the time. It's funny with this stuff—it used to all be paper. Now it's all electronic, although I do actually read the *Washington Post* on paper. I'm an old-fashioned sort of guy. That's the early part of the day. Then once you get beyond that, I'll have to give you a specific example, because it all diverges.

Yesterday, I was in here at seven fifteen. I had a staff meeting at nine o'clock with all the sixteen people who work here, except for the one that had a dentist appointment and the one who had to take his dog to the vet.

Leech: Okay, good. There's some family time. That was my next question.

Dennis: I had a staff meeting. Then I had a phone call because I'm taking a client out to NIH later this week. I had a phone call from somebody from the National Cancer Institute who wanted to talk about that visit to NIH. Because we're pitching a prospective new client later today, we had a planning meeting for that in the afternoon yesterday. In between that, I'm answering e-mails. I'm writing memos often requested in those e-mails, like, "Could you do a memo for me on such and such piece of legislation."

Leech: The memo will be for a client or for someone in government?

Dennis: Either. For example, I did a memo yesterday for somebody on the Hill to use as the basis for a letter for their boss to send out to other members of Congress. The memo laid out the facts. When you take an issue to Congress, the more you can offer to do, the better the chance that they're going to be helpful. Because the staff is so overworked and they've got so many issues and so much going on, the more things you can bring them as close to a finished product as possible so they can just do a cut-and-paste, the better the chance you have that they're going to actually be helpful. That's not any great secret. That's just the way it works.

We had a planning session for the meeting with the potential client that we have later this afternoon. Then I was back to answering e-mails. I get about one hundred and fifty e-mails a day, which sounds like a lot, but some of them are read-and-delete. Some of them are very quick, some of them are more involved. In between, there are phone calls with clients, with the staff, all of that. That took me through to, say, six o'clock last night. I went home. I had some dinner. This is really interesting. I took out the trash, by the way.

Leech: Good. You were supposed to.

Dennis: Then I got back online and started answering more e-mails, the ones that had come in from the time I left here at six o'clock until I got back online at about eighty thirty last night. Now, don't feel bad for me because I did have the All-Star game on TV and I have an office at home, so I'm very comfortable.

Leech: Is that usual for you to be checking, and working, and eating, and watching like that?

Dennis: Yeah. I work every night, usually an hour to two hours until my wife screams. Although increasingly she doesn't scream anymore.

Leech: She's used to it.

Dennis: Then just to take it one step further, today I went to a fundraiser in the morning. I had a conference call with a client, a patient advocacy group that wants to be supportive of an issue coming up before the FDA because the pharmaceutical company involved is making a drug that will help the advocacy group's patients. We did that at eleven o'clock. I have this meeting with you. Then at three o'clock this afternoon, two senior vice presidents in the firm and I will be pitching a prospective new client.

We'll do that meeting with the new client. Then one of my partners and I will do an annual review for one of our employees. That will end about five o'clock. I will answer e-mails, and return phone calls and whatever until six o'clock or so. I'll go home. I'll eat dinner. I'll bring the garbage can in and I will get back online and watch the All-Star game while I'm answering e-mails.

Those are typical kind of days. Now, there are atypical things as well. Medical groups and physicians groups all have annual meetings and they are not located here.

Leech: Hawaii, I'm thinking.

Dennis: I wish. It's not bad places. So far this year, I've been to Orlando, San Diego, Los Angeles, New York twice, Boston once, Chicago. Those are the ones that come immediately to mind, and those are virtually always on the weekends. What that means, of course, is that I'm working seven days a week during those weeks because I'm in the office Monday through Friday. Then Friday afternoon, I fly to Chicago, fly home Sunday night, and Monday go back to work. I'm probably away ten to twelve weekends a year.

Leech: What are you doing at those meetings? Are you presenting?

Dennis: It varies a little bit from group to group. For example, I mentioned the liver doctors before. When I go to their meeting, I do a presentation. Sometimes more than one, depending on how they have their agenda set up. I usually have one or two PowerPoint presentations, which means before I go, I've got to actually produce those presentations.

Leech: Are these meetings a place to get new clients, to make people more aware of what you do?

Dennis: Sometimes. But usually it's more valuable in terms of retention of the existing client than it is in terms of recruiting new clients. The recent meeting in Chicago was for a group that we don't represent, but it's tangentially related to one that we do represent. I did have somebody come up to me after that meeting and say, "Hey, I want to talk to you about the possibility of doing some work with us."

I was at a meeting in Boston last week, or two weekends ago, because of a patient advocacy group we work for, and a guy came up to me and said, "I'm from such and such a company and we are interested in this particular disease and would like to talk with you." Now, in that case, I will listen to him but I probably won't ultimately represent that company because there could be a conflict between the patient group and the company. We're very careful about that.

Leech: Even down the line, such a conflict might develop.

Dennis: Right now, everybody may love each other, but if it turns out that the company wants to get the FDA to allow something and the patient advocacy group doesn't think is safe, then we would have two clients in conflict. We go to great lengths to never get ourselves in that position because that is another thing that could destroy credibility in a hurry.

Leech: If the firm is hiring a new associate, what are you looking for?

Dennis: What we're looking for is knowledge and experience. With very few exceptions, we don't hire entry-level people. One of those exceptions is Tiffany at our front desk, who was an intern from Rutgers who we kept on to take over our front desk when somebody else retired and we moved our front desk person to become a vice president for administration. What we're generally looking for in the folks who are doing the legislative work or agency-related work is Hill experience or relevant agency experience.

For example, we just hired somebody because we're going to do more work in the defense area. We're trying to go where the money is, and the guy we hired just retired after twenty-seven years in the Navy. He was also the Navy's congressional liaison, so he knows virtually every member of the House or Senate who's ever traveled on a Defense Department trip to visit some base somewhere. He knows the Pentagon, knows all the admirals, and knows people in defense firms.

Another of our lobbyists was a legislative director for a member of Congress who lost the election. She had worked in some areas that were really relevant to what we do. Most of the people here have worked on Capitol Hill. I was there twelve years. Other people were there shorter or longer times.

We have one guy who worked for a member of Congress from Philadelphia for fourteen years, the last seven as chief of staff. I've got another person who worked at GAO [Government Accountability Office] for about five years and then was lobbying for an association. She was running a coalition and I went to the coalition meeting and saw her in a meeting with congressional staff. She was so good that I came back here and said to my partners, "I just met our next vice president." We hired her, and she's been fantastic.

We look for people who have relevant experience, good smarts, want to work, and have a little bit of that entrepreneurial spirit. Because essentially what we are doing every time we meet with a client is a job interview. We're selling all the time. When we pitch a prospective client, we're saying, "Hire me. I'm the best one for this job."

In the meeting this afternoon with the prospective client, I will go in and do five minutes on the background of the firm, how big we are, how long we've been around, and about our philosophy. Two of our lobbyists will talk about the substance of what's going on in higher education and in defense, and how we see those communities intersecting. Hopefully, I won't have to say another word.

Leech: What advice would you have for someone who thinks they want to be a lobbyist?

Dennis: The first thing is to get some experience, even though the Hill is enough to drive you nuts. It's not mandatory, but it's really helpful to have an inside understanding of how decisions get made on Capitol Hill, not just what you learn in your political science classes because it doesn't work that way over here anymore.

If you're inside it and you get to know the people, and you've got the TV with C-SPAN on all the time in the office, and you're meeting people from other offices, and you're involved in issues, and you're reading legislation and trying to figure out what makes sense and where your boss' positions have been, then all of that is a good foundation for working the system from the outside.

It's very different from the outside. Information is harder to come by. People who returned your calls for years won't return your calls or don't return them as quickly. You're struggling sometimes to put together the real story: "Why did they change their position on this? Why did they vote that way?" I think working hard inside Congress or inside an agency is very valuable, and easier than trying to learn it from the outside.

Leech: Even after the revolving-door glow disappears, that time inside is still helpful?

Dennis: Yeah. The concept of the revolving door is interesting. My experience is that it often only revolves one way. I was on the Hill for twelve years, then I left and never went back. I know some people who have done literal revolving: on the Hill as legislative director, out for a couple of years to lobby, then back on the Hill as chief of staff or committee staff director, out again to lobby some more. There are people who do that. It does raise eyebrows because it raises the question, "Are you trading on your inside information?"

It is, however, harder to trade on information now with the one-year or two-year lobbying bans for former government officials. A lot changes in a year. The turnover on Capitol Hill is twenty percent a year. By the second year out, two-fifths of the people are different.

Leech: Do you think the career of being a lobbyist is conducive to having a family?

Dennis: I have a wife, two grown kids who are both married, and two grandchildren, with a third one on the way. It can be difficult. But I'm in maybe a better position than some because I'm a partner and no one is going to say, "Why are you leaving?" or "Why weren't you in on Friday?" I just spent the middle of last week, the Fourth of July holiday, at the beach with my son, daughter-in-law, and grandson who is three months old.

Then on Thursday of that week, I drove to my daughter's house in New Jersey. I was basically out of here all of last week. But Congress was in recess and it was a holiday week. I probably was only getting seventy-five or eighty e-mails a day last week, because it slows up.

Leech: Because everyone was on vacation?

Dennis: Exactly. You can have a life. I went to Aruba for a week in April. I went to the beach Memorial Day week for the entire week, with both sets of kids and grandkids. You can do it. You have to manage your time well. If I'm going to take a vacation, the two weeks leading up to it are a pain because basically I have to anticipate what's coming up that week I'm going to be away and how much of it can I get done.

The other thing that we do here—and I think a lot of firms do this—is to run it kind of like a medical practice. Everything is a team-based approach. If I'm gone, liver doctors can call Erika and they know that she works with me. If she doesn't know the answer to whatever they're asking because it's something I've been working on, she can get the answer. My partners and I cover for each other, so it's manageable. You can have a life and do this, but you also can let it consume you. There's always something else you could be doing, and sometimes you have to just say, "Okay, the world is not going to end if I miss that meeting on Tuesday night at eight o'clock. I need to go home."

CHAPTER

7

Dale Florio

Founder and Managing Partner
Princeton Public Affairs Group

Dale Florio *is the founder and managing partner of Princeton Public Affairs Group, Inc. (PPAG), the largest state lobbying firm in the country. Located across the street from the State House in Trenton, NJ, the firm employs 13 professional lobbyists, including a former state Senate president and the longest-serving speaker of the state General Assembly.*

Florio has been named several times as one of the most influential people in the state by local magazines and news outlets. He has long been active in local politics: in 1979, when he was just 24, he was elected to the Borough Council in his hometown of Somerville, NJ. He later served 18 years as chairman of the Somerset County Republican Organization. He was appointed by Governor James Florio (no relation) to the New Jersey Building Authority, he was a member of Governor Christine Todd Whitman's transition team, and he served on the Finance Committee for the election campaign of Governor Chris Christie.

Before founding PPAG in 1987, Florio worked briefly as an administrative assistant in the General Assembly, and then in government affairs for the National Association of Manufacturers and for Philip Morris Companies Inc. He has a bachelor's degree in economics from Allegheny College and a law degree from Seton Hall University Law School.

Beth Leech: You have a degree in economics and a law degree. What made you decide to become a lobbyist?

Dale Florio: I had two gentlemen in my life who had a huge influence. One was a state legislator at the time, Walter Kavanaugh. He was in the state assembly in New Jersey, from my hometown of Somerville. The other individual,

Frank Torpey, was in public affairs for Johnson & Johnson, which has a significant footprint in the state. They were best friends. I was very active in athletics throughout my high school career, and they just took an interest in me. We went to the same church and they knew my parents, and so I would find myself in their company quite a bit.

Through Frank Torpey and Assemblyman Kavanaugh, I had a chance to observe the dynamics of elected politics and public affairs work. So, at the age of 24, at Kavanaugh's urging, I ran for Somerville Borough Council and was elected. However, before my first term was over, I realized that being an elected official was really not what I wanted to be.

Leech: What didn't you like about it?

Florio: At twenty-four, I was probably too young to be an elected official. I didn't enjoy the scrutiny. I remember during the first or second year of my term, I had a New Year's Eve party at my apartment, and the police came to the door and said that neighbors were complaining about the noise. And here I was an elected official in town—and it's probably not the kind of notoriety that you want. I decided that the microscope placed on a public person was not for me. I just wanted my privacy. At twenty-four, I did not want everything I did to be measured in the context of being a public official.

Leech: Was being a council member your full-time job?

Florio: No. I was working for the National Association of Manufacturers [NAM], the largest industrial trade association in the country. In the third year of my three year term, I started working for Philip Morris USA in New York City, doing government relations for the company. I really liked government-relations politics more than my elected official role. In May of my third year on council, I was married. My wife, Leslie, was already living in New York City. So you can say I left elected politics for love when I moved in with her!

Leech: What did you do when you worked for the National Association of Manufacturers?

Florio: NAM had regional offices around the country. We were the grass-roots arm of NAM. We kept New Jersey members aware of what was going in the nation's capital on issues that affected manufacturers, arranged meetings with members of Congress, and encouraged companies to join NAM.

Leech: Then you went to work for Philip Morris and you were based in New York. What did you do in that job?

Florio: This job change was a pivotal experience for me. I was twenty-seven, and Philip Morris was just beginning to create a public affairs unit in the tobacco side of the company. The individual who recruited me and became my boss, Bernie Robinson, was just a master at the art of public affairs. I learned a lot from him. I traveled the country to different state capitals, getting to know state legislators and other contract lobbyists. I participated in all the national conferences, such as the National Governors Association and the National Conference of State Legislatures. During that time, I had a chance to see the country, visiting forty-five different state capitals.

Leech: What year was this?

Florio: I worked for Philip Morris from 1982 to 1987. I was there at a time when secondhand smoke first became an issue among public policy professionals, when it was first argued that that secondhand smoke could be harmful to nonsmokers. Up to that point, the basic argument about smoking in public places was: "If I choose to smoke, it should be up to me." But now there was a new argument for the opposition, saying: "That's fine if you smoke, but maybe your secondhand smoke affects me as a nonsmoker." We also dealt with other issues, including taxes on cigarettes and tort reform issues. But during my time there, the debate about smoking in public really heated up.

Leech: How, as a lobbyist, do you deal with an issue like that—when a product is clearly bad for people?

Florio: Maybe it's part of my upbringing, but I am definitely somebody who believes you should be able to make your own decisions on what is best for you. I never smoked cigarettes but my mother did. My father would smoke an occasional cigar. So I made a determination that I wasn't going to be a smoker. Unless a product is outlawed, I have never liked the namby-pamby society of people telling me what to do. But it was tough because the secondhand smoke issue made it much more difficult.

Leech: My question, then, is how does one go about advocating to state legislators about an issue like that?

Florio: We basically said employers should make the determination about smoking in the workplace. We don't need the state, or the city, or the county making those rules. People think of a restaurant as a public place, but it's not a public place. It's a place where the public's invited. If you're in the hospitality business, you will make decisions in the best interest of your business, whether that is smoke-free or smoking sections. Back in the eighties, we definitely were defending the freedom of the entity to make its own decision. The country went through a period of people always being asked, "Do you want smoking or nonsmoking?" sections in the restaurant, and "Do you want to sit in the back of the plane or the front of the plane?"

Leech: Yes, I remember that separation of smokers and nonsmokers.

Florio: We were behind all those arguments.

Leech: When you were working for Philip Morris, you were going from state capital to state capital. But when you arrived in a city, you wouldn't necessarily know anybody, so how did you choose whom to approach?

Florio: What you're touching on is a reason why I eventually migrated to what I'm doing today. You're correct that when I went into Albany or some other state capital, I wouldn't necessarily know anyone or at least the people that were making the decisions on my issues. What you do is hire the principal public affairs group of Albany to work with you. Or you might join a trade association to help you stay informed or introduce you to key decision makers. At the end of the day, however, you probably need to hire a local public affairs consultant. The tobacco industry was under constant attack, so we had lobbyists in every state, which made it an expensive operation. So part of my job was to manage the consultants in my states. I worked in conjunction with my local lobbyists and provided them with recommended white papers, suggested testimony and research.

I soon learned that the only way to earn more money in the company was to move up the corporate ladder, which had the opposite effect of taking me out of the field of statehouse politics which I enjoyed so much. I was now being placed in a position to manage the people that were having the direct contact with legislators and lobbyists.

I decided that, given my entrepreneurial spirit, maybe I could be a statehouse lobbyist in New Jersey. I was from New Jersey and knew a lot of people there, so a buddy of mine, Pete McDonough, and I started the Princeton Public Affairs Group in February of 1987. Philip Morris and Essex County were our first clients.

Leech: That's interesting. Essex County obviously is a part of government itself, so why does it need a lobbyist?

Florio: I think people misunderstand why a public entity, or private entity for that matter, needs an advocate. County officials certainly know the state legislators from their area. But interactions with state legislative staff, and monitoring of legislative and agency processes need to be done on a daily basis. For example, the county needs to make sure that an appropriation that it wants for roads is included in a pending piece of legislation. Or it needs to keep track of where a roads project is in the approval process at the Department of Transportation. Somebody needs to keep an eye on all that and continue to push it along. Essex County could certainly assign somebody from the county to do that, but it's what we do full-time.

Leech: It might cost them more to have a staff person do it.

Florio: It certainly could, but now New Jersey Governor Christie has discouraged the notion of public entities using lobbyists. It's not a major part of our marketing efforts to have public entities as clients. The paperwork is often voluminous, and there are politics involved in getting hired or rehired. Essex County was one of our first clients because my original partner had just run the campaign of the county executive at the time, so there was an existing relationship.

Leech: Nowadays, I know you have a wide range of clients. But would you characterize your client base in any particular way?

Florio: No. Unlike federal lobbyists where you'll have a firm that specializes in transportation or budget, at the state level, we tend to be generalists. Some of my partners are subject-matter experts and are known throughout the state for their expertise. Our client mix ranges from nonprofits to some of the largest corporations in the country, and from law enforcement unions to the building trades. If there's a major legislative battle going on in New Jersey, we like to be in that fight no matter what side. It's good for business. It shows that we have the people power to help any client make a difference.

Leech: Just a couple of weeks ago you were very busy because the New Jersey budget was just about to be approved—or maybe not. Could you walk me through what happens during a time like that?

Florio: The budget period is an odd time in any state capital. But this is the first time in over twenty-five years that we've had a governor of one party and a legislature of another, so it's made for interesting budget discussions for the last three years.

The economy has been sluggish for the last five or six years, and, they're not giving away money—and I'd put "giving away" in quotes—like they used to. It was easier pre-2008 to argue for a line item for a nonprofit or for a new program. Due to the economy, it is very difficult now, so prospective clients and existing clients don't necessarily come running to ask, "Gee, is it possible to get $500,000 for the new Children's Hospital?" The governor has put out a budget, and this year it's $31 billion. The legislature is likely to work within that number and just end up moving money between and among line items. Increasingly clients are in the mode of just protecting what they have.

Leech: So how do you go about trying to preserve that?

Florio: The process starts in September or October before the governor makes his budget announcement the following February, because that's when the executive branch starts to prepare its individual agency budgets. If there is a particular state program or line item that affects one of our clients, then we work with the relevant state agency to get a sense of how the agency feels about the program, and whether the agency had been using all the money in that line item. We want to find out if there are any red flags. If there are issues that the agency has with the program, we try to figure them out, so that the agency can recommend to the treasurer that the program continue at the present funded amount.

Leech: How do you go about doing that? Do you set up meetings with people in the agency, or are you talking to them informally?

Florio: We start with informal conversations. We have some clients who may want to have a meeting, but then there are other clients who prefer that you handle the matter. It's a very informal process and requires a significant amount of intelligence gathering. If we can get a sense that things are going smoothly and absolutely the agency intends to recommend the same amount as last year, then usually the client will be fine. If we sense that there are issues, then we want to bring the client in and make sure that there's not a misunderstanding or a reason why the administrators of the program are uncomfortable. In these difficult economic times, maintaining funding can be difficult even if the program is widely supported and running well.

Leech: So do you call over there or does one of your lobbyists on staff call over there? Are you walking through the building? Are you popping into people's offices? How does the process work?

Florio: For the informal exchanges, it's often a matter of just picking up the phone and reaching the appropriate staff person.

Leech: Because you know these people already.

Florio: Most of the time someone in our office is going to know who the decision-maker might be. There are two types of people in state government: there are individuals who have come in with the new administration, and there are government professionals who have been there through multiple administrations. They might be civil service, but they also may be people who've demonstrated a value to the agency. In our business we want to know both groups of professionals. Fortunately, we have a group of lobbyists at PPAG who have far-ranging networks throughout state government, which help us navigate to the right staff person. So, we'll task the person who has the best relationship to check in with the appropriate person in that agency to find out: "What's going on? Do we need to bring the client in? What's the deal?" If it requires a meeting, fine, but it's like geometry—what's the shortest distance between two points? A straight line. But sometimes you have to be a little bit more strategic.

So there's not a lot of magic to it. The magic that does exist is the relationship that you've developed over time and how you nurture that relationship. It makes a big difference that people in the agencies know that if a client is with me or anybody on our team, that they will get very straight, direct answers to their questions. Administrators who don't know us do know of our reputation of being reputable brokers of information, and that's also helpful. A lobbyist's reputation really matters a lot.

If the program's having a difficult time or you expect the allotted amount to be reduced, we'll formally find out when the governor makes his budget announcement. But the legislature can propose to increase or restore funding, and so in March, April, May, and June when the legislature is reviewing the governor's budget we schedule a multitude of meetings with legislators, especially with those legislators who are on the Senate and Assembly budget-writing committees.

We find out early in June after all of our meetings if the legislature is going to push for the inclusion of additional dollars in the governor's budget. In New Jersey, when the governor receives the budget back from the legislature, he can use his line-item veto power to "red line" increases. So if the legislature restores funding or increases funding, the governor can cut or reduce the appropriation. However, he cannot restore funds. So, as you might imagine, the politics that get played during this time can be interesting. Two years ago, the governor wreaked havoc with the legislative budget when they tried to restore funds in a major way. The governor made major changes to the legislature's priorities. It was a little smoother this year. There were more discussions between the legislature and the governor, because nobody wanted to go through that again.

Leech: What is a workday like for you? Can you describe what you would do in an average day?

Florio: The first thing I do is get up and get on my stationary bike—that's my coffee in the morning. I need that to get ready for the day. In addition, I do some light weight training to keep muscle tone.

Leech: Do you ever ride on road?

Florio: During the week, I ride in place just because you can actually get a pretty good aerobic workout in about forty minutes. If you go on the road, you need more time, and time is precious during the week. During the summer on weekends, I get on the road for some long rides.

Let's take today. In the morning, I am meeting with you, and then I need to prepare for an eleven o'clock a.m. meeting. We represent a coalition of environmental groups that are hoping to get an amendment to the state constitution on next year's ballot that would dedicate a certain amount of money to funding open space. They had hoped to get it accomplished this year, but it does not appear that the politics and the economy will allow for that to happen. This morning, we're going to meet with senior officials in the governor's office. Last year, because the state revenue picture was not good, we all agreed that we would wait, and so we're beginning discussions now. Remember, I said September or October. It's not even August yet, and we're actually beginning to go back to people to remind them of the importance of looking ahead to next year. So we would hope to get it on next year's ballot.

Leech: What steps need to be done to get an issue put on the ballot? How will your office be involved?

Florio: We believe this issue will be a nonpartisan issue. The legislature and the governor are very supportive of open space. With the shoreline that we have and because we're the most densely populated state, people are sensitive to space and water. The issue really then is how can we fund it, and we're looking for a permanent dedication of money. It's a big step, because economies go up and down, and any dedication of funds takes the money off the table for future generations. But again, open space is a major issue here in the state and we know that the governor and the legislative leaders have both expressed interest. The question, then, is timing. After we meet with the governor's office, we'll go and meet again with legislative staff. We would need to get legislation passed by early September of next year authorizing the constitutional amendment to be placed on the ballot.

Leech: If you succeed and it gets on the ballot, would you also be involved in the campaign to pass it?

Florio: Hopefully, yes, and that'll be the fun phase of developing the messaging to the public as to why they should be supportive.

Leech: You are pretty involved in politics or have been pretty involved in politics in addition to your role here as a lobbyist. You have been on lots of boards and commissions. You were chairman of the Somerset Republican Committee for a long time. How do the official politics and the advocate policy sides work together?

Florio: Although I realized that elected politics was really not my interest, both lobbying and being a party official allow me to play a role in political affairs. As I said earlier, I grew up in Somerville, and after I returned to New Jersey from living in New York City, I saw the county party chairmanship as way for me to be helpful to my home base party but still not have the demands that are required of elected officials. I helped raise the money and select candidates, without having to be a candidate myself. I became chairman in '92, right when Christie Whitman was looking to run for governor—and she was from Somerset County. I felt the pressure as a new party leader to make sure that Somerset County performed well in terms of votes for her.

Having the governor be from our county certainly raised the profile of the Somerset County GOP and gave me a chance to meet people that I might not have otherwise met.

Leech: Was there a perception that your firm therefore had an inside track to the administration?

Florio: I don't mean to sound naïve, but it took me a while to understand the relationship. I didn't plan it that way. I ran for county chairman because I wanted to do it and help lead an organization. But it became clear to me over time that there was a perception that enhanced the reputation of the firm. We had and still have many key Republicans and Democrats at PPAG, but my dual role as a founder of the firm and a Republican associated with the Whitman administration was certainly a plus.

I was always careful not to mix the two. I think, quite frankly, that although there were certainly pluses to the connection, there were also burdens. It became difficult to work publicly against any of Whitman's initiatives, and we tried to avoid those kinds of public clashes. That's why I made an early determination that the firm would not represent any clients that had anything before county government in Somerset County. I didn't want anybody questioning my motives or interests. I wanted county and municipal office holders to rely on me for political advice and counsel. I wanted them to feel like my advice to them was always in their best interest and the best interest of the party and not some hidden personal interest. It really served me well. It was something I wanted to do right at the outset of my chairmanship, and it helped tremendously.

Leech: So you didn't have that conflict of interest?

Florio: Exactly. We do a lot of county and local work for various clients around the state. It's very common for firms like ours. I just stayed out of Somerset County. It was the best decision I ever made.

Leech: We were talking about your day.

Florio: I only gave you half the day.

Leech: Yes, we are only up to your eleven a.m. meeting. What happens after that?

Florio: The Norwegian ambassador to the UN is here for a brief meeting on energy.

Leech: And why are you meeting with the ambassador?

Florio: We represent NRG, which is one of the largest energy consortiums in the country. They're headquartered here in New Jersey, just up the road in Princeton. We are having some preliminary discussions about Norway becoming a business partner with NRG. Then, I'm going to hop in my car and do a one o'clock p.m. conference call with several preschool providers. These companies provide services to school districts. There's an issue of funding that they want to discuss.

Then, I'll head to a meeting at the Sports and Exhibition Authority near Giants Stadium at two p.m. That meeting is with a client that provides interactive services for horse racing that makes sure that when people wager, the bet goes through. The Sports Authority helps oversee and manage the horse-racing facilities.

Leech: What sorts of things would a client like that need help with?

Florio: They want to talk about maintaining and expanding their services that they presently provide to the Authority. We anticipate that sports betting is coming to New Jersey. Last year, we worked on the successful referendum to allow for sports betting. We also helped pass the legislation to implement the question that was placed on the ballot. So the client wants to discuss what the world might look like in New Jersey should sports betting become a reality. We also want to discuss the number of off-track wagering sites for horse racing. Only two have been built. I think we're authorized for twelve. The client has some ideas on how the state can realize the full potential of off-track wagering.

The meeting at the Authority will likely last from two o'clock p.m. to three-thirty p.m. I have a six p.m. meeting tonight at the Adult Day Center of Somerset County, which is one of the boards that I serve on. I hope to catch up on phone calls between the time I leave the Authority and the six p.m. meeting.

Leech: How did you happen to get involved with adult day care?

Florio: Politics can ring hollow at times. You have some clients that treat you as a commodity. You have political friends, and then you have real friends, and so I was looking for some other meaning. I inquired of a woman who ran the human services division in Somerset County, "Is there a nonprofit for battered women and or a children's nonprofit?" And she said to me, "Dale, everybody who's looking to be a volunteer always thinks of kids and women. Nobody really thinks of senior citizens. If you really want to have an impact and be helpful, why don't you go and join the board of the Adult Day Center of Somerset County." She was absolutely right.

Leech: Do you have other things after this? Or are we at the end of the day? When do you usually go home?

Florio: This will be the first time in a while that I'll probably get home by seven-thirty p.m. Last Monday, it was eleven p.m. and last night I arrived home at ten p.m.

Leech: Wow. So one of my questions was whether lobbying at the state level is conducive to family life. Is the answer no?

Florio: I actually think it's much easier at the state level than it is at the federal level. One thing that is different in New Jersey compared with a lot of other states is that legislators go home at the end of the day. They don't stay overnight which helps reduce the number of evening activities in Trenton, although there are political fundraisers throughout the week, usually around the state in the home districts of legislators. In a lot of state capitals, the legislators sleep over because it's too far to go home.

The state also has a very strict laws requiring disclosure of meals with legislators and gifts for legislators. Years ago, when I first started, you could go out to dinner with legislators on Mondays and Thursdays, when they were in session. You would spend time and discuss what happened that day. Now you are required to report these activities, so it's really reduced the social side of the business, which is unfortunate. I think the interaction between and among legislators and public affairs consultants is a good thing. The public has deemed it improper and has demonized these kinds of activities.

Leech: Because the legislators don't want that record?

Florio: Yes, legislators feel intimidated by the reporting process. Quite frankly, I don't blame them. But in terms of family life, again, I think it's a little bit easier for my generation to say, "Hey, I've got to go to my kid's Little League game." I think it was harder for my parents to do that, but I think it's easier now, which is good. It makes you a better person. It rounds you out. I have always worked hard to find the time to make sure family life doesn't suffer. I have great spouse who has made up for those times where I just couldn't be there. Believe me, I've put in a lot of time and I've worked hard, but I made sure that I was coaching the boys and going to my daughter's gymnastics meets.

Leech: What do you end up spending the most time doing in your job?

Florio: Fifty percent of the time it's managing client expectations. Then there is the administrative side of running a business, which is my responsibility as managing partner, and which can take a good bit of time—a good twenty-five percent. The remaining twenty-five percent involves actually interacting with the public, and county, and state officials. The time spent meeting with the official is minuscule compared to the time spent with the client, getting them to organize themselves properly. For instance, for this meeting at eleven a.m., we first had a conference call with the client to review the talking points and their expectations for the meeting.

Leech: How do you deal with the popular opinion about lobbyists? The public mostly doesn't understand what lobbyists do. And, to the extent that they think about what lobbyists do, they think that it's bad.

Florio: I've gotten beyond that. I don't feel like I've ever been excluded from the neighborhood party because of what I do. I speak to high school groups and college classes a fair amount, and we talk about lobbying, so that they understand that it's more than just who you know. Lobbying has evolved into a much more sophisticated profession than it once was. But whenever a lobbyist gets in trouble, there's always going to be the perception that lobbying is unnecessary. If you look at our marketing materials you'll notice that we refer to ourselves as public affairs professionals as opposed to lobbyists.

But scandals are always going to surface. There are always going to be bad actors in any profession. Every four years, when all the presidential candidates spend so much money on running for office, it reinforces that idea about what's wrong with politics. But it's the American system, so I've become desensitized to it.

Leech: What qualities do you think a lobbyist needs, and what do you look for when you're hiring a new associate here?

Florio: We have a good reputation for brainpower here. I think it's easy for a lobbyist to get by on relationships. Our people have subject-matter substance. I'm looking for people who really have an interest in the public policy side of politics. Obviously, you have to have a personality. You can't be somebody who has trouble interacting with people. First and foremost, you need to be smart. Second, you need to be socially engaging—not necessarily a glad-hander, but be able to operate in a social setting. Then I look for the two other basics: writing and verbal skills.

I'll give you a good example. We have a young associate here who was an intern for us two or three years ago. The individual met me in a class where I spoke, and asked to intern with us. We accepted the student as an intern. The intern asked to come back in the fall as an unpaid intern, so we agreed. We do not compensate the interns during the school year, but we do pay them during the summer.

One of the projects that the intern worked on involved preparing a table on cigarette taxes for a client. The intern came into the office one day and said, "Dale, I spoke to the director of the New Jersey Division of Taxation"—I didn't tell the person to call the director of taxation—"and I told him that I thought the information they gave me was wrong."

So I said, "What did he say?"

And the student said, "He told me I was right that they had made a mistake. So I showed them what they did wrong and they fixed it, and here's the information."

I was impressed. First of all, I didn't tell the intern to call the director of taxation, but the individual somehow got him on the phone. Our intern found a flaw in the way they were calculating their taxes from quarter to quarter, and needless to say, that person is with us today.

Leech: That's a great story. So you're looking for some initiative, too.

Florio: Yes, a little initiative can go a long way. Sometimes you find a diamond in the rough and you need to hire that person even if you were not looking to add to staff.

Leech: What advice do you have for people who are interested in a career in public affairs?

Florio: I did it differently than most people, because I worked in corporate America. I did have a brief stint working for Walt Kavanaugh, the state legislator I mentioned earlier. But most people get their experience in government or on a campaign, and I think that's the preferable way to do it because it gives you a chance to meet the government decision-makers of tomorrow. I was lucky. As it turned out, my original partner was somebody who had been working for the legislature, and I had the corporate contacts to help us generate clients.

But again, I don't care what your major is—verbal skills and writing skills will always be important. We don't write as many letters as we once did, but we're certainly doing e-mails and memos that you attach to e-mails. Communication skills are critical, because clients want information. I tell young people to write and take public speaking classes. Most people are nervous about speaking in public. Colleges now, and certainly high schools, are encouraging more and more public speaking, and they require students to do more of it, which I think is good. I used to say, "You are as good as your Rolodex." Of course, today young people look at you and say, "What's a Rolodex?"

Leech: Now it's your list of contacts.

Florio: Now I pick up my cell phone and wave it and say, "You're as good as your contact list."

Leech: Thank you very much for taking the time to speak with me.

Florio: I envy you on your project. I keep saying that I'm going to write a book when I head out the door. We're celebrating our twenty-fifth anniversary as a firm this year, and we've booked a weekend at a historic hotel on the beach in Cape May, New Jersey. Everybody will take off on Friday and bring their significant other and their kids if they want. We have somebody here who is making a movie about our twenty-five years. We pulled out old newspaper clips, and we were looking at the many legislative battles that we engaged in and saying, "Wow, we did that."

Leech: You've been involved in a lot of issues over those twenty-five years.

Florio: One story we found was from the *Bergen Record* newspaper back in the mid-nineties, before all the pay-to-play laws that restricted gifts from lobbyists. We had a client that was sponsoring an event at the Super Bowl and wanted me to see whether maybe some legislators wanted to go. I was just starting out, and I remember giving out one of my business cards, and across the top of it I wrote, "Do you want to go to the Super Bowl?"

I don't know what happened, but the *Bergen Record* did a five-part series on lobbying in the state. A picture of my business card with the Super Bowl message ended up illustrating one of the installments in the series. So I learned how to be more discreet. That is one of the stories that I had forgotten all about until they were going through our archive of clips for our twenty-fifth anniversary.

CHAPTER

8

Christina Mulvihill

Director, Government and Public Affairs Sony Electronics USA

***Christina Mulvihill** is the director of government and public affairs at the consumer electronics giant, Sony Electronics USA. It's a relatively small office for such a large company—just two registered lobbyists—but Sony makes use of hired lobbying firms in addition to its in-house staff. In 2011, Sony Electronics reported total lobbying expenditures of $500,000.*

Before coming to Sony in 1998, Mulvihill was special assistant to the US ambassador to the Organization for Economic Cooperation and Development (OECD). She was the senior legislative assistant to Sen. Mike DeWine (R-OH) and held several staff positions with members of the House of Representatives, including Rep. Ileana Ros-Lehtinen (R-FL).

Mulvihill holds a bachelor's degree in English literature from Sweet Briar College and a master's degree from Johns Hopkins' Paul H. Nitze School of Advanced International Studies. At the time of this interview, she was on maternity leave from Sony and managed the interview while simultaneously feeding, burping, and entertaining her two-month-old daughter, Reagan.

Beth Leech: How did you begin your career?

Christina Mulvihill: If we go way back, it probably started when I was very little and I would go with my mother to work the polls during elections. She was very active in local politics. I would always go into the voting booth with her. At home, we would have political discussions at our table. From a very young age, my parents discussed politics and how the government worked with us. I knew the House of Representative and the Senate before it was taught to me in school.

Leech: Where did you grow up?

Mulvihill: I was born and raised in Miami. I lived in Miami until I was twelve. Then we moved to Georgia, and I went to college in Virginia. While I was in college, I came up to Washington to intern like so many people do, but I didn't work on Capitol Hill. I interned with a trade association that worked on issues related to higher education. Many trade associations have bits and pieces that deal with Capitol Hill, but they also deal with bigger issues that are specific to what their members do.

I knew early on that the sexy jobs and the people that everyone looked up to were the Capitol Hill staffers. Of course, that's what I wanted to do. So after college I got a job working the front desk in a congressional office, the lowest of the lowly in a House office. When I started, my take-home pay was a little over $400 a month. I couldn't even make my rent. My parents had to help support me even though I had graduated from college. From there I moved up, and I've worked for a lot of different bosses. Jumping from job to job on Capitol Hill is not seen as a bad thing. In the professional world, the downtown world, your longevity with a company is admired, but that is not always true on Capitol Hill.

My first meaty job—beyond fluff work as a Capitol Hill tour guide—was with Congresswoman Ileana Ros-Lehtinen. In the last session, she was chairwoman of the House Foreign Affairs Committee. She just left that recently. I was with her for several years. I was on her personal staff and she took me over to committee, which are two very different experiences on Capitol Hill.

Leech: Could you describe that? How is committee staff different from personal staff?

Mulvihill: When you're in a personal office of a member of Congress, you're really dealing with constituent issues. I don't necessarily mean helping somebody get a Social Security check that never showed up, although that is one function that the office will serve. As personal staff, you deal with policy issues from the perspective of that constituency. On committee staff, you're dealing with the aggregate-level policy effects. Even though your boss's position will go into it, the way the system is designed, the responsibility of a committee staffer is to look at the overall policy area and become the subject-matter expert on whatever committee it is. There's a different focus when you're personal office versus when you're on committee.

I left to go to graduate school in Chicago and missed Capitol Hill and politics terribly. After a short while, I came back to Washington and spent a year in the House. Then I decided that, to make my record stand out, I would go to work in the Senate. Capitol Hill staffers usually pick a chamber—either the Senate or the House—and stick with that chamber. I wanted to have both experiences. That's when I went to work for Senator Mike DeWine from Ohio.

Leech: How long were you there?

Mulvihill: I was with him when he first started in the Senate in 1995. I stayed there for two years. Working the Senate is very different from working in the House. I jokingly say that it's like moving from the junior varsity side up to the varsity side, because as a staffer, you have so much more responsibility. Senators' schedules are just so incredibly busy. It was a different experience that I felt fortunate to have.

Leech: There are fewer senators, they're on more committees, and they have more responsibilities. So do the staff as well?

Mulvihill: Yes. I always advise people who want to work on Capitol Hill that the best way to start off is in the House, because there are few staff members in each office. At some point, your boss will be super busy and will look to see who has the least amount of work at that moment, and give them an interesting responsibility. For example, you might not be the press secretary, you could be a legislative assistant, and your boss has a speech or several speeches to give. If the press secretary is busy, the legislative assistant might get to write the speech. In the House, a staffer gets that broad experience. In the Senate, that would never happen. A staffer's job in the Senate is very well-defined, and there is less room to move up the ladder.

So I tell people, "Start off in the House. If you like it, if you find you like a certain issue, then you will know where to focus." In the Senate, a lot of staffers have been there for twenty or more years. They almost have, dare I say, more power than a House member. They wield that kind of power.

Leech: Why do you think that is?

Mulvihill: I think part of it is longevity and that they become the experts. There's no way that a senator can sit down and read through every bill, know every issue, and negotiate every deal. So that responsibility falls to these staffers who often have a lot of experience. In the House, you have some members who may only be elected for one or two terms, and they just don't have the pull or experience that a very senior staffer in the Senate has.

Leech: Staffers are more likely to stay longer in the Senate because . . . ?

Mulvihill: It's a very well-respected position here in Washington. When you're at a cocktail party and you are the chief of staff to a long-serving Senator, you are viewed as having a lot of power.

Leech: While you were in the Senate, what was your position?

Mulvihill: I was a legislative assistant for DeWine. I did his committee work, although I was not paid by the committee. There was a lot of change happening in the Senate. A lot of the senators at that time were old school. They came from a time period when there were a lot of friendships across party lines, and deals were made based on personal relationships. It's more contrarian up there right now—there is a lot more infighting. The Senate, historically, never had grenade throwers. In the House, they have always had grenade throwers, these outlier members of Congress who show up and want to stir the pot.

In the Senate things were different because senators would sit down, have a glass of wine together, figure out a bill, and that bill would pass. That was how work was done in the old days. Things slowly have changed, and now things are dramatically different. It was the end of that older era when I was in the Senate.

Leech: Why did you decide to leave?

Mulvihill: I was a little burned-out and I had a great job offer. I left. I'll tell you, it's very difficult to leave as a staffer, because you really just get sucked into that lifestyle and it is a twenty-four-hour, seven-day-a-week job. I remember my first free weekend after I stopped working in the Senate. I didn't know what to do—because as a staffer, I would work every weekend. If you walked into my office on a Saturday, it would look like it was a Tuesday afternoon because everyone was there working. I adapted and changed lifestyles, but to this day, when I go up to the Senate, my heart beats a little bit faster because I kind of wish I was back there. How crazy is that?

Leech: When you left the Senate, you worked for the Organization for Economic Cooperation and Development in Paris. How did that come about?

Mulvihill: A woman I know became the US ambassador to the OECD. I had a personal relationship with her, and so I became her assistant even though she was of a different party. There are lots of friendships and relationships in Washington that go beyond parties. For instance, I know plenty of Republican women who love and admire Stephanie Cutter—who was Obama's deputy campaign manager—and vice versa.

Leech: Those sorts of connections are not partisan, which I'm assuming is helpful for you in your job?

Mulvihill: Yes. We sit back and we kind of laugh about it. It's like that old cartoon with the wolf and the sheepdog clocking in, then fighting, and then at the end of the day, clocking out and going for a drink together. It's exactly like that.

Leech: What brought you back to Washington?

Mulvihill: I got the opportunity to start Sony's Washington office. And there are a lot of positives about working for a big-name company here in Washington. I've never been denied access to any office. And that is despite the fact that Sony does not have a PAC and we do not give any corporate money. We don't play the money game at all. That is a separate game that's played here in DC. Obviously, I'm aware of it, but I've never been privy to the access that goes with having one of those huge, multimillion-dollar PACs.

But working for a name company provides its own access, because there are Sony constituents in every congressional district in the country. Everyone knows Sony as a brand. That makes my job a lot easier.

Leech: What skills did you have that allowed you to get that job and to transfer over to the lobbying side?

Mulvihill: The skill set I use today, working at Sony, had to be developed. It didn't necessarily come with me from Capitol Hill. On Capitol Hill, you learn the process. You learn the flow, but you don't necessarily have to learn the issues because you're dealing with so many issues and they change all the time. The issues you deal with are whatever's currently on the radar screen. I created a PowerPoint presentation to give at Sony to try to explain the Capitol Hill process in business terms, because at Sony, I'm dealing with businessmen. They spend all day with pie charts and graphs. They have no idea how things work on the Hill.

I called it the "public policy life cycle," because business people are used to dealing with products and products have life cycles. A policy life cycle starts with the media. The media will pick up on something and there will then be public outrage. An example a few years ago was when the story broke about lead in toys coming from China having poisoned some kids. The public was outraged. There were stories on the news every night and in the newspapers. People are following the story and Capitol Hill feels under pressure to react.

Congress does one of two things. Either they ignore the situation completely or they act with a sledgehammer. If it's the sledgehammer, then the entire time the story is in the news, Capitol Hill staffers are working behind the scenes to put together a congressional hearing to milk the story for more publicity for their boss and/or they are putting together legislation to address the issue. That legislation will pass quickly and really without full due process because they don't really always vet things. They pass and then later they go back and look at what they've done.

In the past few years, Congress has kicked a lot of the practical application of policy to the agencies. As a result, we have to focus on agency rulemaking procedures. The case of the toys went to the Consumer Product Safety Commission. Then the focus for the downtown lobbyists moved from Capitol Hill to the various agencies that were regulating. For corporate lobbyists like me, contacting people on Capitol Hill is really about fifteen percent to twenty percent of the job. The bulk of the work is off the Hill now, and possibly further. Some issues might even end up before the Supreme Court.

Leech: Are you dealing with that whole range of issues from all three branches of government?

Mulvihill: Oh, yes, and most corporate lobbyists do unless they work for a big powerhouse of a company. The company would have to have a very sophisticated operation, with fifty to one hundred people in Washington working either as Capitol Hill lobbyists or as specialists to deal with regulation on an everyday basis. They might be specialists in customs laws, or if it's a telecom company, it will have several Federal Communications Commission specialists on staff. There's really only a handful of companies that do that. Most companies have one person or one group that deals with everything.

Leech: How big is your office?

Mulvihill: With our assistant, there are three of us. We also hire a lot of outside people, consultants, and lobbying firms.

Leech: What do these lobbying firms that are on retainer for Sony do for the company? What tasks are they put on?

Mulvihill: For a company that doesn't have access, the lobbying firm will provide access. This is what I always ask people who want to hire a lobby firm. My first question is, "Do you want access?" Meaning, "Do you want access to a certain member, or senator, or leadership?"

Or are you looking for expertise? Sometimes expertise is not an issue because, frankly, companies are full of experts. There's no one in Washington who is as sophisticated as people outside the Beltway on issues related to what the company actually does. I ask if they need experts on governmental process once the issue leaves the Hill—for example, dealing with a small agency within the Department of Transportation or dealing with the FCC. Different lobby shops will have different experts on staff. Those experts might not know the issue at all, but they'll know the process.

Leech: Can you walk us through an issue that you've worked on relatively recently, explaining how that came on your radar and what steps you had to take along the way to deal with it?

Mulvihill: There are so many. I'm like triage. I see problems come in and I figure out how we solve them as a company. It might not be with me. We might have to hire a special law firm or a special lobby shop. This is happening constantly. The other thing I jokingly say is that I can speak two languages. I can speak Washington and I can speak business. I act as a translator between the two. The people I deal with within Sony are businessmen. They're in the business of making a product and making profits. They look at people in Washington like we have horns because logic does not often play into how Washington works. The business people are usually very practical, logical people.

The same thing is true for Washington. There are very few people I have ever come across in Washington who truly understand how a business operates. When I make references to things like supply chains, my business guys know exactly what I mean. Capitol Hill has zero idea what I'm talking about. I recently was dealing with a senior staffer from the House Ways and Means Committee, which deals with taxation. That staffer said to me, "I need you to explain to me why we need these Sony jobs."

I replied, "Really? You need me to sit down and explain why we need jobs for the country?"

This was a staffer who really should understand. This was not some twenty-two-year-old in a first job.

Leech: How did you manage to speak both languages? How did you learn the other language?

Mulvihill: I had to learn corporate as an adult because I went to a liberal arts college and corporate was not taught there. I learned a little in graduate school, when I studied international economics. Working on Capitol Hill, you only learn to speak Washington. It shocks me sometimes how little the two groups are able to communicate. There are few people who really do the translation well.

Leech: What was a recent issue that you worked on?

Mulvihill: One issue that is still going on and will be going on for the next ten years is regulating energy use by consumer electronics products: how, for example, your TV uses energy while it's on and also while it's off. That issue started with a few members of Congress and Senators who were lobbied by a nonprofit organization called the American Council for an Energy-Efficient Economy. These members of Congress said, "Hey, you know what? These products are energy vampires and we should regulate them. We should introduce legislation that would limit the amount of kilowatts that a television or any other product could use." They started with a list and introduced a bill. Our industry had not been heavily regulated, the way the energy and telecom industries are and have been for a long time.

Leech: Consumer electronics not so much?

Mulvihill: Not so much—but on some things, yes. In fact, one exercise I did while at Sony was to look at the number of agencies that regulate the sale of a television. How many agencies do you think have a finger in trying to sell a TV to a consumer?

Leech: I can only think of three possible ones right now. How many is it?

Mulvihill: About twenty.

Leech: Oh, wow.

Mulvihill: Everything from the IRS, which affects how it's taxed, to agencies that get involved in where products come from and how products interact with one another. There is the Department of Commerce, the National Institute of Standards in Technology, and the Consumer Product Safety Commission. We also deal with the Department of Transportation, because we have to transport the TVs, and the Department of Agriculture because it regulates the paper on which the warranty and product information are printed. The list goes on. It's pretty crazy.

After the legislation to regulate energy use by consumer electronics was introduced, the nonprofit organization that raised the issue went to the two major agencies that regulate energy use: the Department of Energy and the Environmental Protection Agency. At Sony, we did what I'm going to call the "state dance," because some of the state legislatures started introducing similar legislation.

Then the industry and the trade associations started meeting to figure out "How are we going to address this problem?" Some of the proposed legislation at the state level was very prescriptive. It was going so far as to tell us what the design of the TV was going to be. Of course, that's what makes a Sony TV different from a Sharp or Mitsubishi. If the government standardized design, obviously that would be a problem for our company. Sony's philosophy is that the government should not be picking technology winners or losers. In TVs, there is plasma versus LCD versus LED. There are so many different options. We didn't think the government should come in, and through legislation or regulation, ban one or the other.

Leech: So this issue comes up and all these agencies are involved. What do you as a lobbyist actually have to do?

Mulvihill: My first stop would be going to see staff in the senator's office or the House member's office who introduced the bills to explain the issue to them. There's no way a staffer could possibly understand what one of my internal engineers does. It's just not possible—even if they have expertise in issue X, whether it is a foreign policy issue or a regulatory issue—that they're going to know as much as the people who spent their entire careers dealing with that topic. I would start there.

I work a lot with our trade associations, because we don't have the resources to do it all ourselves. We could have three full-time staffers dealing with this.

Leech: What trade associations are you particularly allied with?

Mulvihill: For us, the Consumer Electronic Association [CEA] is very important. There are a lot of others: the Digital Electronics Group [DEG], the

Blu-ray Disc Association, the Renewable Energy Markets Association [REMA], and the Institute of Electrical and Electronics Engineers [IEEE]. Each has a different mission. Some, like REMA, do a lot of political activity. Some, like IEEE, are more what I would call "industry associations"—meaning they do certification, and training, and a lot of things other than policy.

The politics and policy part is very small in the CEA. It does the big annual electronics trade show that just happened in Las Vegas. Most of the members of that organization don't follow or understand the policy part at all. Instead, they are interested in how to install a new car stereo and who is allowed to train the installers at Best Buy. Then, we have other trade associations that really do nothing but focus on Washington. Even within the trade association political world, there can be a big difference with regard to Washington. Some associations are very sophisticated and some are not.

There's a trade association for every possible group you can think of. I hired a professional organizer to help me organize my baby's room. There's an organization of professional organizers.

Leech: Of course there is.

Mulvihill: Somebody should write a funny book about all the different associations and their interests.

Leech: One of my favorites is the National Frozen Pizza Association.

Mulvihill: Trade associations are important politically because they do follow issues and file comments on proposed regulations. One recent regulatory issue that Sony was involved in dealt with the transport of lithium ion batteries. These are the batteries that are in every smartphone. These batteries are everywhere. I remember doing a double-take on one comment filing.

Leech: To clarify, when a regulation is proposed, there is a period in which anyone can formally submit information and comment in support of or against the regulation.

Mulvihill: Yes, and this comment was from the National Association of Funeral Home Directors. I wanted to know why funeral home directors would have an interest in lithium ion batteries and transporting them. It turns out that because the way the rule was written, it affected bodies that had to be transported, because some of them would have pacemakers or other devices with batteries in their bodies.

Leech: And the funeral home trade association was on top of things and realized that.

Mulvihill: It never would have occurred to me that a regulation would apply to a dead person, but it did the way it was drafted. So the funeral home directors had to file comments.

Leech: So, like the funeral directors and the batteries, you would turn to your trade associations for help with the issue of regulation of energy usage in consumer electronics.

Can you talk a little bit more about what happens during the notice and comment period within an agency?

Mulvihill: First, you and/or your attorneys will put together a huge package of comments. Comments can be just a simple typed letter, but more often, there's an economic impact study, industry statistics, and sometimes a public relations component. It can take months to put together a comment package.

Every agency operates a little differently. As a result, it's a good idea to hire a lobby shop that has somebody with expertise in that particular agency to help you through the process. Some agencies operate very quickly. They'll put out a notice of proposed rulemaking, you have to get your comments in within the month, and almost immediately there's a new rule. In other agencies, it can take years. In yet other agencies, they'll put together a study group. They'll look at an issue. They'll discuss it. The administrative rulemaking process is just so bizarre—I have no other way to describe it. In addition, once a rule has been proposed, you can no longer talk to the agency. The one time you should be talking to them, you're legally barred from doing so.

Leech: What do you do instead?

Mulvihill: You go see people at the White House. You go to the Office of Management and Budget. They'll have somebody there who can listen to you, but they can't do anything. That's it. If the proposed rule would have an economic impact of over $100 million, then it also would go through an interagency review process.

Leech: Is there anything else you would be doing?

Mulvihill: At the same time, I would be working with people internally to explain what's happening, what's been proposed, what the impact would be to our company, and to explore possible solutions. There's always more than one solution. We run through the list. Businesspeople want to know time frames, cost, and specifics. Here in Washington, people don't really think in those terms. If an issue lingers on for two or three years, then it lingers on for two or three years.

Leech: What does an average day look like for you when you're back at the office? How much of your time would you spend on different types of tasks, and what would those different sorts of tasks include?

Mulvihill: Lots of e-mail. That's really new. In the last couple of years, there have been a lot of media reports on how congressional staffers prefer to be contacted via e-mail rather than meeting because they're so busy. So I do a lot of e-mailing. I often have several events to attend, although the work is cyclical—so, depending on the congressional schedule, my schedule will be different. It depends on whether Congress is in session.

Leech: What sort of events?

Mulvihill: Fundraisers or meet-and-greets. It depends on the member or senator as to what they have. If they're senior, they probably going to have an expensive fundraiser in the evening. If they're not senior, they're going to have a meet-and-greet in the morning to meet people so that they can raise money.

Leech: You'll end up going to these despite the fact that Sony doesn't have a PAC?

Mulvihill: Right. I will give individually to people whom I support personally. It doesn't necessarily have to benefit Sony. It depends. Of course, we're at the stage now where a lot of the staffers that I knew when I first went to Capitol Hill are now running for office themselves, so there is a personal relationship to support. You don't have to support, but obviously if a friend of yours runs for big office, you're going to go to their fundraiser.

Leech: Okay. We're walking through your day.

Mulvihill: My days at work usually start at eight a.m. I might go to an eight o'clock meet-and-greet somewhere and then I would go back to the office. I would read the inside-Washington publications: *Politico*, the *National Journal*, and *Roll Call*. If it's a Monday, I probably have trade-association conference calls in which we plan the week ahead. If it's during the week when Congress is in session, there would be several hearings that you might want to monitor, watching at your desk on C-SPAN.

Sometimes, for a big hearing, I'll go up to the Hill. There is a networking component. You really want to physically interact with people, both colleagues from the industry and government officials, when everybody is gathered at one place. It is a chance to establish rapport with colleagues in industry, with the staffers who are there, and the members or senators involved. If it's a very hot topic, I'll want to sit there and listen, not just to the statements, but to the questions and answers. I would be looking for things like: How hostile is the member or senator in their questioning? How friendly are they? Are they asking questions that seem appropriate? I remember one congressman who asked the same three questions at every hearing, no matter the topic. He obviously didn't fully understand the issues.

Then usually there are lunch meetings with trade associations. There are a million different organizations. Obviously, I'm female, and I do a lot of female-in-politics-related events. They have luncheons or afternoon gatherings. I do more e-mails. I'm on a lot of conference calls based on the current issue.

I'll touch base with any outside lobbyist or law firm. I'm always reporting back to the home office in California.

When Congress is in recess and members and senators go back to the district or state, I might set up meetings out there for them. When Sony had a lot of manufacturing in the United States, we'd want them to tour our plants—have them see it in person. We can say we have five hundred jobs in city X, but until a member or senator actually sees it, it doesn't really have an impact on them. At one point, we had a huge manufacturing plant in Pennsylvania with six thousand employees. I invited one of the two long-serving senators six or seven times a year to visit that plant, and never did he come. We were a huge employer. I was able to get the secretary of the Treasury to come once, but I couldn't get that senator.

Leech: Okay, we're in your afternoon now. What else is happening in this day?

Mulvihill: I like networking. I think it's an important part of the business here. I make up a call list every week and I try to get through to everyone on that list. Usually it's at least ten people that I want to touch base with, to reach out, find out what's happening with them, and where they are job-wise, especially after a new Congress is sworn in. You want to just be current on where everybody is.

Then I get ready for the crowd of five o'clock receptions or events. Usually, I have those maybe two nights a week, sometimes three or four. If I really wanted to do an event every night, I absolutely could.

Leech: Are these mostly fundraising events?

Mulvihill: No. They would be group discussions, conferences, and speakers. Some have a huge impact. I either show up just to listen, or I might be participating in some way, shape, or form. The Council on Foreign Relations, for example, does events all the time: breakfast, lunch, and evening. There's no fundraising involved, but they allow me to keep tabs on what the discussion is on a particular policy matter. Some of the evening events are fundraisers, but they tend to be very high-dollar events if they are for dinner. I don't get that involved with those because we don't have a PAC.

Leech: Given these evening events, how conducive would you say lobbying is to family life?

Mulvihill: My husband and I are both lobbyists. I think it's helpful if you're a lobbyist married to another lobbyist, because you both know you're going to have a lot of late nights. In fact, I know of marriages that came apart because the lobbyist would be out late and the spouse was waiting at home at six o'clock. That's hard. I think it can be conducive to family life, but you have to make it that way.

Leech: Right now you are on maternity leave. Is this your first?

Mulvihill: This is number one.

Leech: Congratulations.

Mulvihill: Thank you.

Leech: How long will you remain on leave?

Mulvihill: I'm going to take a really long leave because I know that I only get to do this once. I'm probably going to be out for six months. Three months paid by Sony, three months unpaid as part of the Family and Medical Leave Act.

Leech: How old is Reagan now?

Mulvihill: Reagan is two months old yesterday. She's little. I don't know a lot of female lobbyists. It can be done but it's overwhelming right now.

Leech: Especially in the corporate world, I would imagine.

Mulvihill: Especially the corporate world. I deal with electronics and technology, which are heavily male industries to begin with. There are some issues that just attract all women and some just attract all men. For instance, take education. Almost everyone I ever worked with who deals with education policy is female. There are a handful of men.

Leech: How do you adjust or how do you cope with the heavily male aspect of your world?

Mulvihill: I walk in and kind of muscle my way in no matter what. I went to an all-women's college, and I think that helped me not to care, not to worry. I think it's very hard for a lot of young women. They're very intimidated. I tell them, "You've got to put that intimidation aside." If you are the only female in the room, then you just have to work twice as hard. I don't think the gender imbalance is going to be solved anytime soon. Politics in both parties are male-dominated.

Leech: What other advice do you have for someone who is thinking about getting into policy advocacy and corporate lobbying?

Mulvihill: I tell people that there are three different types of political animals. First, there are people who deal with pure policy. They work in academia, they work in think tanks, and they simply deal with the nonreal world of pure policy. Somebody over at the Cato Institute can sit in his cubicle and dream up how policy should work and write a paper on it.

At the other end of the spectrum there are people who deal with politics. They are in the business of getting people elected. They do fundraising. They do messaging. They do demographics. They get on work cycles based on the election cycle. If they're in off-cycle, usually there's a referendum in some city and they go off to work on that. This is like James Carville. These are the political hacks.

In the middle, there are people like me who deal a little with policy and a little with politics. We have to balance the two. We deal with policy but also deal with the real world. But in my world, we have almost no contact with the people in the James Carville basket, and you would never hire somebody from the pure politics world as a lobbyist.

Leech: They wouldn't be able to get it done.

Mulvihill: Yes, there definitely are three different groups. If somebody tells me that they are interested in politics, I'll explain my different baskets and ask them which one appeals to them. There are some people who really do love policy, just pure policy. That's great. I would say, "Go work in the think tank. Don't become a lobbyist."

Leech: What is your favorite part of your job?

Mulvihill: For me, it is the person-to-person interaction. I think for a lot of people, some of it becomes a game: Who can win? I think there are other people who are very passionate about their issue and lobbying is their way of giving back to society. It is their public service.

Leech: What do you like least about your job?

Mulvihill: I don't like the money aspect. I don't know if I would ever work for a company that had a PAC. Working for Sony, if someone asks me for a contribution, I can say, "We don't make PAC contributions. We don't give out any money. If you do something for us, you're doing it because you're helping the company and helping create jobs." To me that is a better reason to act than getting a $2,000 campaign contribution.

Leech: If someone's dream is to become a corporate lobbyist just like you, what advice would you give them?

Mulvihill: Go to Capitol Hill. That's the first stop. You have to understand how the system works. It's nothing you could ever learn in a classroom. You really have to be up there and see how the everyday of Capitol Hill works.

Leech: What in your education or training, besides Capitol Hill, do you think helped you do what you do?

Mulvihill: A lot of politics is instinctual. I don't think it's anything you can really learn. I have a friend, a colleague from Capitol Hill, who is very smart. He went to University of Chicago undergrad, University of Chicago for his MBA. He didn't understand politics. He could read about it and understand it from a historical perspective, but he couldn't quickly see the ramifications of an issue and which parties it would affect. Capitol Hill just wasn't the right place for him. I don't know if it's anything you could possibly learn. I think it's just a personality trait.

CHAPTER

9

Leslie Harris

President and CEO

Center for Democracy and Technology

***Leslie Harris** is the president and CEO of the Center for Democracy and Technology (CDT), a nonprofit organization that advocates on behalf of Internet freedom. CDT was part of the 2012 efforts to derail the Stop Online Piracy Act (SOPA) and the PROTECT IP Act (PIPA), which CDT argued would have chilled online innovation and expression. CDT educates and speaks out on issues related to online freedom of expression, online privacy and security, intellectual property, and Internet architecture and openness.*

Harris has been named one of Washington's "Tech Titans" by The Washingtonian *and was listed as one of "10 Female Tech CEOs to Watch" by* The Huffington Post. *She is a senior fellow at the University of Colorado's Silicon Flatiron Center for Law, Technology and Entrepreneurship.*

Before joining CDT in 2005, Harris ran her own public interest consulting firm, Leslie Harris & Associates, which represented nonprofits, foundations, and tech companies on issues related to the Internet. She was chief legislative counsel for the American Civil Liberties Union and public policy director at People For the American Way. She has a bachelor's degree in sociology from the University of North Carolina and a law degree from the Georgetown University Law Center.

Beth Leech: This book is called *Lobbyists at Work*. Do you even consider yourself a lobbyist?

Leslie Harris: Well, not as the public understands that term. It's unfortunate that the term has become a pejorative label, used principally to refer to people who make lots of money representing large corporate interests seeking tax breaks or earmarks. "Bridges to nowhere" and the like.

I'm also not a lobbyist as defined by current law, although I have been at various points in my career. I'm a lawyer and an advocate for policy issues that I care about. As a result, I have spent much of my career testifying in front of Congress, drafting bills or amendments, commenting on rules, and supporting or opposing bills and amendments. So how I would describe myself is as a public interest lawyer and a civil liberties and Internet freedom advocate.

Leech: Earlier in your career, you were officially a lobbyist. How did you start your career? Did you start off wanting to be a policy advocate?

Harris: No, I started out wanting to be a lawyer, probably a civil rights lawyer. I grew up in the South. I was a child in Atlanta during much of the most visible civil rights movement activity. My synagogue was bombed when I was a small child because of the civil rights activities of our rabbi. Later, I was inspired by books like *To Kill a Mockingbird* and activities that the ACLU was involved in, including a lot of the landmark voting rights cases. I saw myself in that work and could imagine my career path emulating that work, but it was a pretty inchoate desire. There weren't many lawyers that I knew, and none who were women.

My high school counselors also were very discouraging about the idea of my becoming a lawyer. They believed that nobody would hire me. And as far as wanting to be a policy advocate when I grew up—that didn't occur to me because I didn't know any policy advocates. Today's high schools have a lot of organized advocacy groups for high school activists, but that simply wasn't the case back then, at least in the South.

Leech: So in high school you thought you wanted to be a lawyer but you were discouraged from it. Did you go ahead with that plan anyway?

Harris: I didn't see that path forward. I don't come from a professional family. I was encouraged to go to college—that was the big goal. But that was about it. I didn't start moving into advocacy work until after college, when I came back to Atlanta from North Carolina. Atlanta had elected its first black mayor, Maynard Jackson, and Jimmy Carter was still governor and both of them were aiming to make progressive change.

As I look back, I didn't have a plan, just a set of issues I cared about, with civil rights and women's rights at the top of the list. I know people with master plans. I was not one of those people.

I got a job with the Corrections Department out of college. Governor Carter had brought in a reformer to lead the department. They were developing drug and alcohol intervention programs and programs dealing with sexual abuse in the women's prison. I was a junior person working within these programs. It wasn't advocacy, but it was reform from the inside.

After that, I went to work for the city council when Mayor Maynard Jackson was first elected. Again I was an inside person, not an outside advocate. I was a very junior person working on issues like police brutality. I started to meet people and get involved in local organizations. The National Organization for Women [NOW] was still a young organization, and I got very involved in the local chapter. I was part of the effort to set up the first battered women's shelter in Atlanta. We were advocating for the Equal Rights Amendment before the Georgia Legislature.

Leech: That was a hard haul, I'll bet.

Harris: I didn't know what I didn't know. We would invite these legislators to lunch and talk about whether they would support the ERA. They would address me as "little lady." I find it kind of laughable now. You have a lot of courage when you don't know anything.

Leech: That's actually pretty inspiring.

Harris: Kind of goofy.

Leech: That's why we like young people, right?

Harris: It's why I love young people. But back then, I wasn't the slightest bit sophisticated.

I really found my voice through NOW. I discovered that I could speak, that I had a voice, and that people listened. I was shaped by the injustice I saw around me as a child. I had no outlet for that, and suddenly I found myself making speeches. And I was good at it.

I became thoroughly involved in the emerging civic life of the local community, which was very vibrant. It was the beginning of what we believed would be the New South. It was in the couple of years leading up to Carter's election as president, and it was the beginning of a new black-white coalition in the South, and Atlanta was where that was all happening. And so I was at meetings and events with John Lewis, Julian Bond, and all these people who had been my heroes.

Most of my early experiences as an advocate were around women's rights. I started to feel empowered and I started to see a path forward, although at that point, it was not very specific. It did eventually lead me to law school. But first, I was the associate director of a rape crisis center.

Leech: You were involved in a lot in those early years.

Harris: The rape crisis center was one of the first in the country. We did training for other rape crisis centers in the South. I was doing the traditional rape counseling, training, and management. But I was also the person responsible for policy, working with the city council and the state legislature to try to reform rape laws.

Leech: So you were already working as a policy advocate.

Harris: I was doing it then and I was doing it in my work for NOW. I was doing policy on the other side of the table in all of my just-out-of-college jobs. I was just starting to see the place that might work for me. So I came to Georgetown University to go to law school.

Leech: How many years was it before you headed to law school?

Harris: I was twenty-six when I went to law school. I picked Georgetown because it was in Washington, DC, with lots of interesting work. I worked my way through law school. It was very difficult. I should have opted for the four-year evening program. But at the time, I believed I needed to "catch up" with my peers who went to law school right out of college. I didn't want to spend an extra year. But I did have some interesting jobs.

I worked for the Justice Department for a long time. I also worked for Chuck Morgan, who had been the head of the ACLU in the South during its halcyon civil rights days. He had a small firm in DC and I worked for him for a year on a big case. I learned a lot.

I had a lot of fire in the belly for the issues that I cared about. At that point, women's issues were number one. And I suppose if you'd asked me what I was going to do when I went to law school, I fully expected to join one of the emerging small law firms that were mostly women who were doing a lot of the early litigation and representation around employment and emerging women's issues. That's what I would have predicted. One lesson here is—don't predict.

Leech: Well, even if the prediction is accurate, by the end of your career, you may be someplace different.

Harris: My favorite quote has always been, "To travel hopefully is a better thing than to arrive." It's Robert Louis Stevenson.

Leech: You went to law school, and after you graduated what happened?

Harris: I had this terrific offer to stay in the Justice Department in the Honors Program, and I had an offer from a terrific law firm. The law firm—Wald, Harkrader and Ross—was known for its commitment to pro bono work and its stellar leadership. I chose the law firm. My entering class at the firm was the first one with an equal number of women and men.

I discovered fairly early on that even though these were some of the most extraordinarily interesting, and bright, and wonderful people in Washington, that I just couldn't make myself care about a lot of the work. For me, my legal skills had to be placed in a context of something I cared deeply about. I really struggled with it. I was not sure what I was going to do, and I saw a job posting for the ACLU and I applied. I didn't expect to hear from them. I was two years out of law school. But I did.

There are moments when roads diverge and you have to make a choice. The ACLU offered me the job and, frankly, I panicked. People just didn't leave a prestigious law firm after two years. I persuaded myself that I needed to stay at the firm. I wasn't sure I was ready for risk, so I turned down the offer. The board member who called me, the late Jim Heller, actually got quite angry and said to me, "Fine, go have a nice, safe life." I was stunned, but I thought about his words all night, and called back early the next morning and accepted. I remember saying, "You know, Jim, I don't want a nice, safe life." So that's how I joined the ACLU. I am forever grateful to him.

I had a great career at the ACLU for thirteen years. Most of that time was spent in the Washington office, which is basically the legislative and policy arm of the national ACLU, and I did a lot of good, old-fashioned lobbying. But it was at a time where Congress was less partisan, more productive, more open to working across the aisle. I worked on several important civil rights bills. I led our efforts against the nomination of Robert Bork to the Supreme Court and against the constitutional amendment on burning the flag. I worked on a range of reproductive rights issues, the death penalty, habeas corpus, free expression, religious liberty, and more.

Leech: I had initially thought that you were in the litigating arm of the ACLU.

Harris: I was never a litigator. I worked on cases in the law firm and when I worked for the Justice Department, but I was not a litigator for the ACLU.

I worked on critically important issues, learning how to navigate Congress, develop bipartisan support, and bring together coalitions. Being a good lawyer and a trusted source for members and staff mattered. But being a good strategist was equally important. I was lucky to have wonderful mentors, including Morton Halperin, whom I still rely on for advice all these years later.

Leech: The way you describe your interactions with Congress suggests that perhaps things are different now.

Harris: It is different now. It's much more driven by party politics. Pre-9/11, it also was a more open environment. Back then, if it was late at night and something you were working on was being debated on the Senate floor, you and other lobbyists would be right there, standing in the Senate antechamber or at the door to the House floor, places I haven't been in years. At a key moment, the senator, or staff, or both would come out to discuss what was happening and how to respond to possible amendments or other developments. I had to understand strategy as well as the substance of the issue. I had to know how to create coalitions around issues and powerful messages. It took inside knowledge about how Congress worked and the rules for floor debate. Today, almost every bill that comes to the Senate faces a filibuster and there need to be sixty votes to get the issue on the floor to start the discussion.

In those early days, a filibuster meant that the senator stayed on the Senate floor and talked. I can no longer remember the issue, but I recall bringing a civil rights casebook to the late Senator Paul Wellstone to read on the floor during a filibuster. He stayed all night and so did we.

Leech: That's interesting.

Harris: I was lobbying on the Hill at a time when there were a lot of important civil rights and civil liberties issues. I had an opportunity to contribute to a lot of them and learn an enormous amount about how to be an advocate—how to be a principled advocate. By that I mean advocacy grounded in intellectual rigor, deep expertise, and a respect for the facts, not just the message. And I'm very grateful for those years. They were really important and fun.

I also had a lot of opportunity to appear before the media. I am not sure young people have the same opportunity to learn media skills as I did. They learn to blog and tweet, but there are fewer opportunities to be in front of a camera and make your point. But when you are called on to debate Rudy Giuliani on a crime bill on *Crossfire* when you are three years out of law school, as I was, you have to learn to do it. Broadcast and cable media today rely less on substantive expertise and more on political partisans.

Leech: Interesting. Where are we in your story? You've been at the ACLU. Why did you decide to leave?

Harris: First, the Clinton administration came in and I worked in the Clinton Justice Department transition. It seemed like the right time for my own transition and I had an offer from People For the American Way to head their public policy shop. I was there about three years. Again, I had great experiences. I played a lead role in drafting the law that protects women's access to abortion clinics. I was part of the leadership of the Campaign for Military Service, which was the coalition fighting against Don't Ask, Don't Tell. And I was part of the leadership of the coalition fighting against the Communications Decency Act.

At the same time, I became fascinated by the Internet and its capacity for free speech and democracy-building, as well as its potential power as an advocacy tool. There were seminal questions about whether the Internet would be available to low income and rural communities, which led me to play a leadership role in a coalition that successfully advocated for a new universal service program that subsidized Internet access in schools and libraries. It was an early program to address the digital divide.

I also saw that many of the questions and many of the issues that I had worked on for a number of years were going to get played out again over this new technology. It was too early to understand that it was going to be a platform for everything. We thought it would be a platform for democracy and for equal opportunity. We didn't know it was going to be a global platform for human rights. I became intrigued and discovered my inner geek. I was already an early adopter of technology—largely because the guys I worked with at the ACLU all had computers.

Leech: They were there.

Harris: And I knew then that computers were one more thing the guys were going to get that the girls weren't, and so I joined in to see what it was about.

So my interest goes back a long way. In the mid-1990s, we were starting to see that the new technology raised equality issues and access issues as well as free expression issues. We did not yet fully realize how important privacy and government surveillance issues would be in this new space. No one at the time completely understood what the Web would be. Once again, I took a risk and left People For the American Way to set up my own firm.

It was one of the first consulting groups to focus on the Internet and new technologies, and probably one of the first founded by a woman. We were mission-driven—our mission being to harness the power of the new digital age for social good. We did some lobbying, for example, on free expression issues for the American Library Association—including Patriot Act issues, new content-filtering laws, and new questions coming up about intellectual property. We also represented groups like the National Center for Accessible Media at WGBH on disability and technology issues and educational technology groups on emerging issues and funding.

But Congress was not the only place that these new issues were emerging. For example, the question of how to make the Internet accessible to people with disabilities was facing companies as well. My firm worked with America Online to create a disability advisory council to look at new products and services. We also helped forge a partnership between the company and the Leadership Conference on Civil Rights to build their technology capacity and to explore the potential value of the new technologies to the mission of member organizations.

Leech: So your advocacy, in part, was between and among organizations, not necessarily organizations-to-government?

Harris: Yes, I helped foundations learn and develop programs in the area. I did some direct coalition building and management for foundations as people started to work in this space. And I built partnerships between industry and nonprofit groups. I also began to represent clients before agencies like the Federal Communications Commission.

Leech: How does one go about building these coalitions?

Harris: I had no idea where to begin, but many people I had worked with over the years either became clients or opened the door to them. For example, one of my colleagues at People For the American Way went on to join AOL, eventually leading its Washington office. She reached out to me on a specific policy project and introduced me to the AOL Foundation, which was looking to build partnerships with communities I had worked with for years.

I realized that I had this enormous network and it was gratifying to discover that my firm had something valuable to offer them. It was an incredibly diverse portfolio, but the thread that tied it together was technology and the public interest.

What I resisted doing during those years, and what I think I needed a break from, was being a very visible public advocate. I really enjoyed the break from that. It takes its toll. But the firm thrived for about ten years and had ten employees at its peak.

Leech: So when you did leave your firm, you came to CDT?

Harris: Yes. CDT was created by people who also came out of the ACLU.

Leech: I did not realize that.

Harris: Yes. CDT's founder, Jerry Berman, was one of those guys at the ACLU who were already into the policy implications of technology when the rest of the world didn't know what a desktop computer was. I was always close to the organization. I headed CDT's public interest advisory group back when I was still at People For the American Way. I ran that group with John Podesta, who later created CAP [Center for American Progress], and who earlier was Clinton's chief of staff.

And so I was very close to the organization as an advisor and consultant. My firm did a couple projects here and there for CDT. And when Jerry retired, CDT approached me about the job and I was ready to get back in the game.

When you're an advocate in Washington you're always putting yourself out there, and that was true even before people were 24/7 on Twitter and Facebook. But being an advocate is always being in the public eye, with testimony, media, speeches, debates, and constant meetings.

At my lobbying firm, even though we were very active and I had ten employees, I actually backed away from public visibility so that I had some flexibility in my schedule. It was a strategy for how to deal with life during ten years when my children were growing up.

Leech: A nanny can't do it all, right? Nannies can't go to ballgames.

Harris: Well, they can—and mine sometimes did. But I didn't really want to have someone else do that for me. Some people do, and that's fine. I just know what worked for me. But when my children were older, I was ready again for a big challenge in taking a very good organization to its next level. There were nine people at CDT when I joined. We're now around twenty-five. We have offices in California and Brussels. And the issues are really interesting and compelling.

Leech: So, could you explain in a nutshell the mission of CDT?

Harris: The mission is to keep the Internet open, innovative, and free. That's the world's shortest mission statement to be sure. But what that means in practice is that we aim to ensure that the technical, legal, and policy framework for the Internet continues to provide for an open platform for free expression, democracy building, and innovation. To do that, we have a team of lawyers, policy professionals, and technologists.

Leech: What sorts of things do you do to try to fulfill that mission?

Harris: We support measures to increase online privacy and believe the United States needs to enact a comprehensive privacy law. Having said that, it is hard to get it right in an environment where innovation is fast outpacing law. That is why we also work with companies to ensure that privacy is built into the design of products and consumers have more tools to control the use of their own data. At the same time, we are fighting against surveillance and increased data collection that violates privacy and security.

We work on intellectual property and we were a very major part of the big uprising that happened last winter against SOPA, a bill that would have imposed a variety of obligations, including blocking and filtering content—something that we just don't do in the United States. Of course, we work on traditional free expression issues. We also work on Fourth Amendment privacy issues related to surveillance, cybersecurity, and national security. The Patriot Act years were very busy and I have to say not as successful as I would have liked. We bring a lot of expertise to the table. We're asked to testify a lot. We draft analyses and reports and participate in agency proceedings. We're called by congressional offices, the FCC, the FTC, the Departments of Commerce and Homeland Security, and other agencies to come talk to them about issues. We convene diverse parties around issues to find consensus. We are often asked to serve on agency advisory committees. We don't do that much lobbying.

Leech: Because if they ask you, then it's not lobbying.

Harris: Well, it's more complicated than that. But we keep our hours very carefully to determine whether we have reached the threshold for lobby registration.

Leech: Where does your concern about not getting to the point where you'd have to register as a lobbyist come from?

Harris: Part of the concern comes from the limits on the amount of lobbying that 501(c)(3) charitable nonprofits can do, and part of it comes from the complications and restrictions associated with being a registered lobbyist, owing to the many scandals involving corporate lobbyists over the last decade—think Jack Abramoff.

It's become a very difficult situation to navigate. The public interest advocacy community has been hurt by being herded into the same cattle pen with the enormous corporate interests. The work public interest advocates of all political stripes do is constitutionally protected. We are supporting citizens' rights to petition the government. I worry that has been lost in the debate.

Leech: In the case of the Stop Online Piracy Act, how did CDT first become involved?

Harris: We first became involved at least a year and a half before it became a big public issue, when there was a similar but more narrowly written bill introduced in the Senate. One of the first things we did was to meet with Judiciary Committee staff about what our concerns were in the bill language.

Leech: And how had you heard about the issue in the first place?

Harris: In this case, I am pretty sure that Senator Patrick Leahy's office had asked us to look at the bill. But it's a big community. Long before that bill was introduced, drafts of the bill were circulating among the advocates and companies who work on intellectual property and Internet policy. It's really hard for me to say how we first knew about it.

In this case, we were in strong disagreement with Senator Leahy. We have worked with the senator on many civil liberties and Internet matters over the years, so it would not be surprising for his staff to reach out and get our views early. And we had enormous problems with the early drafts of that bill.

CDT is known as an organization that has a lot of expertise. And so our first action is not to go to the press. Our first action is to write a short, understandable, serious memo on what's wrong with the bill and try to make sure that a lot of people see that memo quickly, including the office involved. So we wrote a memo and shared it broadly with other organizations, companies, and congressional offices that were interested in the bill.

Looking at that bill, and especially its treatment of domain policy, we saw concerns about security. We saw concerns about free expression. We saw concerns for the rest of the world in terms of how global content would be treated in the United States and what kind of precedent it would set, particularly in the developing world that hasn't really established policy around the Internet.

So then we did a lot of outreach. We reached out to the top technologists and security experts who we thought would share our concerns about how the bill planned to block domain names. We reached out to human rights groups. We reached out to intellectual property advocates, to domain name registrars and experts, and to Internet companies. There are a lot of different communities, and we weren't the only people at that point to sound the alarm. But our involvement began very early on.

At that point, there wasn't really a lot of grassroots involved in it but there was a very active coalition in Washington that was working on the bill. It seemed unlikely that we would be able to stop the bill, so one of the strategies was proposing lots of amendments to try to narrow it. But members of our coalition also were talking to other members of Congress to try to get somebody to object. And that somebody turned out to be Senator Ron Wyden. So there were lots and lots of meetings with other members of the Judiciary Committee to express concerns, and then with other members of the Senate who were known for caring about civil liberties on the Internet.

Leech: How often do you end up working in coalition with other organizations in the work that you do at CDT?

Harris: An enormous amount of our work is in coalitions, both formal coalitions and informal working groups. We facilitate several ongoing working groups at CDT focusing on consumer privacy, freedom of expression, and government national security/civil liberties issues in which advocates, academics, and companies participate. Those groups are one of the places that our work gets shared and discussed. But on this issue in particular, another organization, Public Knowledge, coordinated the loose coalition around intellectual property.

Leech: And so when a coalition like this comes together, how often do you meet?

Harris: At least weekly, and as things heated up, much more. There was a lot of thinking about who else needed to be involved to slow the bill down. The first iteration of the bill didn't move at all in the Senate. It came back in a slightly different form and moved out of committee without a hearing involving any civil liberties or Internet advocates.

CDT held a press briefing early on, which lead to a few editorials, articles, and analyses, and some of the key bloggers picked up the story and started writing about it. This is a full year before SOPA and PIPA became national news and lots and lots of people became involved.

When the bill came to the House Judiciary Committee, the circle began to widen. There were efforts in New York and in Silicon Valley to start bringing the venture capital community together and getting more technology companies involved in the bill. And that was when the important online campaign began to come together.

So the circle started getting wider and there started to be venture capitalists who came into town to meet with members of Congress about their concerns with the bill. People from our coalition went to the White House quite a few times over the course of a year and a half to meet with different people about our concerns. Because the administration did not have a position on the bill at the beginning, the White House was an important target for advocacy—particularly regarding cybersecurity concerns.

There were a lot of meetings and discussion about what the bill might potentially look like, but it took the House a very, very long time to come up with the bill. We didn't like the bill in the Senate, but at least Senator Leahy was open to talking to us about our concerns and making changes. In the House, they wrote a bill but would not show it to people or get any kind of feedback from outside. I think the House bill was so bad that it finally started a drumbeat that developed over time as more and more influential bloggers talking about the bill and writing about the bill. Then people started talking about it or reading about it on Reddit and other social media spaces, building strong interest outside of Washington. And it was at that point that grassroots groups and DC advocates began to join together in the effort that led to the online campaign and the Internet blackout.

Leech: Oh, very interesting. And during this time, what was CDT doing?

Harris: It was no-holds-barred at that point. CDT was writing and working with the online activists as well as the DC-based opponents. We were building resources for the grassroots who were developing their own campaign, putting together an online resource that mapped the growing opposition to the campaign, and participating in endless meetings on the Hill, including regular strategy meetings with key Congressional opponents. There were meetings in the White House, as well. CDT was also working with technologists on an influential report, taking them around the Hill and encouraging companies to get involved.

Leech: That's interesting that you needed to encourage them. Historically, computer and Internet companies were known for not being politically involved and not really being super-savvy about Washington. They assumed that if there were an issue that affected them, they would be asked by the committee for their opinion. That assumption seems to have changed.

Harris: Obviously, the big companies have a presence in Washington now, but a lot of companies still tend to work through their trade associations so that they don't have to visibly take aggressive positions in Washington. That's partly the culture, but it's also good politics. Nobody wants to be in an aggressive position opposing the chairman of the committee. But soon there was a deluge of opposition from engineers, entrepreneurs, companies, and activists.

Leech: So CDT was essentially acting as a think-tank and as a resource?

Harris: I would not say think-tank. We were certainly lobbying and participating in the development of the strategy. But CDT has a particular voice and that voice comes not just from the advocacy position that we believe in, but from our expertise. That's kind of our brand. We were the expert resource for a lot of what was going on in the grassroots at that point.

Public Knowledge did a great job of being the resource on the policy process itself: "Here's what happens in committee. And here's what it means when amendments are offered." What CDT would add is expertise on how the technology works and how particular legal obligations would play out in practice. We talked about what the implications would be for Internet users and for companies.

In November 2011, the first grassroots call-in day was organized, where constituents would call their members of Congress to express opposition to the bill. CDT's basic memo explaining what the bill would do was downloaded thousands of times that day.

Leech: Wow. Was your server ready for that?

Harris: No, but it survived. And on then the big Internet blackout day—January 18, 2012—a number of sites, including Google, had links to some of our key resources. I was very afraid that the amount of traffic was going to bring our site down entirely.

There are people who spend a lot time arguing about which role is most important: grassroots, inside strategy, or outside strategy. I just don't see things divided like that. I see them as highly integrated and, if they're done right, each part of the advocacy campaign plays a role that strengthens every other part of the campaign. Full credit needs to go to a whole set of people who ran that online campaign, who did a completely brilliant job. And it built from the initial work that was done for the previous year and half here. I would never pick any one piece of the big campaign and say it was because of this piece or that piece that the legislation was defeated. I don't believe that's ever true.

Leech: Including the Internet blackout.

Harris: Oh, the blackout was critically important. But it didn't happen in a vacuum. It happened in conjunction with a set of senators who had already said they were going to filibuster the bill. It happened in the climate of a press that was, by now, highly educated about and hostile to the bill. It happened in the context of analysis that was widespread and heavily read about what the implications of the bill were, and a technologists' report that set out the security dangers. But the blackout was critically important. Do I think that's why the White House took the position it did against the bill? I know it wasn't, but I also know the blackout forced them to finally act.

Leech: Why do you think the White House took the position they did?

Harris: They were very, very worried about cybersecurity implications, but I think their number-two concern was global Internet freedom. And there were hundreds of thousands of people around the world protesting this bill, because they knew that if the United States were to start blocking and filtering Internet content, something we have never done, that it would be "game over" for the rest of the world. We would have no moral authority to fight for global Internet freedom.

And so the administration had a lot of crosscurrents. It is an administration that has strong beliefs in protecting intellectual property and with strong ties to Hollywood—so they certainly didn't do it for political reasons. Whoever they made happy, they also made a lot of people unhappy. And I was pleasantly surprised to see that at the end of the day, traditional politics didn't block them from saying what they believed to be true. They came out with their position over the weekend before the blackout.

Leech: Before the blackout.

Harris: Yes, but everyone knew that there was going to be a tsunami unleashed the next day. There are many different pieces to a successful campaign. And in an Internet environment, there is no command and control: there's only consultation. There were so many different elements. There was a very high-level meeting at the White House that brought in CEOs and top-level people from industry, which I participated in. That was very important in terms of White House thinking. So there were just too many pieces, all happening at once, to be able to claim which moment in a series of moments was the one that somehow won it. The blackout was critically important, that is clear. And I think the blackout also has created an opportunity for a much broader set of individual organizations and companies to work together on these issues. That's probably the best thing that's come out of it.

Leech: I'd like to have you walk me through what your average day looks like. And given that I'm guessing there is no truly average day, maybe you could pick a day last week and tell me how it went.

Harris: Well, I tend to come in the office early because I don't like to stay as late as a lot of my staff. Remember, I run this organization, so there are a lot of things I have to commit my time to every day that are not terribly fun: fundraising and management take up a fair amount of time. I check my e-mail every minute, so I can't say there's a time to check my e-mail.

Leech: Got it.

Harris: I would love not to do that, but I do. I also usually run upstairs pretty regularly, because we're on two floors. I call it "making rounds." CDT has grown dramatically over the last five years, so we have to work to remain cohesive and keep the culture of a small organization.

There is no such thing as an average day, so let me look at my calendar and tell you some of the things that happened last week. On Monday, CDT held a press briefing in our office on Internet governance related to an upcoming treaty renegotiation at the International Telecommunications Union. We are playing a lead role in organizing several groups around the world in understanding and reaching out to their own governments on this issue.

So fairly early in the day, we had a press briefing. Since it was Monday, we also had a staff meeting, which gives us a chance to catch up with each other and try to figure out if there's an issue that we ought to be discussing—either on the Hill, in a regulatory proceeding, or something in the news about what a company or a country is doing. It's not unusual for us to pull together internal meetings to discuss what our position might be on an issue that's arising. On Fridays, we reserve lunchtime so that people can get together to try to do that kind of meeting.

Then last week, the Senate cybersecurity bill was about to come out, so we had a pretty long meeting to discuss the substance of the amendments that were being offered to address the privacy concerns that we had, and the complicated question about what our position should be on the bill. We were successful in getting a lot of important changes. So did we still oppose the bill? What were we going to say to the grassroots groups? What were we going to say to the sponsors of the bill?

Later in the afternoon, I had a fundraising meeting. If I wasn't running the organization, I might be lucky enough to be purely an advocate and not have fundraising meetings. But I have lots of fundraising meetings with funders and potential funders.

I went out to a State Department meeting where they wanted some advice about an Internet conference, and who should attend and what issues they might suggest to the country that was hosting the conference for countries from all over the world. My schedule is going to disappoint you because I haven't been on the Hill in the last few weeks.

Leech: Well, that's good to know. Sometimes advocacy is not only about the Hill.

Harris: Actually, I don't go up there very much.

I spent a couple of hours writing a keynote speech that I was going to be giving at a conference. We're hiring a CDT director in Brussels, and I spent about forty-five minutes to an hour talking about candidates and résumés for that job. Then I had another meeting at the State Department. This is not all in one day. I'm just trying to give you some ideas.

Leech: Your average week.

Harris: There's not a lot that's moving in Congress because it's an election year and things tend to shut down. So, except for the cybersecurity bill that's moving ahead, there's not a lot of legislative activity. Agencies continue to have proceedings, but by summer in an election year, it does slow down here.

Another day, I had a meeting at a company where they wanted to get our view on a new product they were rolling out and how they were trying to protect privacy. They wanted our feedback and suggestions as to whether or not we thought they were doing the right thing. We actually do a lot of that.

Leech: What sorts of products would you be asked to consult on?

Harris: In this case, it had to do with the collection of people's personal data and what kind of protections they're putting on that data. Are they going to hold on to that data? Are they going to share it with third parties? The fact that the Internet is driven by an advertising model makes this a constant and very big issue.

Leech: That's interesting that you consult with these companies. Is that something you do as part of your advocacy, or is that also a moneymaker for the organization?

Harris: It's part of our advocacy. We advocate with companies because what they do in this space has a lot of implications for people's privacy and rights to free expression. I should be clear here that we are funded in part by companies who participate in our working groups. We believe in consultation and dialogue, and working toward consensus where possible.

The other thing that would happen in the course of a week is that one of our working groups would meet. For example, we have a Digital Privacy and Security Working Group, so our director of that project and the people who participate in that working group—advocates, companies, technologists, and academics—might get together around something specific—like the cybersecurity bill—or around a longer-term goal. For example, a major priority is reform of government access laws because the government has much easier access to your personal information online than it does offline. What you store in your desk requires a warrant. What you store online in your social media, or e-mail, or search browsers often does not.

So we have put together a very big coalition to try to amend the law, which includes advocates from across the political spectrum and a growing number of companies. The senior lawyers here who are project directors are focused all day every day on whatever issue is in front of them. They'll be on the Hill. They'll be meeting with other groups. They'll be drafting memos. They'll be drafting amendments. That's basically what I did for a very long time. But it's not necessarily what I do when I'm running an organization.

I spend a lot of time going back and forth among my projects, checking in, offering advice, seeing where work that's being done on one issue overlaps or has a potential to conflict with work that's going on in another issue. And there's a lot of staff management, hand-holding, and conflict resolution.

Leading the organization has a different set of activities and a fair amount of high-level luncheons and meetings with government officials and people who lead other organizations and people in companies. It's about relationship-building and looking for opportunities to work together. And raising money.

Leech: Your day would wrap up usually about when?

Harris: It really depends. I'd say six thirty is average for me, but that doesn't mean I don't go home and just start up again. I'd say almost every night I'm working, and I tend to work most Sundays, although not all day. But it really depends. This time of year, it's a lot slower. And people tend to have different biorhythms. If I have a lot to do, I'll start working at six in the morning. The younger staff will work at twelve at night.

Leech: Are most of your younger staff lawyers?

Harris: There are a lot of lawyers. We have technologists—mostly people with master's degrees or PhDs in computer science from the information schools. Some people have a lot of experience doing policy, but are not lawyers. We also have a communications team, including a person who is managing social media, and a director for campaigns.

Leech: Let's focus in particular on the people who do policy. If you're hiring someone like that, what are you looking for in that person?

Harris: We don't have the opportunity to train people who don't know anything about this area, so almost everybody who comes into CDT is either going to have a strong civil liberties background or, if they're coming out of law school, they've already taken lots of courses and shown a strong interest in the issues that arise from the Internet. They're going to have to be really, really good writers and thinkers.

Leech: And why in particular is good writing important?

Harris: Because it's part of our brand that we are producing understandable memos, issue briefs, and blogs that people in positions of authority can take and use and have trust in when they're making policy decisions. Part of our brand is making sure that when people look at our work, they say: "This is serious work done by serious people and we can rely on it." So, writing skills are important.

Leech: What else are you looking for in that person?

Harris: The person needs to be highly creative because there isn't one reliable way that the policy process always operates. There isn't a beginning, middle, and end that always happens.

A passion for the work is really important. You can't do this kind of work without caring about it and having a reason for doing it. You really have to care about how technology intersects with civil liberties. It's not the kind of job you just come into to produce documents. You have to be excited. You have to care. And, of course, almost everyone comes in to CDT with a strong grounding in technology.

Leech: What advice do you have for someone who would like to be a policy advocate?

Harris: Get a good education and start with what you care about. Volunteer or do internships in relevant organizations. If you are in college, look at ways to be involved in the organizations that exist on campus. For people who are interested in coming to Washington, a lot of people start on the Hill.

I never did spend time on the Hill. Also, Washington is not the world. It is an interesting place to work, but there are real trade-offs between trying to work in an advocacy organization here versus one in a city. I started my career working in a city. In a city, you know everybody, and you get to see the fruits of your labor a very direct way. I think it's much harder when you work in the national level.

There is a difference between wanting to do politics and wanting to do issue advocacy, and Washington is as much about politics as issue advocacy. So if you can't stand the politics going on all around you, this is probably not the place to do advocacy.

The most important thing is to know what you care about. There's no such thing as "I want to be a generic advocate." I think that's meaningless. What do you have passion for? What do you want to achieve in the world?

So I think people should think really broadly about what they care about, what their skill set is, and what the different venues are to work on the issues they care about. Washington is a really interesting place to be, but it's not the world.

CHAPTER

10

Mark Burnham

Vice President for Government Affairs Michigan State University

***Mark Burnham** is vice president for governmental affairs at Michigan State University. He is based in Lansing, with responsibilities that involve local, state, and federal affairs, but before his promotion in 2011, he worked full-time in Washington, DC, as MSU's associate vice president for governmental affairs. Before coming to Michigan State, Burnham was director of federal relations for research for the University of Michigan.*

Close to 100 different universities maintain their own lobbyists and offices in the Washington area, and many more than that hire lobbying firms to represent them. MSU reported spending $340,000 on lobbying expenses in 2011.

Burnham has bachelor's degree in political science from the University of Michigan and a law degree from Boston College Law School. Before going to law school, he spent four years as a staff member for Rep. Marcy Kaptur (D-OH). After earning his JD, he worked for the law firm Jones Day and then for Lewis-Burke Associates, a lobbying firm whose clients include many universities.

Beth Leech: How did you become a lobbyist? How did you enter this line of work?

Mark Burnham: I knew I had always wanted to go into public policy. Even before I finished my undergraduate degree, I knew. I didn't communicate that too well to my parents, though. At the end of my junior year, I had an internship set up in Washington, and I was moving my stuff back to my parents' house. My mom and dad sat me down and said, "We're a little concerned because we don't know what you're going to do." I looked at them and said, "Oh, I guess I didn't tell you."

I laid it all out: "I'm going to move to Washington and do this internship. I'm going to work in one of the House Office Buildings and start building my career." Dinner came and their jaws were sitting on the table. I just started eating. It's funny now.

Leech: What was that first internship? Where did you work?

Burnham: I worked for Congressman Dennis Hertel. I had a wonderful summer. It was a tremendous experience and I got the bug, that so-called Potomac Fever. I knew what I wanted to do. I finished my senior year and I started applying. I sent résumés all over Capitol Hill. I was applying for jobs that only existed in six buildings in the entire United States, and I got a lot of rejection letters. I have enough to paper a wall. For some reason, I kept them. It's kind of entertaining to read them because I now know most of these people.

Leech: You kept all the rejection letters?

Burnham: I did, though I am not really sure why. I had gotten a rejection letter from Representative Marcy Kaptur, but I kept pounding the pavement, walking door to door in Capitol Hill. I went to Marcy's office and I said I appreciated the courtesy of her response because not everybody bothered to respond. I was curious if they knew of any other jobs that might be open in the area that I could apply for. The guy behind the desk said, "Well, actually, I'm going back to grad school, and the office didn't know that when we rejected you." So, he took my résumé again, and they had me come back to interview. Then I drove to DC to do an interview and the chief of staff had been called to a meeting in the district office, which was in Toledo. So I went to Washington in order to have a phone interview with the chief of staff, who was in Toledo.

I was hired and started at the front desk, which is where most Hill staff start their careers—opening mail and answering phones. By the time I left, four years later, I was a senior Appropriations staffer who had also worked on issues related to NASA, Veterans' Affairs, and a variety of other topics. Every legislative staffer has a list of about twenty things that they're responsible for, far more than most people would imagine.

At the end of the four years, I decided to go to law school. What convinced me in part was that Marcy wasn't a lawyer. She's an urban planner by training. She had a couple of cases where she was really struggling because she didn't have an attorney on staff and she wasn't an attorney herself. I learned from that and decided, "I think I want to know what the law's all about."

I went to law school with the idea of coming back into public service. The people and the program at Boston College really fit me and I was one of those odd ducks who really enjoyed law school. After graduating, I knew I wanted to get my feet wet in actual court work first. It took a little while to find that first law job, in part because some employers didn't believe a twenty-something could actually have had the scope of responsibility I had had on Capitol Hill.

Eventually, I spent about three years doing litigation for Jones Day, which at that time was still Jones, Day, Reavis, and Pogue. I was basically a traveling attorney doing major litigation in Minneapolis, Florida, and all over the place.

Leech: Any particular area of expertise in litigation?

Burnham: I was staff attorney doing document support for major product liability litigation, but I knew I wanted to continue doing public service. You do law firm work for a while and then you get really tired of it, at least I did. I reached back to a colleague whom I had met my freshman year of college. He had worked for a member of Congress, for MIT, and for the University of Michigan.

He helped connect me to a small niche firm called Lewis-Burke Associates, which was run by a woman whose name was April Burke but her maiden name was Lewis, so Lewis-Burke was all her. I had an interview early on in my search, but it didn't really go anywhere. It turns out that I was a little early for her. She wasn't ready for a new person.

A few months passed. I got married, went on my honeymoon. I came back from my honeymoon and two weeks later, I got a call from the Lewis-Burke office saying, "Are you still interested in a job in this field?" They had a staff person leave. Once again, first rejected, then I got in.

Leech: You stayed in the game.

Burnham: It seemed to be a pattern at the time. I started working for April and one of her main clients was the California Institute of Technology—Caltech—so my experiences working on NASA appropriations when I was back on the Hill became very relevant very quickly. I still had contacts. One of my really good friends from early days on Capitol Hill (when we were both maintaining our office computers) was now the senior Appropriations staffer for the chairman of the subcommittee that funded NASA. He helped me understand the details of the NASA budget, and that led to me being able to speak intelligently about the budget issues with the client. So that's the story of how I got into lobbying.

Leech: A lot of the clients that you worked with at Lewis-Burke were universities.

Burnham: Yes. Lewis-Burke is a niche firm that represents universities and science consortia. It was either directly working for the university or the science consortia, which are almost all university-based. For example, the National Center for Atmospheric Research, which is managed by a group known as the University Corporation for Atmospheric Research [UCAR], is really a group of about seventy research universities around the country. As a result, we ended up doing a lot of work with the federal science funding agencies like NASA or the National Science Foundation, as well as with Congress.

Leech: You went from Lewis-Burke to Michigan and then Michigan State. How does working a lobbying firm as a lobbyist differ from being in-house the way you are now?

Burnham: There are significant differences and advantages to both. Let's back up and look at lobbying. I think there are two types of lobbying. One is based on relationships that are there because you know the legislator or their key staff. You might have known him or her when you were growing up, or you worked for him or her for a number of years, or some other affiliation like that. You're not really substantively based. You're relationship based. A lot of lobbying firms rely primarily or exclusively on that kind of lobbying.

The other type of lobbying is when you really come up through a particular area or field and you become very knowledgeable in that area, and then you use that knowledge to develop the relationship, because that subject area happens to be important for that member of Congress. Lewis-Burke is a little different than your typical lobbying firm. Lobbyists there had some relationships that they had built, but we did most of our lobbying based on substance.

At Lewis-Burke, we had a depth of knowledge about the politics of higher education and science funding, but a less robust understanding of the client, because we represented many clients. I might have a meeting with an Appropriations staffer, so first I have on the Caltech cap, and then I'm wearing the UCAR cap, and now I'm wearing the University of Cincinnati hat. I was very deep in the policy and had in-depth relationships in Washington on all of those issues. I didn't necessarily know any given university nearly as well as I do now, nor did I have to deal with things other than funding for those universities' research agendas. That said, I probably did some of my best policy work while I was with Lewis-Burke, since it is one of the few really skilled policy shops working in the sector.

When I started representing the university as a whole, I had to develop a much more comprehensive understanding of the politics within a university and the many roles the university plays in the world. When I first started at the University of Michigan, I worked directly for the vice president of research, so in theory, I still was limited to the research portfolio. Even then, I ended up getting a much broader understanding of the mission of the institution, a much better understanding of the institution itself. For example, when I worked for UM, I was the face of UM in Washington (not the only one of course). This meant I had to be prepared to discuss everything from athletics to admissions issues—even when those weren't my area of responsibility. On campus, I didn't just report to one point of contact—but now I was a part of the office and was representing the Vice President for Research with the faculty. That creates an entirely different dynamic than when I was merely a consultant to the university.

I went from there to MSU's Washington office, and then I had to deal with the full breadth of the university's activities. Now I'm a vice president of the university and I'm located on campus, rather than in Washington, and I have an even more in-depth relationship and understanding of the institution, and the people, and the direction the institution's going. I don't quite have the same level of engagement with the agencies and the Congress as I did when I worked as an outside lobbyist, although of course, I still retain a lot of that knowledge and I work to keep those relationships fresh.

Leech: How long have you been back in Michigan?

Burnham: Two years in February 2013.

Leech: Let's talk a little bit about why a university would need a lobbyist.

Burnham: First and foremost, because places like Michigan State or Michigan, or even Caltech, are institutions that are so large that they become some of the biggest employers in their areas. At MSU, we have our own power plant. We're a two billion–dollar entity with sixty thousand students and staff, so we're very much like a small city. There isn't an area of federal, state, or local government that doesn't impact the university or where the university cannot play a role.

On top of that, at a place like MSU, the university receives about $295 million a year in base support from the state of Michigan, $300 million a year in federal research dollars, and another $400 million a year in financial aid that goes to the students.

There's a lot of need to manage the relationships with the congressional delegations, the congressional committees, and the federal agencies—whether it be because of funding issues, immigration status for faculty or students, regulations about where and how to store hazardous chemicals that might be used in scientific, or agricultural, or power plant operations, or how the university deals with emergency response if there is an active shooter situation on a campus of fifty thousand students.

A university also might need a lobbyist to keep on top of proposed changes in labor regulations or regulations that affect fundraising efforts, such as changes in tax laws that deal with charitable contributions. These are just some of the issues that come to play on a regular basis.

A lot of my job now is about trying to keep government officials and the public informed. For example, a lot of people think state universities are still funded the way they once were back when they went to school, and assume that universities have been getting funding increases. Public universities nationwide used to receive about seventy-five percent of the cost of undergraduate education from their states. However, today, state financial support for MSU has declined to twenty-two percent, and if you look around the country, some schools are as low as four percent. The world has changed in terms of public financial support for public universities. They're a lot more dependent on tuition dollars, competitively awarded research dollars, and federal higher education financial aid dollars.

Leech: At this point, you split your time between attention to Lansing and attention to Washington. How do state and national lobbying differ and how are they the same?

Burnham: Whether or not a university has permanent staff in Washington depends a lot on how much research funding the university has, because general higher education funding is primarily dealt with every five years during the higher education reauthorization, but research funding is an annual process. The more research dollars you have, the more likely you are as an institution to have somebody full-time in DC.

At MSU, I'm lucky to be able to have somebody in Lansing who is doing the day-to-day state lobbying work and I have somebody in Washington who is doing the day-to-day federal lobbying. At the state level, where we have term limits, there are a lot of elected officials who are very new and have very little base institutional knowledge of the university or even of the legislature. You have to do a lot of educating quickly. It used to be that legislators would have enough time to learn these things. They really don't these days, and there is very little incentive to bother.

Congressionally, we don't have term limits on our elected officials and that allows us to have members of Congress who stay long enough to really start to understand where we fit in the process. A lot of the difference is that I don't have to retread the same ground on who we are and why we exist, but I can get more into the substantive details. It's harder to get into that level of detail at the state level.

Leech: How many people are in your office?

Burnham: I have two professional staff in Washington, myself and four professional staff here in Lansing, and a couple of support staff.

Leech: Let's slow down a little bit to talk for a while about a recent issue that you've been involved in, because I think it might help if we went step-by-step-by step through how it arose, what you and your office did to try to address it, and to explain to the general reader how something like this comes about and the sorts of things a lobbyist actually does. If you can think about something you've worked on recently, let's just pick it apart for a minute.

Burnham: The most common issues we deal with relate to funding, including some big projects that are multiyear and multidimensional, but ultimately revolve around funding. But we also have policy issues that pop up unexpectedly, and then we have to deal with that issue.

There was a proposal in the lame-duck session of the state legislature at the end of 2012 to change the rules on gun-carry permits. The proposal would allow people to carry concealed weapons in places that up to now have not been allowed, including churches, theaters, sports arenas, and on campuses.

As soon as the bill was introduced, we spent time talking with the bill's sponsor, asking him, "What is it that you're trying to accomplish by expanding the concealed-carry law?" We also talked to senior-level folks on campus to clarify what are our concerns were. Our biggest concern was that regardless of how responsible an individual person might be, we have a lot of eighteen-year-olds on campus and a lot of them drink. The mixing of eighteen-year-olds, alcohol, and firearms is not really a good idea. And even if the person with the permit is responsible, there could be a problem with their roommate or their friend getting access to their gun.

We had a serious concern about the potential for bad accidents to happen on campus if concealed weapons were allowed. We spent our time talking, both in person and on the phone, to the legislator who proposed the bill, to the legislative leadership, to the committee that was going to consider the bill, to opponents of the bill, and to our other colleague universities about what positions they were taking and whether there were other allies that we could work with.

Leech: At this point, are you just collecting information during these talks, or are you already arguing the university's position?

Burnham: We're doing both. We would start with an inquiry: "Why are you introducing it? What is your intention?" And we would follow with, "Here are our concerns." We try to explain our institution's particular perspective.

Leech: How do you come up with that perspective? Where does it come from?

Burnham: Usually it's done in dialogue with senior-level folks on campus. In this case, it included our chief of police, the university president, other senior academic and administrative leadership, and the university's lawyer, its general counsel. The general counsel was important because in the state of Michigan, the public universities are "constitutionally autonomous." Of course, there's always the question of what does that mean in practice?

Leech: Conceivably, the university could make up its own rules and govern itself?

Burnham: Yes. Actually, that was the tack we were able to successfully use. By meeting with the proponents of the bill and talking about the concerns we had, they agreed that they didn't want to be advocating for people having guns in inappropriate circumstances. They were willing to accept putting language into the bill that acknowledged the university's autonomy and that it would be within the authority of our Board of Trustees, who are publicly elected, to pass an ordinance to continue to keep concealed weapons off campus, out of our stadiums, out of our dorms, and our academic buildings.

In some of our conversations, we would make the point that the Department of Homeland Security, which does work with the university pretty regularly, is concerned about what we allow in our stadiums because our stadium holds more than seventy thousand people. The federal government is telling us not to allow purses in the stadium to prevent people bringing dangerous things inside, and now we're going to allow concealed weapons in the stadium?

Between the fact that we are autonomous, the fact that legislators did agree that they're not trying to mix guns and alcohol, and the potential for public safety issues in crowds like at football games, we made our point. So the legislators included the provision to allow us to make our own choice. Now, we supposedly already have that authority, and they were simply acknowledging it, but it was a greater acknowledgment of our autonomy than has been recently made. The bill passed in the state House and Senate, but then the tragedy at Sandy Hook occurred, and the governor, I think rightfully, vetoed the bill. But this will probably come up again in the future, although I don't know how quickly they'll be interested in taking it up.

What we as lobbyists actually do is talk. It's a lot of sitting down with public officials, making the suggestions, and in some cases making written proposals or simply critiquing what they have written. It's having dialogue with our allies and making sure that we talk among ourselves. It sometimes can include trying to get lots of alumni to call their legislators, but a lot of times, that's not an effective approach, because if you've gotten to that tactic, you've probably already lost the fight.

Leech: That's a tactic to use when you're feeling like the underdog.

Burnham: Exactly. If a lobbyist is approaching advocacy the right way, it will include three things. There will be direct, face-to-face conversations that help legislators understand the university's position and the university to understand the legislators' position. There also will be discussions like that with university leadership, donors, and people who are important in their communities.

If you're getting into a grassroots situation where you're trying to mobilize alumni to call in, that can work, but efforts like those are a blunt instrument and need to be used judiciously. We want to move the ball, but we want to do it in a way so that we can still come back tomorrow and have another conversation with the policymakers, because tomorrow it's going to be a different issue. We can't use the blunt instrument of having two hundred thousand alumni jam the statehouse phone lines every week. We have to save that power for when we're in a really tight situation and at a point where we have to go all in. No one can go all in on every item.

Leech: How does working on an issue that pops up, like concealed handguns, differ from what your office does day-to-day in terms of funding?

Burnham: The big difference is the time line. When an issue pops up—especially in a legislature like ours where the same party controls both houses and the governorship—things can move really fast, so you have to be incredibly nimble.

In contrast, the appropriations process has a cycle. There is a known pattern. The president/governor's budget request is going to come out in the early part of February. Then there will be hearings, and the university will provide testimony. Lobbyists from our office will look at what was proposed by the Adminsitration and suggest changes at the level of the House and Senate subcommittees. You'll have a point where the House will vote and the Senate will vote, and then they'll go into conference committee. There's a series of points in time when you have conversations with the same people and find that sometimes your allies on Day 1 are not your allies on Day 7 because they want something different, and on Day 14, you're allies on a different part of the bill. So you have to be flexible and nimble, but there's more of a steadiness to it.

It's a lot more methodical and a lot more nuanced as you try to work your way through the appropriations process. You never are dealing with one single issue. Every appropriation bill will have multiple issues that affect the university, whether it be the base funding line, or the funding for a special project, or reporting requirements. In an appropriations bill, our office is always dealing with at least four or five different issues. We can't push one too hard without putting some of the other issues at risk, so we have to be very careful in our approach. You have to balance the overall interests of the university. And often when the governor's budget comes out, or the House acts, or the Senate acts, one or all of them may have introduced something new that our office wasn't aware of before, that we then would have to decide whether to support or oppose.

At the end of the day, you're trying to get the best overall outcome for the university, with the fewest oversight requirements, while at the same time getting as much money as you can. There's always a midpoint and you've got to accept a certain amount of oversight for a certain amount of funding.

Leech: Now that you've explained these issues, could you walk me through an average day so that we can get a picture of how you would spend your day at the office?

Burnham: First, there's no such thing as an average day. There are things that happen which are planned, like a visit by a legislator or a governor for a tour. Both Congress and the Statehouse tend to work Tuesday through Thursdays, so those are "session days" when our lobbyists are down at the Capitol a lot or on the phone with legislative staff. There might be a basketball game or a football game that I've invited people to come to. There might be an issue where some legislator's constituent didn't like their interaction with the university—for almost any reason. Our office has to try to figure out what happened and what, if any, resolution there can be, and try to make sure that it is resolved in the best way possible. There's a lot of casework like that. Mostly, we spend our time trying to figure out what the legislature is likely to do next, and whether that will benefit or harm the institution. That requires a lot of rounds of communications between university officials and legislative officials with our office serving as translator and to some degree the train conductor.

Leech: Where do the local officials come in?

Burnham: For the local stuff, our office also has to deal with the traditional town/gown issues, where there are neighborhoods that don't like the fact that university kids who live nearby are drunk and disorderly at two in the morning and leaving trash all over the street. The neighbors want to know what the university is going to do about it. We work hard with our communities to resolve those types of issues quickly and help both our neighbors and our students to understand and respect each other's needs.

Our office also might get involved in local development plans involving property we own. Right now, we're working with the city, and the county, and the local transit authority to get a new train station, a new track, and a new platform to upgrade our Amtrak station. There's economic development at the local level. There's "How do we work better with our community?" And new local officials are being elected every cycle, so our staff have to get to know them and their issues.

We work on all of those levels simultaneously. Today, I started the morning with a conversation with the governor's office about the State of the State address. We have a major initiative we're hoping to launch and we have leadership meetings that I need to schedule. So I needed to make sure that if I schedule those meetings, I wasn't going to get surprised that the initiative didn't get funded in the budget.

Then I met with a visitor from US Senator Debbie Stabenow's office who came to campus to tour the site of our new Facility for Rare Isotope Beams, funded by the Department of Energy's Office of Science.

After that, I had a meeting with a newly elected councilwoman for the township that's adjacent to the university. I had staff meetings, and this conversation with you, and then I have to brief our faculty and our graduate students on what's going on at the federal funding level. I'm meeting with the budget group on campus to talk about the university budget. That's just in one day. Tomorrow may be totally different.

Leech: When do you normally come in to the office and when do you normally call it a night?

Burnham: I have to say that one nice thing about working for a university is that I usually can get in around nine and I can usually go home between five and five-thirty. Except, of course, when I'm here on weekends or weeknights because we have important visitors to entertain.

When I go to Washington for the presidential inauguration, it may sound like a lot of fun, but actually, I'm going there to work. There are a whole bunch of folks I need to talk to, and I'll have them all in one place. By and large, the quality of life is not bad, but there are some weeks when I don't get free time even after hours.

Leech: That leads into my next question, which is about whether lobbying life is conducive to family life.

Burnham: Two points, Number one, I just finished a divorce, so there's a reasonable question of how much my job might have something to do with that. That is probably so. Secondly, being a lobbyist for a public entity like mine is very different from being a lobbyist for a lobbying firm or a company where political action committee [PAC] fundraisers and campaign events take up most of your life. That's one of the reasons why I enjoy working for universities. By and large, we don't have any federal PACs and we have a very small state PAC, so I'm not spending my nights at campaign events. I will say that many of my colleagues who work in private-sector lobbying are spending four or five nights a week out until ten or eleven o'clock talking to people who are campaigning.

I personally question the value of that, because I have done PAC work before. The legislators and members of Congress just want more money. At the end of the day, you're not really getting much influence. You're just getting calls for more money. And especially if an organization isn't a big campaign contributor, the only way it's going to get attention is if it has reliable information. For a university like MSU, we aren't going to get someone's attention because of a campaign contribution; we have to be the source of good information on a whole number of subjects.

We also have to be telling them something that matters. Information is the only currency that really matters in Washington and here. Integrity is critical, because if officials find out that we're not being truthful with them, they're not meeting with us the next time. As much as the public perception may be that lobbyists are one step below lawyers—and sure, there are always some bad apples anywhere—most lobbyists know that if they don't have integrity, they're not getting very far for very long.

How does it all hit your family? A lot of that depends on your ability to balance work and home life. I'm very lucky in that with my job, I'm able to spend time with my kids—certainly more so than my other colleagues who work in the private sector. Lobbying, like a lot of jobs in Washington, is really a full-time, full-contact sport, and it can take up your entire life if you let it. I think quality of life for a university or a public sector lobbyist is a lot better. Of course, those jobs don't pay quite as much, but that's okay. I think it's still worth it.

Leech: What is your favorite thing about your job?

Burnham: Engaging with students and working with them, and showing them what's going on. It's also a lot of fun getting to talk about a university doing research. I'm talking about the future, how things are changing, how things are getting better. I'm talking about being hopeful going forward. It's a lot of fun because we are always looking at what's on the horizon – and some of it is pretty amazing stuff.

Leech: What things do you like least about your job?

Burnham: Surprises. If I know what's coming, I can pretty much deal with it. It's the six a.m. text message that unexpectedly throws off my whole day. It's the surprise turn that completely changes what our office needs to do for the course of the next legislative session. Those things happen and it's hard. You can lay out a whole great plan, and then something that's outside of your control happens and you have to deal with it.

Leech: You said you like talking to students. If one of them came to you and said, "Hey, I want to be a lobbyist when I grow up," what would your advice to that person be?

Burnham: Learn to write and speak well. That is always a big challenge. Find a job on Capitol Hill, or on the state legislature, or on a campaign early on, because those are jobs that are hard to take once you already have a graduate degree, and life, and kids, and work, and all of that, because those jobs don't pay very well. Most good lobbyists have spent some time working on the other side—working in the legislature, working for the administration, working on Capitol Hill—and they understand how the system operates and what the rules and procedures are, what the committees are, and why they are set up the way they are. Once you have some institutional knowledge, then you can go on to graduate school or law school if that's what you choose to do.

Leech: A couple of people have mentioned to me the importance of writing well. Why is it important for lobbyists to write well?

Burnham: Lobbyists need to be able to prepare their presentations. They have to know how they're going to say something. Lobbyists have to be able to condense their arguments to one page, because legislators and staff are just not going to read more than one page. Lobbyists have to be able to articulate what it is they want, why they want it, why it's the right thing to do, why it's in the best interest of the official they are talking to, and why it's good for the state, the nation, or the institution. Lobbyists have to say all that succinctly and in a way that is compelling. That's hard to do in one page and it runs completely contrary to how faculty members have been taught to organize their arguments.

Leech: What other qualities would you say are important or useful as a lobbyist?

Burnham: You have to be curious. You have to want to understand why things are the way they are, why things work the way they do. You want to always be learning. You've got to have the personal skills and the personality to be able to go up to a perfect stranger and start up a conversation. You have to be able to handle people yelling at you, usually for things you had nothing to do with, and not reply in kind.

Leech: Is the yelling coming from people within government or people outside of government?

Burnham: Yes.

Leech: [Laughs.] Is there anything else you'd like to say about your job?

Burnham: I think one of the biggest challenges for people who do this job is the public sentiment that somehow lobbying as an enterprise is inappropriate or tainted. I can appreciate in the world of post–Jack Abramoff why people would feel that way, but I would remind folks that anybody who speaks to power and seeks redress of grievances is doing what a lobbyist does. The only difference is that a lobbyist has decided to do that as a profession. Whether you're talking about the Boy Scouts, or the Red Cross, or NOW [National Organization for Women], or any citizen organization of that size, they all employ lobbyists. There's no interest that isn't a special interest. They're all special interests.

Leech: It's only a special interest if you disagree with them. Otherwise, it's an interest.

Burnham: That includes raising taxes, lowering taxes, pro-guns, anti-guns, balanced budget, against balanced budget—whatever. Those are all special interests. A lobbyist can speak on behalf of good things, and unfortunately, they also can speak on behalf of bad things, depending on who the client is. Both sides employ lobbyists. It's like lawyers: it's understandable why people would not like them unless they need one, but everybody likes their own lawyer. It's a part of the process. If the lobbying is based entirely on relationships and not on substance, I can appreciate that is unsavory. Most good lobbyists are not like that.

CHAPTER

11

Danielle Her Many Horses

Deputy Executive Director
National Indian Gaming Association

Danielle Her Many Horses *is deputy executive director at the National Indian Gaming Association (NIGA), where she has worked since 2005, beginning as legislative director before being promoted in 2012. The NIGA is a trade association that represents Native American tribes that have casinos or other organized gambling on their lands. In 2011, it reported spending $465,000 on lobbying.*

Trade associations make up about one quarter of all of the interest groups active in Washington, because virtually every industry in the United States has one or more trade association to provide information, networking opportunities, and often political representation to their members. The NIGA's membership includes 184 Native American tribes, many of which also hire lobbying firms to lobby for their particular tribes. These lobbying relationships gained notoriety in 2005 when Jack Abramoff and other contract lobbyists were accused of fraud for overcharging and creating lobbying opposition to their tribal clients.

Her Many Horses has a bachelor's degree in finance and a law degree from the University of New Mexico.

Beth Leech: How did you begin your career? How did you come to be a lobbyist?

Danielle Her Many Horses: In 1997, when I was just out of college, I began working for a newly elected senator, Tim Johnson of South Dakota. I've always been interested in public policy, but I began work as his tribal liaison in his Rapid City office. I worked for him for two-and-a-half years and during that period I fell in love with public policy.

Leech: What did you do as tribal liaison?

Her Many Horses: I helped constituents from the tribe with issues related to things like transportation, roads, education, veteran affairs, and the Missouri River. Constituents would call into the office, and as a congressional staffer, I would try to help them with their federal issues where possible. Sometimes they might need the senator's office to talk to a federal agency on their behalf, because something was getting stalled for some reason. And I would work directly with the tribe as well to see how things were going and where the senator could be of more assistance.

Going through all of that and learning about the legislative process, I ended up deciding that I really wanted to go to law school.

Leech: Why did you think law school would be useful?

Her Many Horses: My bachelor's degree was in finance. As I was faced with different issues that tribes were dealing with, I would see proposed or existing legislation—and I did not have the technical expertise to read it. I had trouble understanding the committee reports, legislative history, and case law. I wanted to help the tribes, but realized I didn't know enough about the law itself.

Leech: So, you went to the law school at the University of New Mexico.

Her Many Horses: Yes, because they have the best Indian law program in the country.

Leech: While you were in law school, were there any internships that helped build toward your becoming a lobbyist?

Her Many Horses: The summer after my first year in law school, I got a wonderful internship with the Mohegan Tribe in Connecticut, which operates one of the largest gaming facilities in the country. Although what I was working on was not gaming-related—I worked on issues related to internal tribal government—I got to see a lot of how things worked, and gaming became very intriguing to me.

Leech: Where did you end up after graduating from law school?

Her Many Horses: I went to work for the Navajo Nation Department of Justice in Window Rock, Arizona. I worked in their Economic Development Unit because they wanted somebody who had a business background and also a law background. So I was a perfect fit. I did contract reviews, looking at different development proposals to see whether the proposals fit within the legal structure of the Navajo Nation. We had to evaluate what federal action might need to happen for a project to take place on Indian lands.

One of the main projects that I was assigned was gaming. They wanted to see what it would take to develop a Navajo Nation casino.

Leech: What did you have to do to see if that would work?

Her Many Horses: Well, I helped make sure that we had the appropriate tribal laws in place, in particular the Tribal Gaming Ordinance. I had to do a lot of work with the different chapter governments, as well as with the Navajo Nation Council, trying to get what they wanted done, while fully complying with the law.

And even though that wasn't "lobbying" under the legal definition, there definitely was lobbying involved in it. Passing any type of legislation in any government requires consensus building. There always are some people who want something to happen and other people who don't share that vision. I learned to find ways learn from and educate different shareholders to develop consensus.

Leech: When did you move on from there?

Her Many Horses: In 2005, when I was hired by the National Indian Gaming Association as their legislative director.

Leech: How would you describe the mission of the National Indian Gaming Association? What are you advocating for?

Her Many Horses: Our mission, really, is to protect tribal sovereignty and to ensure that tribes have adequate means and ways to develop sustainable tribal economies.

Leech: And how do you do that?

Her Many Horses: One of the things that has really worked as an economic boost has been gaming. NIGA spends a lot of time and energy making sure that there aren't any incursions into the tribal right to conduct gaming activities on Indian land.

We work particularly with the National Indian Gaming Commission, which is an independent agency within the Department of the Interior, to ensure there is a proper regulatory balance between the federal government and tribal governments, who are the primary regulators of tribal gaming. We also work with the Department of Interior on trust land acquisition policy and revenue allocation plans. We also work with the Department of the Treasury on bonding and taxation issues, and work with the Department of Homeland Security as well.

Leech: Why does Homeland Security get involved?

Her Many Horses: The Department of Homeland Security is concerned about the fact that casinos draw a lot of people, especially if there is an event like a concert. Any large event like that is a potential target for a terrorist group, and so the Department of Homeland Security becomes involved. Additionally, because of the large amount of security and surveillance that tribal casinos maintain, they work with Homeland Security to make sure that everyone's adequately trained to recognize potential threats.

Leech: That makes a lot of sense. Maybe at this point it would make sense to talk about a recent issue that you worked on, and you could walk us through how you approached that issue, and the sorts of things you did to advocate on that issue.

Her Many Horses: Our association, the National Indian Gaming Association, has one hundred and eighty-four tribes that are members, and those members really set the agenda for what we do.

Whether the issue is an attempt to limit a tribe's ability to game on acquired land, or whether the issue is unfair taxation, what we've found is that the best strategy for our members, the Indian tribes themselves, is to contact their members of Congress.

Our office might notice an issue first or the tribes might bring an issue to our attention. Then our office will analyze the issue and bring that information back to the tribe so that they can make decisions on how they want to go forward. We do all of their work in conjunction with the tribal attorneys and the lobbyists the tribe has hired, to make sure that we're all on message.

We also want to make sure that if there is a chance that some issue will move forward on really short notice, we are ready for it. In the upcoming lame-duck session for instance, we are concerned that everyone has all of the information that they need, all of the talking points, and all of the contacts that they need to make sure that nobody's caught flat-footed.

Leech: And do you contact members of Congress and their staff as well, or do you try to keep that to the members?

Her Many Horses: We make the contacts, as well. We talk daily with different member offices.

Leech: How do you make decisions about whom to target? Obviously, there are a lot of members of Congress, and you can't talk to everybody.

Her Many Horses: We focus on senators on the Indian Affairs Committee, the Finance Committee, or whichever committee any relevant legislation is going to go through. And in the House, we focus a lot of our activity in the Natural Resources Committee and the Indian Affairs Subcommittee. It really does depend on the issue. There's a strong Native American Caucus on the House side.

Leech: People who are ethnically Native American?

Her Many Horses: No. There's only one Native American in the House: Tom Cole of Oklahoma. But there are a lot of members who are interested in supporting tribal issues.

Leech: Are they interested because they have a lot of constituents who are Native Americans?

Her Many Horses: Some because of their constituent base and the states that they're from, and others because they actually have a genuine interest. If you look at some of their backgrounds and the districts that they're elected from, there is no possible constituent interest they could have in Indian country, so they must have a genuine concern.

Leech: What percentage of your time ends up being spent on issues that are legislative in nature versus issues that have to do with regulations and the gaming commission?

Her Many Horses: It really can depend. Sometimes the National Indian Gaming Commission [NIGC] is very active in pushing regulatory changes. A lot of the changes that they're making are good changes that keep up with the industry. I don't want it to seem like we're in constant conflict with NIGC, but sometimes they overstep. And then sometimes it's Congress that's active.

Leech: It sounds like a lot of the contacts you make in Congress are people who are already in your corner.

Her Many Horses: Yes.

Leech: And why is that? Can you explain to a person who's not in the lobbying business, why you would spend time talking to people who already agree with you?

Her Many Horses: A lot of those people who already agree with you are in positions where they can influence a lot of other people, and those other people may not be as inclined or interested. Sometimes there are people who just don't have tribal sovereignty in their world view. But because we have relationships with other members of Congress, we can have the members who are already on our side talk to those other members on our behalf.

Leech: That makes sense. What people read about lobbyists outside Washington is connected to campaign finance, including the dinners, receptions, and breakfast fundraisers. Do you get involved in that that scene at all?

Her Many Horses: There's some of that. It is part of the Washington, DC, culture, but they are not daily things for me. I might have a reception here, a reception there.

Our work at NIGA is more focused on stopping by congressional offices and calling congressional offices. We have relationships with members of congress and their staff: talking with them, keeping in touch, learning about where things are moving—or if they're not. Also important is making sure that our tribal members, the constituents of those members of Congress, are also making those contacts. We're definitely not a fundraiser-focused, reception-focused kind of organization.

Leech: That leads me to the question of the negative popular opinion about lobbyists, who are viewed as typified by Jack Abramoff. How is reality different from that public perception?

Her Many Horses: As a lobbyist working for a nonprofit association, I can tell you that we're not all big spenders making more than members of Congress. For many lobbyists, it's not about how much they have to spend but about what they know. A lot of people who go into lobbying have a lot of knowledge about specific issues.

Leech: As do you.

Her Many Horses: We do have a lot of knowledge here about how Indian gaming works, how it has benefitted tribes, and what is going on in Indian tribes. That knowledge needs to be conveyed to lawmakers who, if they didn't have that information, might do something that could negatively impact tribal sovereignty and the tribal gaming industry.

Indian gaming employs about 625,000 people. That's a lot of people whose livelihoods are dependent on the Indian gaming industry. If NIGA and the tribes are not actively making sure that Congress isn't tinkering in a way that is going to cause Indian gaming facilities to shut down or to lose market share, people are going to lose their jobs.

Our tribal members are very cognizant that they are putting people to work, and they want to protect those jobs and those people. I'll use my own tribe—the Oglala Lakota Sioux—as an example of the many tribes across the country. We have a very small casino, and we don't employ very many people. But the reservation where I am from has an unemployment rate of eighty percent. If there are three hundred people who have jobs because of this tribal casino, that's three hundred people who weren't working before.

That makes a difference in day-to-day lives. What we're trying to do is make sure that those people, who may not have been employed before, are continuing to work. The casino industry also employs a lot of retirees who are supplementing their Social Security income. They're trying to get by, and we want to help them continue to get by.

Leech: So NIGA advocates by explaining to policy makers the impact their potential decisions would have on real people?

Her Many Horses: Yes. They need to know that a decision could affect their constituents, the people who voted for them.

Leech: Why do policy makers listen to you?

Her Many Horses: They listen because we make them understand the issue—not necessarily from the technical aspect, but from the human aspect.

Leech: How is what NIGA does different from the lobbying firms that some tribes hire to represent them as well? I'm thinking of the Jack Abramoff case, which turned out so badly because Indian tribes were defrauded, but obviously not all hired lobbyists turn out like Jack Abramoff.

Her Many Horses: No, not all hired lobbyists are like that. NIGA itself has a hired lobbying firms on retainer. NIGA is a nonprofit organization, so our in-house staff is only a bitty, tiny lobbying shop. But NIGA also hires outside lobbyists from lobbying firms who work on our behalf. They're very good at what they do.

Leech: What does a lobbying firm bring to the table? What do the hired lobbyists give you? Obviously manpower, right? You wouldn't have the manpower otherwise, but why would an organization that already has its own lobbyists choose to hire a lobbying firm?

Her Many Horses: Increased access.

Leech: Explain.

Her Many Horses: Many people who go into lobbying are former staff members for people who are still sitting members of Congress, or they've worked on congressional committees. Those lobbyists know a number of different members of Congress. They have a very high level of access.

Leech: So, you have the knowledge about the content of proposals that might affect Indian gaming, given your law degree and your expertise in Indian law, but NIGA might sometimes need to hire someone who has expertise in who the decision makers are and who has access to those people.

Her Many Horses: Yes.

Leech: What does your average day look like now that you're deputy director? When would you get into the office, and what might you do in an average day?

Her Many Horses: Well, let's see. I would wake up in the morning, put on coffee.

Leech: Very important.

Her Many Horses: Sit there, wait for it to get done, read the *Washington Post*, read the *New York Times*.

Leech: Are there any other publications that you read regularly?

Her Many Horses: I also read the inside-Washington publications, *The Hill* and *Roll Call*. It is also very important to keep up with the Indian news media.

Leech: About what time do you usually get into the office?

Her Many Horses: Nine o'clock. I'd get in, go through *The Hill* and *Roll Call* real quick, and then start reading e-mails.

Leech: What are you looking for as you go through these publications?

Her Many Horses: Anything that's mentioning Indian tribes, primarily. Anything about tribes, tribal sovereignty, or gaming.

Leech: How many e-mails will you get in a typical morning, do you think?

Her Many Horses: About eighty. I go through them, see which ones need to be responded to, which ones can be deleted. I sit down and make a schedule of everything that needs to get done that day, making note of whether there's any upcoming travel, and if so, what needs to be prepared for that.

Leech: What sort of travel do you usually do? Are you going out to visit members at their casinos?

Her Many Horses: Yes. We go out to visit member casinos and also to attend conferences put on by regional tribal organizations. The more chances we have to meet more of our members, the better off we are. That way, they know what's going on here and we can learn if there's anything else that we need to be focusing on.

Leech: When you go through your e-mails, are most of them coming from the DC area, or are most of them from member organizations around the country?

Her Many Horses: It's about half and half.

Leech: So you're slogging through the e-mail—I know about that! Then what?

Her Many Horses: Different things will come up. I'd realize our white paper on economic development needs to be updated, so I would do that.

I'd update and rewrite, then look at it and reread it to see if I've glossed over anything or if I've been unclear. Then I turn back to whatever's in my paper inbox: trade magazines, political reports to read, reviews of new regulations that are up for comment.

More e-mails would pop up throughout the day. I would call a member of congressional staff to talk about a current issue. One of the fun things I'm doing right now is planning our legislative summit for July, finalizing our invitation list.

Leech: What will happen at that legislative summit?

Her Many Horses: We will have about twenty different members of Congress come to address their tribal leadership. About two hundred tribal leaders will come to Washington for the two-day summit. One day, we're having a tribal leader policy discussion, where we'll discuss what's going on and develop a strategy for going forward into the lame-duck session. The next day, we'll have our congressional speakers come over, giving each member ten to fifteen minutes to address the tribal leadership about current issues and longer-term issues.

Leech: And, do you do this every year?

Her Many Horses: We do it twice a year.

Leech: So planning for those conferences takes a lot of your time. In this average day that we are discussing, are we still in the morning or have we moved on to afternoon by this point?

Her Many Horses: Oh, it's probably afternoon by now.

Leech: Will you typically go out for lunch or do you work at your desk?

Her Many Horses: I work and eat at my desk most of the time.

Leech: Those three-martini lobbyist lunches aren't for you?

Her Many Horses: No, not for me. I spend about ten minutes running to the little buffet where they sell lunch for $6.85 a pound, picking up something, and coming back to my desk.

Then in the afternoon, there will be more e-mails, more planning for upcoming trips, more updating of different PowerPoint presentations, or writing a white paper that needs to get prepared for Hill meetings.

Leech: Will you spend much of that time on the phone, reaching out to congressional staff?

Her Many Horses: Some of that is done by phone, but a lot of it is done by e-mail. Everyone is very busy, and it's hard to reach people.

Leech: So, would you reach out to the congressional staff person in charge of the issue area that you are interested in and send a white paper or some other information?

Her Many Horses: Yes. I'd e-mail to say, "We're currently working on this issue, and I just want to give you an update." Or, "We're expecting this, this, and this to happen, and we'd certainly love your office's support."

Or I might be responding to an e-mail from them. The staff member might e-mail me saying, "We've just received a call with questions about Indian gaming. Can you help us? We need some statistics on how much money tribes are making." I would compile that information and e-mail it to the congressional office.

Leech: How often do those requests for information come into your office?

Her Many Horses: About twice a week.

Leech: The classic idea of lobbying is that lobbyists are always talking directly to a member of Congress, not to the staff of that member. In a year, how often do you actually interact with the actual member of Congress?

Her Many Horses: That's why we hold our legislative summits. We get a lot of face time with individual members.

Leech: But in an average week, would you get the chance to meet with a member of Congress in his or her office?

Her Many Horses: Some weeks are very intensive with Hill meetings, so we will have 10 to 15 member meetings that week. The next week may be spent with a lot of phone calls and e-mails with staff people. Each week brings its own challenges and priorities. It is also subject to the schedule of the House and Senate.

Leech: What qualities make for a good lobbyist? What characteristics, training, and background are necessary to be a good lobbyist?

Her Many Horses: From our perspective, it's really being able to tell the story of Indian gaming. If you can craft the story, tell that story consistently and make it resonate. That is the most important skill.

Leech: What sorts of things help make a message resonate with members of Congress, or staff, or agencies?

Her Many Horses: When you turn an abstract issue into a story about people's lives. If you can tell a member, "This is how this is going to affect people's lives...," it makes a difference. The stories come from our members. That's why we work so hard to have good relationships with our members—to be very responsive to them.

Leech: Are there other skills that a person needs to be a good lobbyist?

Her Many Horses: A good memory for names and faces.

Leech: Why is that?

Her Many Horses: Because Washington, DC, is like a small college campus. Especially up on Capitol Hill it's good to be able to have sight and name recognition when you're just walking down the street or buying a cup of coffee, because you never know when you're going to be standing in line behind a member of Congress and you could have a couple minutes to chat.

Leech: There you go. So you could take advantage of that opportunity.

Her Many Horses: Yes.

Leech: I have heard Washington described as being an old boys' club. Is it more of a challenge to get ahead as a woman? Or do you think that's changed?

Her Many Horses: There has been change, but that old boys' club is not completely gone. Women are still vastly outnumbered in Congress, and it's often easier for guys to get along with guys and be able to talk about shared and similar experiences. I think that's just human nature. But substantively, I don't think that there's much difference in how women are treated. As long as the person knows what she's doing and what she's talking about, people will have respect for that.

Leech: How about the personal side of being a lobbyist? Is being a lobbyist conducive to family life?

Her Many Horses: I have a two-year-old daughter. Working for a small trade association is not an impediment to me having a good relationship with my daughter. There is a lot of travel and a lot of work and long hours, but I'm not at receptions every night. It's a much different experience to be an in-house lobbyist for a nonprofit than it would be if I were working for a large lobbying firm.

Leech: What advice would you have for someone who is starting out and thinking that they might want to be a lobbyist or a policy advocate of some kind? What would you say to that person?

Her Many Horses: Know your subject matter. Be prepared for long hours.

Leech: Is it important to have worked on the Hill?

Her Many Horses: It certainly helps.

Leech: How about having a law degree? Is that crucial?

Her Many Horses: I wouldn't say that it's crucial, but from my perspective, it's what I wanted. I wouldn't say it's absolutely necessary, but a law degree helps because, for example, the degree would help you get a better committee position. Then later on, when you decide you no longer wish to be in government employment, you can choose to become a lobbyist and you'll have greater access than you would have had otherwise.

Leech: What's the best thing about your job?

Her Many Horses: My favorite thing about my job is working with tribes, with the members of NIGA.

Leech: Is there anything you're not so fond of doing?

Her Many Horses: No. I actually really enjoy all aspects of my job.

Leech: There's no part that makes you say, "Oh, yes! Now I get to delegate that!"?

Her Many Horses: Filing.

Leech: You have moved out of the entry level most definitely.

Her Many Horses: Yes.

Leech: When you are hiring someone to work as a lobbyist at NIGA, what qualities are you looking for in that person?

Her Many Horses: A good base of knowledge about Indian gaming is one good positive, and also if they've worked for tribal government, or a tribal gaming facility, or a different inner-tribal organization. That would mean the name and face recognition curve isn't as steep. Beyond that, a lot of it's going to come down to your personal interview.

Leech: Why is that?

Her Many Horses: We're a very small operation, and it helps to be able to work well with others who are in that small organization.

Leech: Any other particular skills that you would be looking for in such a person?

Her Many Horses: Someone who's articulate. And very down-to-earth.

Leech: Why is that helpful?

Her Many Horses: Because the members of Congress and the tribes that we work with are very no-nonsense. It's certainly not about flattery. The more down-to-earth a person is, the more able they are to communicate the narrative of Indian gaming.

This conversation has been interesting because I don't often think about how different what I do is from how lobbying is viewed by the public. It's important to talk about. I hope conversations like these can dispel some of the myths about what lobbyists do and how they do it. For me and for NIGA, lobbying is very grassroots-oriented—and not about expensive fundraisers.

CHAPTER

12

Timothy Richardson

Senior Legislative Liaison
Fraternal Order of Police

***Timothy Richardson** is senior legislative liaison at the Washington office of the National Fraternal Order of Police, the largest organization of law enforcement officers in the world. The FOP serves as a union as well as an educational and advocacy resource for its more than 330,000 members. In 2011, the FOP reported spending $250,000 on lobbying; in the 2012 election cycle, it made $41,250 in campaign contributions—95 percent of them to Democrats.*

Richardson has been with the FOP throughout his career, beginning as a legislative assistant in 1996 and being promoted to his current position in 2001. Both his father and his grandfather were police officers. He has a bachelor's degree in English/professional writing and political science from Elizabethtown College in Pennsylvania.

Beth Leech: How did you begin your career? How did you end up working for the Fraternal Order of Police?

Timothy Richardson: Good timing. After graduating from college, I found a paid internship—which nowadays do not exist—working for the Senate Republican Policy Committee. It was the time of the federal government shutdown of 1995 and 1996, after President Clinton vetoed the budget the Republicans sent him. "Nonessential" government workers were on furlough for almost a month, so the committee was really squeezing every ounce out of their interns. We interns had more of an opportunity to be engaged in how the Senate and legislative process worked.

I worked for the committee for about six months, and it just happened that the FOP, which had selected a new executive director in 1995, had finally gotten money to hire another staff member.

Leech: In Washington?

Richardson: In Washington. I saw an advertisement about the job in the basement of the Russell Senate Office Building. My grandfather and dad were police officers. My dad at the time was chief of detectives and his most senior detective was the state lodge president of the Fraternal Order of Police. I had known that detective since I was two or three years old. He knew I was interested in the position, put in a good word for me, and my résumé made it to the top of the pile pretty quickly. They interviewed me in May and I started here in June 1996.

Leech: You have been at the FOP ever since?

Richardson: I have been here ever since. At the end of that first year, my boss had said, "What do you think? Do you like it?" I said I did. He was a good mentor and taught me a lot about advocacy, about lobbying. I told him, "I'm probably not going to stay past the next Congress, but I'm going to commit to staying the entire next year for sure." That was in 1996.

Leech: What was the learning curve like? You knew a fair amount about police officers in general, having grown up with them, and your degree is in political science. How ready were you to be on the ground, in the real world?

Richardson: Most of the learning curve was about the approach. Because of my work in the Senate, I had a very good grasp of procedure and the basics of how a bill really becomes a law. As a staff member, I also watched advocates who were coming to the committee to say, "This is important. Here are the merits of this." I had seen lobbyists advocate, and now that's what I was being asked to do. That was the only really tough part of the curve.

Leech: What was hard about it?

Richardson: Learning how to approach a staffer, not as another member of the staff, but as someone who wants something. For my first three or four months at the FOP, I was in the boss's pocket. He had a lot of experience, so I followed him from office to office and learned by doing and watching. He had been an assistant director at ATF [Bureau of Alcohol, Tobacco, Firearms, and Explosives] and he was in charge of their congressional relations for the last ten to fifteen years of his career. He was very savvy about how the policy process works and how best to be an advocate.

It didn't take too long for me to figure things out. I was lucky again with the timing. Back in 1996, it was usual for Congress to take a break—unlike now where Congress goes to Christmas Eve or later every year. It was an election year, and Congress met the last time on September 30 and then not again until January. So I had three months to really learn the FOP's issues in depth, learn where the organization had been historically, and find out how the organization worked. When the 105th Congress started in January 1997, I was prepared.

Leech: The FOP is involved in a lot of issues. I looked at your last lobbying disclosure filing and there were sixteen pages of issues the FOP has been lobbying on. How would you describe this range of issues?

Richardson: A lot of things changed after the attacks of September 2001. The FOP got involved in a whole new menu of issues specific to homeland security. The administration at the time believed that to fight terrorism, you not only needed to access the military, but also domestic law enforcement. Some acts of terror are not necessarily acts of war, but they are crimes that need to be investigated and prosecuted like any other crime.

Yes, we've got an awful lot of issues. There are sentencing issues: locking bad guys up—the longer the better—and identifying where different criminal activities fall in the sentencing guidelines. There are firearms issues, immigration issues, Internet issues—like the criminal acts covered under the Stop Online Piracy Act, retirement issues for our members, and even education issues like the Children of Fallen Heroes Scholarship Act.

The FOP is also a labor organization, but the Grand Lodge, which is the national governing body of the FOP, is not a union in and of itself. We represent unions. Our members are part of local bargaining units that sit down with city mayors and county executives and negotiate contracts. There is always a lot about the labor side of things that needs work.

Sometimes, yes, we find ourselves in the middle of a lot of issues that might seem unusual for police officers. We are very much involved in the online environment now. We were drawn into Internet spectrum issues connected with the National Public Safety Broadband Network, the aim of which is to provide nationwide emergency communications. I sat on the board of directors for the Public Spectrum Safety Trust as a representative of the FOP. We were involved in SOPA [Stop Online Piracy Act], which we supported because it involved curbing fraudulent and criminal activity online.

Leech: How deep does your knowledge need to be of all the various issues that you are involved in, in order to lobby on those issues effectively?

Richardson: For the Internet issues, for example, I did not need technical expertise but rather enough familiarity with the technology that I could make a rational argument. I needed to be able to explain it to a staff member or a member of Congress who didn't have even basic knowledge about how these things worked.

At the same time, these technical issues are not top priorities for the FOP.

What we do often when we have those situations where we need some technical expertise is that we look internally and find someone who is an expert. We have two guys who I rely on quite a bit when it comes to the technological ins and outs of public safety radio spectrum management, how broadband works, that sort of thing. But I know enough. A lobbyist can make a formidable argument without knowing everything down to the last particle, but that lobbyist will be more effective with a working knowledge of the technicalities.

Fortunately, staff and members of Congress are often in the same boat. I will come across staffers, particularly on the relevant committees, who know this issue down to the bones and who could construct a broadband network if you gave them a toothpick and a piece of gum. Then I may meet with staffers who are not on the committee, who have never dealt with this before, and they may not know what "spectrum" means. When I am advocating, it's a matter of knowing my audience as well as the issue.

Leech: These experts who you bring in, are they in your office in DC?

Richardson: One of the guys is retired from the Metropolitan Police Department here in DC. They called him out of retirement to do the secure communications for the inauguration. The other experts are drawn from our three hundred and thirty thousand members. We've got experts in just about anything. It's just a matter of locating them, getting on the phone with them, or having them send me some bullet points about what I need to know.

Leech: How big is your office? How many people are doing full-time advocacy for the FOP in DC?

Richardson: We have the executive director, myself, and one other legislative liaison.

Leech: What are the top priorities for the Washington office?

Richardson: Priorities are set by the membership, although I make a distinction between what we call a "top legislative priority" set by the membership and legislative priorities dictated by which issues are moving on the Hill. The latter are things that can actually be achieved in the current political environment. While we have top priorities from the membership, those may not necessarily involve the majority of our staff's time.

Leech: Because you have to react to what is actually happening in Washington?

Richardson: Correct. Some of our top priorities are very far-reaching and may not realistically be bills that we can achieve in the near future. We have a Social Security issue connected to getting rid of the Windfall Elimination Provision. Police officers usually do not pay into or receive Social Security, unless they work at some other job as well. The Windfall Elimination Provision eliminates up to fifty percent of Social Security for those officers who have worked outside jobs or who qualify for spousal or survivor Social Security benefits. We have been working on that issue since 1997. We also have a Collective Bargaining Bill that we almost got through in 2004 and 2007, but regrettably fell a little short. We could not reduce that shortfall in the last Congress and we are unlikely to do so in the 113th, considering the partisan makeup of the House.

Leech: This is because public safety employees currently don't have a federally guaranteed right to collective bargain?

Richardson: The bill would establish a national floor of what public safety employees' rights are. Those rights vary widely. There are states that have very solid public safety employee laws that govern their labor relations. Pennsylvania and Ohio settled that issue on the ballot. But, as we saw in Ohio and Wisconsin, those rights can also be taken away. We want to put a floor in place nationwide.

Leech: We've talked about a bunch of different issues that the FOP has been involved in. What sorts of steps does a lobbyist take to try to achieve policy goals like these?

Richardson: The most important thing is getting yourself on the radar screen. You first need to find a staff member who will listen to you. You want that staff member to work for a member of Congress who would be interested in your issue and who would want to help—who would want to be identified with your organization and with the policy objective that you espouse. There are a number of ways of picking that person. Obviously, whatever the issue is, you want to first look at the relevant committee and you want to try and get a member with seniority, if you can. Sometimes you may have district or state ties to the member that the organization can use.

That's the first step and that's often the most difficult. Staffers and members are inundated with policy ideas and with constituents sharing their views. It's not magic, but the trick of it is to find the right person. Ideally, you will find a member of Congress who is interested in the issue and who has ties to the organization, either through constituents or because they want to be a champion for the organization. You've also got to make sure that it is an issue on which there is some agreement, or it won't get very far in Congress.

Leech: The general public seems to think that this all happens because of campaign contributions. What role do you think campaign contributions play?

Richardson: I think for the most part that it's just one other way to try to capture that member's attention. I don't think it's any more or less effective than any other strategy. The FOP established its national PAC in 2004.

Leech: Relatively recently.

Richardson: Yes, and having a PAC really hasn't made any difference in how we approach things day to day. It might make a difference for other industries, but obviously there aren't any pro-crime members of Congress, although there are a few who are anti-law enforcement. In general, law enforcement officers are popular. Publically elected officials want to support police officers and help them do their jobs. That was one of the things that attracted me to the FOP. I liked serving on congressional staff and wasn't sure that I wanted to represent a "special interest." But law enforcement officers are out there protecting everybody, whether you make a political contribution or not. That is a *really* special interest.

The chief role of campaign contributions is to get that member's attention, but regardless of the check that you write, unless that individual member of Congress *wants* to work with you on issues, you are really wasting your money. Thus, we are very selective about who we do give to.

Leech: You were talking about the first step in approaching an issue as a lobbyist, and you had gotten to the first step, which is getting a member of Congress on board with you.

Richardson: Right. Let me give you an example. We had a staff member whose husband is a federal officer while she was an employee here. In the Commonwealth of Virginia, they were working on legislation called National Blue Alert, similar to an Amber Alert but only used when an officer is killed in line of duty or severely injured. It worked the same way as an Amber Alert but it relies on the description of the suspect or the vehicle that the suspect used. An alert would go out and light up along highways: "Watch for a red Chevy with a six-foot-two man with a ski mask and a sawed-off shotgun," or whatever the description was, so that the public could alert police.

We crafted some legislation that would make the National Blue Alert a national plan. We have an excellent working relationship with Representative Steny Hoyer, who was majority leader for the House. We took the legislation to him. He put it into bill language, and then Representative Michael McMahon from New York introduced the bill with Mr. Hoyer's support. The plan did not cost any money because it was calling on the resources already in place from the Amber Alert. It was a positive for law enforcement. You had the Fraternal Order of Police, the oldest and largest organization of police officers in the country, saying that this was a good thing, that this was important to us, so the issue started rolling very quickly. This was in 2010, and unfortunately, it was very near to the end of the congressional session, so there was not an opportunity to vote on the legislation.

Leech: Because there is limited space on the legislative calendar, right?

Richardson: Very much so, which is why having someone like Mr. Hoyer on your team is so important. When we got to the 112th Congress at the beginning of 2011, McMahon had been defeated by a freshman Republican, Michael Grimm.

Grimm immediately reintroduced the bill without talking to the supporters and then it became somewhat political. Eventually, we were able to sort everything out and get everybody on the same page and that legislation passed the House during National Police Week. Unfortunately, in the Senate we faced Senator Tom Coburn, who has blocked just about everything we have tried to do in the last two years.

Leech: Any idea why that is?

Richardson: He is very much against law enforcement as a federal concern, and does not believe the federal government should be involved in public safety laws.

Leech: Is that one of the reasons the FOP ends up having more allies within the Democratic Party than the Republican Party? I noticed that most of your campaign contributions do go to Democrats.

Richardson: It depends. When it comes to a lot of the labor issues, we find ready allies on the Democratic side. When it comes to criminal justice to fund crime measures, we find a lot of allies on the Republican side. It really depends on the issue. Dr. Coburn is a unique case. He just blocks us across the board.

Leech: So the Blue Alert has not become law. Do you have any other examples of issues you have worked on?

Richardson: Yes, we also have legislation that I have been working on since my first day or two in here. It's a bill to allow law enforcement officers, active and retired, to carry concealed firearms even when they leave their jurisdiction. This issue crops up frequently in law enforcement because, unlike other nations that have national police forces, in the United States they are broken down into local jurisdictions. There are eighteen thousand different jurisdictions in the United States, although a lot of them overlap. You've got federal, local, and state overlapping jurisdictions. Every chief is a king and every sheriff is a duke, so everybody does things a little differently. Police officers needed the right to carry their firearms when they entered those other jurisdictions.

We passed that as a law in 2004: the Law Enforcement Officers Safety Act. But, of course, you never get everything right the first time. What we discovered after we passed the law is that civilian law enforcement officers working for the Department of Defense did not have a statutory arrest authority—so under the definition of "qualified law enforcement officer" that we built into the bill, they still did not have the right to carry their firearms outside of their jurisdiction. The officers working for Department of Defense could apprehend suspects but they could not arrest anyone, so the law's language excluded them.

We were stuck with that. So we rewrote some language and passed an amendment in 2010 that just said every police officer, as defined by the federal government, who works for the executive branch is covered.

Leech: Problem solved.

Richardson: Well, no, actually. It turns out that the amendment helped the Amtrak officers and some other federal officers, but it still did not cover the Department of Defense officers. What we had to do was go back into the law and add the word "apprehension" and cite the Uniform Code of Military Justice, because that's where the apprehension authority for the Department of Defense law enforcement officers apparently derives.

This was back in the 111th Congress, later in 2010. We got agreed-upon language. We cleared it with the Senate Armed Services Committee and we had it inserted as part of the National Defense Authorization Act at the close of the last congressional session. We had support from Senator Carl Levin, the Armed Services chairman, and from Senator John McCain, the ranking Republican member of that committee. All t's were crossed, the i's were dotted, and then the amendment was stripped out.

I later found out that the amendment was dropped because somebody in the House Judiciary Committee had seen it and said, "Wait, we don't know what this does. We don't know what this is all about. It's got to go." It actually did fall into their jurisdiction. It wasn't just an Armed Services issue.

We had to come back the next year, in the 112th Congress and redo all that. Right away we were meeting with members of the House Judiciary Committee to go over the same ground we had gone over with the Armed Services committee members, and we finally got the language inserted. Senator Jim Webb was a huge help to us, as was Senator Leahy. Patrick Leahy is one of our most stalwart and steadfast champions on the Hill. He does a lot for our law enforcement officers and we were able to get the amendment inserted into the bill. The House Judiciary indicated that they did support the inclusion of that provision, so Armed Services signed off and we finally got it signed into law. It was just signed into law by the president on January 2.

Leech: Wow. When you are checking in with all these people and doing all of this due diligence, is it always through your legislative champions, or do you yourself go to the individual offices to explain what is in the bill?

Richardson: It is mostly staff work, meeting with staff. It is the staff on the Hill who make the wheels go round. The decisions are made much further up the chain, by the members of Congress, by leadership, but all of the ground work and all of the ins and outs of dotting the i's and crossing the t's are done by the staff.

Leech: You must be in constant communication.

Richardson: Yes, absolutely. We build relationships with the staffers and we know what their expertise is, what their strengths are, and—depending on whom they are working for—we also get to know what their political inclinations are and where their policy interests lie, and we use that as well.

Leech: What percentage of your days is taken up with talking with staff and getting to know them versus other things you might do, like doing research, or writing, or working on something internal to the FOP?

Richardson: I would say that the bulk of my day—maybe sixty or seventy percent—is spent writing, be it a simple letter of support for a particular bill, an alert for our membership about the introduction of a bill or about movement on a bill, or an invitation for a member of Congress to speak at a function.

Most of the rest of the time is focused on the Hill. I'll be on the phone with the Senate Judiciary Committee—the folks I work with all the time. Sometimes I am calling just to check in. Sometimes I am seeing what their agenda is going to be for next week. The more staff an organization has, the more lobbyists can be proactive and can get out of the office and go look the congressional staffers in the eyes and talk with them. When staffing levels are lower, lobbyists are more confined to the office, and e-mail, and the telephone. Many staffers now prefer electronic communications to finding a place to meet in a small congressional office.

Leech: Interesting.

Richardson: With the draconian changes to the ethics guidelines and rules of the House and Senate, it's not like it was ten or twelve years ago when a lobbyist and a staffer who knew each other both in the office and away from the office could get a cup of coffee in the morning or have a beer after work. You can't do that anymore. It's just too much of a hassle.

Leech: How has that affected you and the FOP?

Richardson: It is hard to get to know new staff persons as well as I know the dozen or so that have been around since I started in Washington. I had a good friend who worked for a member of Congress. We would hang out very frequently after work and almost never discussed business. This is, I think, something else that most folks don't understand. When we are not working, we don't want to work. There is, obviously, shop talk because that's what you do, but you are not taking a guy to a baseball game or to grab a beer after work because you want to lecture him on the merits of concealed firearms.

Leech: Although you still could do that if the staffer paid his own way.

Richardson: Oh yes, absolutely. Anyway, my friend was off the Hill for a while and then when he returned to the Hill, he had to fill out more paperwork than he knew what to do with just if we went out for a beer after work. And so it is hard to get new staffers outside the office so that you can get to know them.

Leech: But you wouldn't have to fill out the paperwork if he paid for his own beer, right?

Richardson: Yes, that's true if everybody is on their own dime but there is still some negative attention. Staffers are very cognizant of any appearance of any impropriety.

Leech: You were talking a bit earlier about the amount of time you spend writing. Could you expand on that and walk me through an average day? What does a day look like to you?

Richardson: The first thing every day is reading the news from *CQ, Congressional Quarterly*, a service that monitors Congress. Then I check my e-mails on my way into work.

Leech: How early do you start?

Richardson: This town wakes up early, but I live about fifty miles from Capitol Hill, so my day in the office starts about nine thirty. *CQ* will let me know what the agenda is for the committees in the House and the Senate so that I can be prepared to respond to anything that is happening. I scan the news to see if our issues are being talked about so that I am prepared for the day. Normally, that day will mostly consist of the writing I've got to do. Then I try to do at least one call to someone I don't need anything from, just to keep connections open. Sometimes I am able to do it: my rule is three people a week.

Leech: A congressional staffer or somebody from another organization?

Richardson: Yes, just to check in just to see what's going on. More often than not, the communication will be electronic, but for the people I work with quite frequently, I will pick up the phone and see if I can get them on the horn.

Then I also will be working on whatever issue we have at the moment that is near to being introduced, preparing for a committee markup, or trying to get a floor vote.

Because the FOP has such a broad swath of issues, depending on the week I could be talking to the HELP [Health, Education, Labor, and Pensions] Committee in the Senate, the Education and the Workforce Committee in the House, the House Judiciary Committee, or the Senate Committee on Homeland Security. It could be a whole mix of things.

Leech: We were up to the afternoon in your day. When do you usually head home?

Richardson: Normally, my day ends about six thirty. That's the last train out. There are sometimes events that occur after regular working hours, such as events with other organizations for members of Congress, so sometimes my day can stretch into the evening. The evening events are not as frequent as they used to be—again because of the problems with out-of-office interaction, and because the economy stinks and there are not a lot of organizations willing to pay for those large events.

But especially now, with communication being what it is, I am never really off duty. I have my Blackberry with me all of the time. If I can get to the Internet, I can do my job. I was on the phone and doing a lot of electronic communication over the holidays because, in addition to the fiscal cliff, and the tax, and everything else, there was a piece of legislation introduced that directly affected the FOP. The Safer Act was introduced by Senator John Cornyn, and similar legislation was introduced by Senator Patrick Leahy. This legislation would create a public DNA registry using information from rape kits in sexual assault cases. It would beef up the Debbie Smith DNA Act and there was some hope that we could get it through before the congressional session ended, because it began as a bipartisan effort and there was a lot of broad-based agreement. But, unfortunately, we were not able to do it.

Leech: And that issue kept you working right up through the end of the year?

Richardson: Yes, it's the first time I can remember trying to have a policy discussion at seven p.m. on New Year's Eve.

Leech: Ouch. That sort of leads into a question I wanted to ask you: whether you feel that being a lobbyist is conducive to family life?

Richardson: It is. When I was younger, I was not as responsible with my time, but now I think it's like any other job. You've got to make smart decisions about your time. I have a pretty long commute and that does affect home life because sometimes I am not home until eight p.m. because it's an hour and fifteen- or twenty-minute ride home, but we make do. I don't think there are any particular challenges for home life in lobbying or legislative advocacy.

Leech: Do you have kids?

Richardson: I do. One of each, ten and nine.

Leech: What do you think is the best thing about your job? What do you like the most?

Richardson: Dealing with government can be incredibly frustrating, but when you get something done, it is very fulfilling because you have passed a law. My mom used to say, "Let's not make a federal case out of this," but that's what I do every day. I make a federal case out of something. When you get it done and you see how many officers are appreciative of the objective you achieve, it's a very positive feeling. I talk to three or four officers a week who call in with questions about the Law Enforcement Officer Safety Act that exempted active officers from the concealed-carry laws, and they are always so appreciative of what the FOP did for them in making that change federal.

Leech: It sounds like you have a lot of interaction with FOP members.

Richardson: Yes, the FOP differs from a lot of other labor organizations, which are very top-down, leadership-driven. The decisions are made at that upper level. The FOP, by contrast, is organized at the local level, so the local president is sovereign in that locality for decisions about public safety policy. The same thing is true at the state level. State laws are sovereign to state organizations. The national FOP can't come into New York, for example, and take a position on state firearms legislation. We have a constitution and bylaws that prohibit us from doing that. The national FOP only deals with issues and matters that affect all three hundred and thirty thousand of our networks. We don't do local contract negotiations, although we do have support staff that will assist.

Leech: I know the FOP does a member fly-in day. Why do you do that and what does it look like when you are doing it?

Richardson: We do it annually. It started the year before I got here. We call it our Day on the Hill, even though it's about half a week. We ask all of our members who can to come to Washington, DC. We ask them to make appointments with their senators and their representative. We spend the first day briefing them on lobbying strategies, lobbying tips, and the legislation that we are asking them to talk about—our top priorities and whatever pending issues are topical. For example, last year, the House was scheduled to vote on a funding bill that affected the COPS office, which is the Community Oriented Policing Services office that administers the grants to localities that assist them in hiring new officers. That vote was that week. We had about two hundred officers in here and there were twenty-four, maybe as many as thirty votes, that we flipped and I think that's just because we were here in town.

Leech: Yes, because the members of Congress were hearing from their constituent police officers.

Richardson: In any case, we brief the officers on Monday on what they need to know. For that whole week, this office is not doing anything else proactive. We are on standby for the visiting officers. We are here to answer questions for our members and from staff because sometimes staff is going to be hearing about this issue for the first time from officers that patrol our communities. It's a great time. We often get a spike in co-sponsorships of a piece of legislation we are interested in, and for at least the next couple of weeks, those congressional offices are going to be talking and thinking about these issues and responding to the constituents who took their time and spent their money to come to DC.

Leech: What about the popular opinion about lobbyists? How would you say that reality is different from what most people think lobbyists are and what lobbyists do?

Richardson: The perception is a little off. We are not as bad as lawyers, for example. We are paid to represent a certain point of view or a certain group of constituents, so no matter what we are lobbying for, someone is paying us to do that job, and I think lobbying is the sign of a healthy democracy, of healthy public interaction. What can muddle things up is when people make bad decisions. That happens in any career or industry, but with lobbying it is magnified. I think the degree of offense is increased because lobbyists are perceived as having special privileges because of their access to members of Congress.

Everybody has a lobbyist in Washington. When I first got to town, I had to commute past an entire building for the National Snack Foods Association. Not only do snack food manufacturers have a lobbyist—they have a whole building. Everyone has a point of view and if you are organized enough, you can get professional representation to express that message in DC.

Leech: What's the worst thing about your job? What don't you like doing?

Richardson: The only thing I really hate is my commute. I'm sure that's true for about two million people that live and work around this city.

Leech: I'll bet that's true. Why do you live so far out?

Richardson: Mostly the economy. I started out in Arlington, then Alexandria, then Prince William, and I think I might keep going, so I will be in Richmond before too long. My wife is a teacher, so her job also was an issue. We just kept migrating further and further south. It's nice when I'm there. It's a great area, great neighborhood. I can't think of a better place to live in the area, but it's a long commute every day.

Leech: Do you manage to get much work done on the train?

Richardson: I try to avoid it if I can. That's my decompression time. During the morning commute I review any early e-mails that come in. *CQ* does what they call alerts, so when a bill that I'm interested in is set up for action or it shows up in a news story, I get those e-mails. So I probably spend about half my morning commute interacting through my phone. But at the end of the day, I turn the lights out at six thirty unless there is something happening. I try to end my workday at that time. It doesn't always work.

Leech: What are the skills and qualities that someone needs to do a good job as a lobbyist?

Richardson: Be happy and be personable. You have to like to talk. You have to like to interact. You have to have a great deal of patience. One of the not-very-fun parts of the job is that Washington attracts a lot of conflicting personalities. That's just how it is. You also have staffers who are supposed to protect their bosses by not letting lobbyists talk to them. You have to have a lot of patience.

Depending on whom you work for, you may have to be willing to advocate for something that you don't feel very strongly about in your heart of hearts. I came from the Senate Republican Policy Committee when I was hired by the FOP, and two months later, they endorsed Bill Clinton for reelection. I had the twitches and the fits for the first six months I was here. I went from writing Republican screeds to coordinating with the Clinton campaign. It was quite a culture shock. You have to be open-minded in that way. If you can't, then you are better off working for an organization that represents something that you believe in very strongly. If weapons are your thing, then you'll want to work for the NRA [National Rifle Association] or the Gun Owners of America, or if you're interested in social issues go to the Family Research Council if you are conservative and the ACLU [American Civil Liberties Union] if you are not.

An organization like the FOP is not really "special interest." It's the man on the street with the badge and the gun who is keeping your family safe. I think it's easier because everything we do is directed by our members who say, "This is what I need to get this job done well and get it done safely." I'm much more comfortable with whatever that agenda is, because it is to support the officers.

Leech: Your undergraduate degree was in political science but you also had some training in writing. Do you find that's a help in your work?

Richardson: Yes, it was very helpful. I was a double major in political science and English professional writing. I have always had some talent in writing, and I was able to apply it here. I think that's one of the things that made me stand out early at FOP. I had talent as a writer and that has improved. Ironically, the only English course I did not get an A in as a college student was a course in writing for the government and judiciary. I barely passed it.

Leech: That's very funny.

Richardson: The professor and I had very deep philosophical issues and I barely made the final exam. I was not very responsible with my time as a younger man.

Leech: Do you have any advice for people who are college students now?

Richardson: Anyone who is interested in public policy, political science, or politics should spend some time looking at the advocacy side. Whether it is because you are going before your zoning board in your local community or because you want to make the world safe by banning the use of land mines internationally—whatever that cause is or whatever is important to you, you will need to know what it takes to advocate effectively.

I apply the same principles I use on the Hill to every other aspect of life, all the way down to meeting with my kids' teachers or principals. If I have an objective, I use the advocacy strategies there. Anything that you are doing—regardless of whether it is professionally as a lobbyist, or just getting things done around the house, or in your life dealing with other folks—the advocacy approach is going to work. There is some application for it.

Leech: When you say the advocacy approach and how you are using it in other aspects of your life, what in particular are you talking about?

Richardson: Know what you want to get before you sit down. That's the biggest thing. Have your goal, have a goal that is achievable, and then don't let up until you have achieved that goal, regardless of how long it takes. You will need some patience sometimes, but if you know what you want to get, there is no reason you can't get it.

CHAPTER

13

Jonathan Schleifer

Executive Director

Educators 4 Excellence—New York

Jonathan Schleifer *is the first executive director of Educators 4 Excellence's New York chapter. E4E was founded in 2010 by two Bronx public school teachers. Its mission is to "work to ensure that the voices of classroom teachers are included in the decisions that affect our profession and our students." E4E's members are teachers who learn, network, and take action around public policies to elevate the teaching profession and student performance.*

Before coming to E4E in 2012, Schleifer was chief policy officer for Iraq and Afghanistan Veterans of America (IAVA.). Earlier, he was responsible for online communications for former New Hampshire Governor Jeanne Shaheen's successful bid for the US Senate and he served as Rep. Anthony Weiner's (D-NY) senior policy advisor. His first job after college was teaching for five years at Middle School 303 in the Bronx, initially as a Teach for America corps member.

Schleifer has a master's degree in public policy from Harvard's John F. Kennedy School of Government and another master's degree from Columbia University's Teachers College. He has a bachelor's degree from Rutgers College.

Beth Leech: Your bio says that your undergraduate degree is from Rutgers University, where I teach. Were you in political science?

Jonathan Schleifer: No, I was a painter. I studied painting at the university's Mason Gross School of the Arts, and also studied philosophy and women's studies. One of the things that interested me most about painting, besides the expression, was studying critical theory, exploring notions of power and class and race.

Rutgers is a politically active campus and I was involved in SCREAM Theater, which is still around. There was always something to talk about and to be animated around. It's interesting to talk to people who went to less politically engaged campuses, because their college experiences were so different from mine.

Leech: Could you explain what SCREAM [Students Challenging Realities and Educating Against Myths] Theater is, and how it helped lead you into political activism?

Schleifer: SCREAM Theater is a student-led organization that dramatically simulates the moments leading up to, including, and following domestic violence and sexual assault. We share these reenacted moments with students on campus, with the general public, law enforcement officials, judges, and those who are engaged in the courts. It was a theater group, so I played the role of someone who is a perpetrator of domestic violence and sexual assault, which was very challenging emotionally and intellectually. It gave me a chance to teach people about an issue that lives in the shadows. Most people don't know, so they can't empathize and they don't intervene. One of SCREAM Theater's main focuses was to get people to intervene when they see domestic violence.

It gave me a chance to be an educator on a significant public policy issue and to see people's faces as they began to understand an issue that they certainly were outraged by, but didn't know what it looked like or sounded like. I think one of the key lessons I took away from working with SCREAM is the importance of telling stories around policy issues in order to create a community that understands and empathizes with the issue.

Leech: After you graduated, what did you do?

Schleifer: I joined Teach for America.

Leech: What made you decide to do that?

Schleifer: My art studies as well as my work in SCREAM got me thinking a lot about power and how it's distributed and abused. I wanted to move beyond just thinking and talking about it with my friends, to finding a meaningful way to engage with these issues in the real world.

I had two friends at Rutgers who graduated before me and joined Teach for America. They would call me at night and share their stories of the kids and the communities that they were working in. One was teaching in Washington

Heights on the north side of Manhattan and the other was teaching outside of DC. Their experiences sounded incredibly challenging yet so meaningful. I thought I could have an immediate impact by becoming a teacher. I applied and got in. I requested to teach in an urban community and I was placed in New York City. I was assigned to be a kindergarten/first-grade teacher and went through the summer training with Teach for America. When I got to New York, there were no kindergarten or first-grade classrooms available, so they put me in middle school. I went from being trained to teach early elementary and basic reading skills to having to go through puberty over three hundred times with my students. I ended up teaching for five years at Middle School 303, from 2000 to 2005.

Leech: All in the middle school?

Schleifer: All middle school. I taught sixth grade for three years, and then I cycled up with my students. I taught the same kids sixth, seventh, and eighth grade. When they graduated from eighth grade, I graduated from teaching at that school, and I went to graduate school. Through my time teaching at Middle School 303 in the Bronx, I was always looking for different ways to involve myself in the community, and in the needs of my kids generally. I wanted them to become savvier with using the Internet, so I got our school on a sanctioned e-mail system and all my kids had e-mail before other schools were doing that. I advocated for grants to get digital cameras, laptops, and printers for my kids, so they had access to the tools that are really essential for academic and professional success. Toward the end, I required all of my students to have blogs so that they could share their work. It's one thing to put your work on a bulletin board. It's another thing to put it out there where people around the world can see it.

Leech: You were teaching the day of the September 11th attacks.

Schleifer: Yes. It was a really difficult period to be a teacher, in New York especially. I became sensitized to foreign policy in a way that I hadn't before. This is despite the fact that, growing up, I had been involved in the Zionist movement and gone to Zionist summer camps. I started the first high school AIPAC [American Israel Public Affairs Committee] chapter at my high school. Those activities were core to my identity and my family being in Israel than to foreign policy per se. I hadn't really thought about America's place in the world. September 11th definitely changed that for me.

Leech: Because you had a lot of family in Israel?

Schleifer: Yes, most of my mother's family. After the Holocaust, my mother's mother came to the States and her aunts went to Israel. The majority of my family on my mother's side is still in Israel.

After September 11th, I developed a much keener interest in what was happening internationally. I became active in the antiwar movement. I didn't think going into Iraq was the right use of our resources at that time; it was the wrong direction. I learned how to organize from some wonderful mentors in New York, who had been involved in previous organizing movements in the past, around HIV. I learned to be a community organizer, and was involved in organizing some of the larger antiwar protests in New York City and in DC.

Leech: With any particular organizations?

Schleifer: I worked with New Yorkers Say No To War. We had been working tirelessly and the announcement that we were going to war in Iraq was deeply discouraging. We had invested so much time and energy into trying to stop it. It was a profound moment for me, having done so much to try to stop a policy, and regardless of our efforts and how deeply we believed we were on the right side—it happened anyway.

Leech: And yet you decided to stick with it.

Schleifer: Yes, absolutely. I think that's what was transformative. I was in a fellow organizer's home and we watched the announcement. We immediately got back to work again, which is something that I'd certainly learned from teaching as well: facing small setbacks and persevering through it.

That was partly what was so exciting about teaching, and it's one of the things that has translated to the work that I do now: the need to distinguish between what are the true obstacles and what are false obstacles. I remember I had one student who was almost perfect. She always did her homework. Whenever I was having a rough day, she would give me a smile and let me know that it was okay. She would always help other students. She did really well on exams. One day, she came in and she was miserable. She began to become disruptive and stopped doing her homework. She was getting into fights with other girls. I figured out that it wasn't anything pedagogical. She had strep, and she was in lots of pain. Her mother didn't have access to affordable health care, and as a result, she didn't even tell her mom because she knew that her mother couldn't help her, and she didn't want to burden her mother with something else. She just suffered with it. As you know, that's a miserable experience, to have strep and not have it treated.

Leech: And potentially dangerous, yes.

Schleifer: Yes, but thankfully she got the treatment she needed. And I learned two things from that experience. First, to be sure to properly diagnose problems, identifying the root causes without being distracted by the symptoms. And I learned the degree to which external issues like health care affected the work that I was doing in the classroom. This and similar experiences led me to realize that I needed to leave the classroom and see how I could help improve the larger system.

I keep in touch with all my students, and I was talking to one of them about her high school experience. She was assigned a high school by lottery and she ended up in what she described as "a terrible high school" after graduating from eighth grade. Although she did well there—she was valedictorian of that "terrible high school"—the notion that a lottery could decide someone's future in America is shocking. It's like the plot of *The Hunger Games*—not something that should be driving anyone's destiny in a country as wealthy as ours. That's why I left the classroom to go to graduate school.

Leech: You went to the Kennedy School of Government at Harvard, right?

Schleifer: I went to the Kennedy School, which was great. I met my wife. I went there thinking that I'd become some sort of policy wonk. I quickly learned there were so many great ideas and so much wonderful research about education, but I didn't get the sense that there were enough people who were invested, and trained, and skilled in making those ideas real. I worked on developing the negotiation skills, the communication skills, the political skills, and the leadership and management skills that would be required to make a difference. I had a wonderful time in graduate school and was glad I spent time studying economics and statistics, and really filling in those gaps in my experience.

I graduated after two years and left with a phenomenal cohort of classmates, who have spread throughout the world, but many ended up in DC. That's where I ended up, working as a senior policy advisor for Representative Anthony Weiner for nine months. I worked with him prior to the scandal that ended his congressional career.

Leech: That scandal, which involved him sending sexually explicit text messages and photos to several women, must have been particularly difficult for you, given your past history and feelings.

Schleifer: Yes, it was. I think was hard for all of us in the office. It was particularly frustrating because, at the time, he had become a progressive voice in Congress. I was proud to have been associated with the speeches he was giving on the floor about health care, and his wonderful "Click and Clack" speech defending NPR. How the scandal unfolded, what it said about leadership, and the loss of a really important progressive voice in Congress—all that made it hard for me.

While I was in his office as a senior policy advisor, initially I was supposed to help design bigger policy positions for the congressman to take. Because of turnover, I ended up basically managing his DC office for him, and also staffing him on the Judiciary Committee. I learned a lot.

I got the job in Weiner's office in large part because while I was at the Kennedy School, I had a summer fellowship in Senator Barbara Boxer's office. I was on her domestic policy team and met some incredible people there. She has a lot of veteran staff who really took the time to mentor me and help set me up to get the job with Congressman Weiner.

I remember sitting down with my direct supervisor and walking through all the things I would need to get a job on the Hill afterwards: making sure that I wrote policy memos, making sure that I wrote talking points, and walking through that checklist so I had deliverables to show when I was applying for jobs on the Hill later on.

Leech: You used that summer to become trained.

Schleifer: Exactly. I was a policy fellow, which I think made a difference.

Leech: You were able to get that because you were coming from the Kennedy School, and not just off the street.

Schleifer: Exactly. And I asked for specific training and had the right mentors to provide it. One of the skills that I've seen the greatest advocates employ over and over again is that they know how to ask for things. They're not afraid to ask over, and over, and over again. I think that's one of the things that I had to shift in my thinking: from being a teacher, to doing advocacy work, and doing political work generally. There are conventions that insist that it's rude to ask for things. Whereas in politics, you're either asking on behalf of yourself, if you're the candidate trying to raise money, or you're asking on behalf of your boss. If you're a staffer, you're asking someone to support your boss's bill, or you're asking someone to give your boss information. You're always asking for something. Certainly as an advocate, you're asking for specific policy to be made into law and then effectively implemented.

To get that fellowship, I asked for it. I made very clear going into it what I wanted to do. I was happy to take phone calls, but I also wanted to be able to develop a portfolio of material that I could use to get a job later on.

Leech: You were thinking ahead.

Schleifer: At that point, I was an advocate for myself.

Leech: When you left Weiner's office, you moved on to New Hampshire Governor Jeanne Shaheen's campaign?

Schleifer: Yes.

Leech: How did that come about?

Schleifer: She had been a mentor of mine at the Kennedy School. She ran the Institute of Politics. She had previously lost a race. I kept offering to work on her next race, and she insisted she wasn't going to run, but of course, she did. As soon as she announced, I packed up my car and got to New Hampshire as quickly as possible. When I got there, I just offered my services. They didn't need a policy person. They already had someone on staff to do that. They asked me what I knew about the Internet. I had been on Facebook and e-mail, and I had done a little bit of stuff before, but I didn't really know much about it.

What I had learned as a middle school teacher in the Bronx, without formal education training, is that I'm ready to learn anything. If I put in the time, and I think it through in the right ways, and ask the right questions, I can learn it. I can be successful. They put me in charge of the online communications, which included everything from setting up her Twitter accounts to the Facebook account, and sending out the blast e-mails for advocacy, for fundraising, doing the online advocacy, doing the online list-building. We grew the e-mail list more than two hundred times bigger than it was. We raised a good chunk of the overall budget online as well. It was a wonderful experience to be a part of a campaign, working those crazy hours with a singular goal of getting the right person elected.

People too often dismiss the political side of advocacy. The political side that I'm referring to is getting the right people in positions of power, so that they can be vehicles for the policy that you want to see achieved. Just knocking on the doors of Congress, or of the mayor's office, or the councilman's office, and demanding things will only get you so far. There's a tremendous value in being a part of making sure that the right people are elected to the right offices, so that they can get the right policies in place.

Leech: If you don't have support from these people, no amount of asking or arm-twisting is going to get what you want.

Schleifer: Yes. But it doesn't have to be as quid pro quo as that. If you're advocating to the wrong people over and over and over again, because your values don't align, and your interests don't align, then no matter how many creative ways you can come up with to communicate an idea or attack an idea, your values still aren't going to align. The more elected officials that you can get in place who share your values and share your interest, the more elected officials are going to take your advocacy seriously and become advocates themselves for your ideas. Not only because they owe you one—though there's certainly something there. I think more importantly, it's because you're aligned in principle.

Leech: Yes, you fundamentally agree.

Schleifer: It's so much easier to talk someone into something if they agree with you in the first place.

Leech: Well put. What happened after the election?

Schleifer: After the election, I moved back to DC. I spent the time to try to figure out what was next. I was considering going back to the Hill. I was considering getting another campaign. I was really looking for something to capture me. I was looking for my next mission. A consultant who was reviewing résumés saw my résumé for another job, and thought that I'd be a good match for Iraq and Afghanistan Veterans of America. I hadn't heard of the organization at the time, and frankly, as someone who has antiwar work on his résumé, I didn't think that I'd even be considered.

I met with the founder of IAVA, Paul Rieckhoff, and really came to admire him and was blown away by the work that IAVA was doing. I think what was really interesting to me was coming back full circle. Having disagreed with the war initially, I now had an opportunity to serve the men and women whose patriotism and commitment to country and to their community are so profound that they would serve regardless of their position on the war. I think it's an incredible faith in democracy and in the country to say, "I will trust in the electoral process to the point where, if we elect someone who sends me to war, I will go and I will fight in those missions."

I was hired, and I took over their policy department, which does their policy advocacy and research. I just fell in love with the community of veterans and with veterans' work. What's fascinating about veterans' work is that it touches on almost every issue: health care, housing, employment, domestic violence and sexual assault, children's policies, and elementary, middle, and high school education. Then you have foreign policy thrown in as well. Veterans' work is a microcosm that includes every policy issue.

It became a really exciting set of issues to work on, even though I had never considered veterans affairs before. One of the things that I have realized over the years is that I've never met a policy issue that isn't exciting when you start to take it apart. I remember working for Senator Boxer's office, and they asked me to look at an issue around port security in Los Angeles. I was much more interested in domestic policy and things that seemed to directly impact the lives of Americans. I agreed to do it, but I thought it would be a bit boring.

The more I investigated and explored it, I learned the scale to which our economy rests upon the movements of shipments in and out of Los Angeles, and the impact that an hour shutdown can have on our overall economy and what that means for health care, housing, employment, and education. When I learned how vulnerable those ports are—we don't know where these ships are for months at a time until suddenly they show up on our shore, and they want to park. It was fascinating. I had a number of those experiences. The more I got to see the interconnectedness of the issues, the more I became excited and interested in a broader range of issues.

Leech: You went to IAVA and found working with veterans was actually something pretty interesting. What sorts of things did you do when you were working there?

Schleifer: Let me start with the bigger picture. We identified the essential long-term challenge as the closing window for public interest in veterans and their families. As the wars wind down and as veterans age, the country is going to want to think less and less about these two profoundly unpopular wars. Because of this closing window, there was a fierce urgency that we had to maintain in our work. We had to keep our eye on about six major issues—education, housing, mental health, and employment were the biggest ones—and later on, domestic violence and Don't Ask, Don't Tell.

Leech: It was important to keep people's attention on these issues while there still was hope of doing something.

Schleifer: Exactly. We worked to keep the public's attention on these issues in order to keep the political leaders' attention on these issues. IAVA is a membership-based organization, so it wasn't about me or the executive director sitting down and coming up with policies. We would do annual surveys of our membership to ask what they wanted us to be working on. The surveys got more and more complex every year. I think the longest survey was maybe over one hundred questions, quantitative and qualitative, about their policy preferences.

The remarkable thing was that we would get our members to sit there and spend the time to answer. There were an obscene number of questions, but our members were so interested in giving us their opinions that we would have incredibly high response rates and completion rates.

When I left last year, we had a larger sample of the opinions of Iraq and Afghanistan veterans than anyone else. We folded that data, along with focus groups and conversations with political leaders and other organizations that were lobbying on the same issues, into a policy agenda. That policy agenda then became the vision for what a world where veterans were truly supported would look like. From that, we would choose several priorities every year and advocate for those. We'd design discrete campaigns to advocate for issues that were, at the time, of high need and ripe for a campaign like that.

We were successful in being able to pass a major piece of legislation every year. There also were minor pieces of legislation and always being on guard for smaller potential threats.

One of the short-term issues that popped up was an issue with a bill we were pushing. This bill would have protected educational benefits for a few thousand veterans that unintentionally would have had their benefits cut. We got word that some language in the version of the bill that was about to pass was vague and might not have protected all of the vets that we intended. We found out about this on a Friday afternoon. There was going to be a vote on Monday afternoon.

Leech: How did you find out about it? How does that information come to you?

Schleifer: We had relationships within the committee. A staffer on the committee brought it to our attention, told us that the proposal was out there. A big part of the work at IAVA has always been about building and maintaining deep relationships with other organizations that did similar work, and with members of Congress and with their staffs. The relationships between a good lobbyist and the staff are of critical importance. Those staff members will turn to you for information, as well, because congressional staffers will each have dozens of issues that they're working on, as well as needing to monitor another two or three dozen things for the member. They don't always have the opportunity to get the depth of knowledge and understanding that they'd like. That's certainly also true for the member of Congress who has a whole other set of responsibilities on top of that.

A good and trusted lobbyist is actually one of the most valuable sources of information in DC. One of the things that you learn very quickly is that if you confuse advocacy with information sharing, you will quickly lose your credibility. That means that if someone calls you to ask you for a piece of information because they're writing a memo to their boss, and you spin them in that conversation, or you mislead them in that conversation in order to advocate for your position, then you are not going to get a second or third phone call from that person. They are not ever coming back to you for information, because you've lost your credibility.

This is something that I learned when I was a staffer. Congressman Weiner would call me and ask for advice on something. I would have to go out and get as smart on that issue as I could, as quickly as possible. That would require calling experts in academia, experts in think tanks, and lobbyists. I needed to talk to someone who had their head in that issue all the time. If anyone ever tried to spin me, or mislead me, or give me wrong information, that would be the last time I'd ever go to them.

Leech: Even just partial information that left out some important bit would be a problem.

Schleifer: Exactly. For me, what I would try to do in those conversations is to say, "Look, here are the facts as we know it. Here are my sources for those facts. This is what we think it is." I think it's always valuable to throw in what the other side is going to say. "If you call so-and-so, they'll tell you this. This is why I disagree with that." At least I'm giving them the full picture.

So at IAVA, we got a phone call from a congressional committee staffer, who basically said, "Look, we've got a vote Monday afternoon. This will mean the loss of thousands of your members' educational benefits." We're talking about the new GI Bill, which provides almost a free ride to college for veterans of Iraq and Afghanistan. For many of them, that means a huge, huge change in their life—being able to go to college for free. It includes a book stipend and a housing stipend.

Leech: How would the amendment have changed things?

Schleifer: As part of the process of upgrading the New GI Bill, a segment of veterans would have inadvertently had their benefits cut, based on where they had registered for school. Almost immediately after passing those upgrades, we mobilized to get bill that would grandfather in those vets who would lose benefits. We got word on Friday that Congress was going to pass the "grandfather clause" on Monday. Unfortunately, in the version that made it to the floor it was unclear when the grandfather protections would have started; potentially leaving the vets that we were trying to protect holding the bag for an entire semester. We needed to get that bill quickly amended, or get the VA to implement the law at the right time. We quickly organized a war room over the weekend. Members of the policy team, members of our communications team, members of a membership team all got together and designed a rapid response. We started talking to the press about it, to raise the issue publicly. We started talking to our own members, to educate them as to what was going on, so that they could be valuable advocates for themselves. We also started making phone calls to leadership staff and committee member staff, making sure that everyone knew that we were not going to let this happen without a fight.

We needed to create a situation where it would become more politically painful for them to pass this piece of legislation with its flaws than it would be for them to fix it. That meant trying to bring as much public attention to the issue as possible, as quickly as possible, all in forty-eight hours. That included building an online component with Facebook and Twitter. We created an e-mail petition. That was one of our most successful e-mail petitions, where we had our members e-mail the highest-ranking person in the House Veterans' Affairs Committee and that staffer.

The e-mails flooded that staffer's inbox. She made a phone call asking me to turn it off, because she couldn't get any work done. We hadn't disclosed her actual e-mail address. There was a nifty little workaround that allowed us to control the flood of mail. The committee ended up postponing the vote. They postponed it a couple of times. In the end, rather than amending the bill, the VA corrected the problem internally so that we could get the bill passed and it would protect all the veterans it was originally intended to protect. Without our swift action, Congress would have just passed the flawed bill and called it a day.

Leech: One of the other interesting things you did while you were at IAVA was your annual fly-in day for veterans. How did that work?

Schleifer: We would have what we called Storm the Hill, which was an annual event. Veterans would apply to participate. There was a written application and a Skype interview as well, so we could see how they presented themselves. Then we would handpick about twenty veterans and fly them to DC, where we would have two days of training in lobbying, in media, and in the issues that were part of IAVA's agenda. We wanted them to become thoughtful communicators, especially in storytelling, since that is such a huge part of really good advocacy work. How can a veteran tell his or her story in thirty seconds if it's a short elevator ride, sixty seconds if it's a long elevator ride, and five minutes if it's a sit-down meeting? How can they tell their story and their friends' stories in a way that makes it appealing to a congressional staffer or the member of Congress?

We would do two days of intensive training and then spend the next three or four days storming the Hill, having meeting, after meeting, after meeting that we would preschedule. We would identify the most important offices to be in and target those offices. Our office would work for two months beforehand, scheduling meetings. The meetings were in both the House and Senate with the Veterans' Affairs committee members and leadership on both sides of the aisle. We came up with this incredible spreadsheet that had them going to eight meetings a day. They would go in groups of three or four, so in the course of three days, we'd have one hundred and twenty meetings on Capitol Hill.

There are two ways of doing these Hill trips. Some organizations will do the shotgun approach. They'll bus in thousands of their members from around the country, all wearing the same T-shirt, all wearing the same hat, just knocking on doors and trying to get meetings, and putting down written materials in each office. Our approach was much more strategic and targeted. We would choose the offices. We would choose the people. We would have an extensive training. And then we would make sure that they all were talking about the same things, in a similar way.

Because I wasn't a veteran, I didn't do a lot of the direct advocacy work. We had veterans on staff, and I was a registered lobbyist, because I did lobby, but I tend to lobby only on certain issues, and with certain people. The day-to-day lobbying was run by a veteran, because in the end, you can best advocate if you're advocating for yourself, if you're telling your own story. You have a level of credibility with your audience that an outsider wouldn't have.

We needed people who could go into a congressional office and say, "When I served, this was my experience, and when I came back, this was my experience. Therefore, I understand the urgency and the need for my brothers and sisters in arms, and therefore this policy is a good idea and will help people who are like me." As someone who didn't wear the uniform, I just couldn't make that same case. I would be telling other people's stories. As much as I cherish those stories, and value those stories, and respect those stories, they were never my own.

Leech: So instead, you were more involved in strategy and planning of advocacy?

Schleifer: Exactly. I also would go into meetings where there was less interest in stories and personal experiences and more interested in getting down to the policy details.

Leech: It sounds like in Storm the Hill, you did not focus on making sure veterans were connected with their own members of Congress, but rather you focused on members of Congress in key positions of leadership and on key committees.

Schleifer: Exactly. Whenever we'd call to set up a meeting, they would also ask us, "Is there a constituent coming?" I think, at most, we had twenty-four people. With only two dozen people coming through, there's no way we could hit most constituencies, especially on the House side. It just wasn't a priority. We would try to have geographic diversity, as well as in terms of gender and race, but we were not trying to put a constituent in every office.

Leech: How long were you at IAVA?

Schleifer: A little bit more than three years.

Leech: What brought you then to Educators 4 Excellence?

Schleifer: As I described, I was never telling my own story at IAVA. I get sentimental when I talk about that work. My closest friends are the men and women who I worked with there. They flew around the world to Australia to come to my wedding and to roast me the night before. The bonds formed doing this type of advocacy work are strong because the stakes are so high. Protecting veterans' educational benefits can mean all the difference in a successful transition to civilian life. Being a part of passing the new GI Bill 2.0 that extended educational benefits to four hundred thousand veterans was one of the greatest things I have ever been a part of. Advocating for the repeal of Don't Ask, Don't Tell was a great point of pride.

But in thinking about where I wanted to be, I was telling other people's stories. My passion had always been education, and I wanted to get back to my students and their community. I wanted to do similar work, building advocacy campaigns and getting the right laws and policies passed that would be transformative. Educators 4 Excellence was founded by teachers who had a similar classroom experience as I did. They loved teaching, but felt shackled by a system that didn't listen to their voices. They started an organization that in many ways mirrors IAVA, in that it's teacher-led. Teachers define the policies, not the professional staff. We advocate for issues of importance to our members. We involve our members in writing the policy reports and in leading the advocacy campaigns. They are the voices at the rallies and at our events.

While I was still at IAVA, I had a fellowship through Leaders for Educational Equity, which is a sister nonprofit to Teach for America. Its mission is to get former Teach for America alums involved in public policy and in the political world. One of the political leadership fellows I met worked at Educators 4 Excellence. He insisted I meet the founders. I had lunch with them, and at that lunch I was certain that I wanted to be a part of that organization. Their theory of change was so spot-on.

Leech: Now that you are at E4E, what do you do? Are you advocating at the state and local level only, or also in DC?

Schleifer: I came in as the Executive Director of the New York chapter. The two founders started E4E in New York, and now they're expanding it nationally, after teachers from across the country reached out. I came in with a focus on growing the New York team, growing the membership in New York, and growing our impact and building our relationships at the local level. Education policy is very local – it lives mostly at the state and district level – and so we focus our efforts on getting our teachers' voices heard in those arenas.

Leech: Today, even though you are still a policy advocate, you are no longer officially a lobbyist, at least under the law. How is what you do now different from what you did before, and how is it the same?

Schleifer: It's different in that I'm not spending a good part of my time preparing for and directly addressing elected officials. That aligns with the legal definition. E4E is a 501(c)3 non-profit, and we work to educate and inform the broader public conversation about education policy by ensuring teachers' voices and ideas are heard. The things that are the same... A lot of the work that I did as a lobbyist-advocate was about being part of a community—understanding what that community wants and needs in order to realize its vision. For the veterans, that was a healthy transition back into civilian life. For teachers, it's elevating the profession and better serving their students, and figuring out what the best policies are to help them achieve both of those goals. That's consistent. In both jobs it was important to find ways to make the issues relevant to the general public, so that the issues also become relevant and significant to elected officials.

In both cases, it's about building coalitions so that we have strength in numbers. It's about working deeply with the community, not just to understand them, but to help grow a movement so that we can rely upon collective action to influence policy makers and stakeholders at the city and state level when we need something for that community, when we have a specific ask. It's about making sure that I have a team that is excited and trained to do all those things as well. It takes a community of people to realize the goal of executing on these effective, strategic priorities.

Leech: It's helpful to see the parallels that exist between working in a political office, working as a lobbyist, and working in advocacy more generally. There are many similarities throughout the work.

Schleifer: I think I learned to be the advocate in the classroom. I learned so many great political skills as a teacher. Everything from the confidence that's required to stand in front of a room of thirty kids and communicate effectively, to the ability to break down complex ideas and issues in a way that's accessible to them, that understands where they are. I think one of the biggest mistakes people make when they communicate is they don't understand their audience.

To be an effective teacher, you have to know where each and every one of your students are, in terms of what they know and don't know, and what their emotional states are that day. When a student walks in and he has his arms crossed and is grumpy because he hasn't had breakfast, that's going to be a very different day and interaction than it will be for the student who did have a full breakfast and is in a really good mood. Like a good teacher, a successful politician or lobbyist advocates knows how to communicate to many people, meeting them where they are.

Leech: Why don't you pick one of the issues that you have recently worked on and walk me through how you and E4E have approached that issue.

Schleifer: The teachers' union and the City of New York are negotiating a teacher evaluation system. Over a year ago, to win federal Race to the Top funding, the legislature and the governor required that every district in New York have a teacher evaluation system in place by January 17, 2013. Any district that didn't have this evaluation in place by that date would lose a portion of state aid. In New York City, that translates to about $300 million.

Leech: That's some serious money.

Schleifer: Yes, it's serious money. And beyond that, the issue itself is important. One of the early issues that E4E's teachers focused on was teacher evaluation. We believe that the only way a person can become exceptional at anything is to get consistent feedback and support. E4E's teachers created a policy team, which is how we develop our policy papers. We get a group of teachers together and investigate the issue. The group comes up with policy recommendations and writes a paper. Our teachers came together, and they wrote up a recommended teacher evaluation report.

Our concern was that there's a long history of finger-pointing and contention between the union, and the mayor, and the city Department of Education. We were concerned that they wouldn't commit themselves to fully negotiating and the school district would lose both the money and the opportunity to get meaningful feedback and support for our teachers.

Over the last couple of months, we studied the issues again with our members. We had panel discussions, focus groups, and roundtables so that more of our teachers got involved in the issue. Our teachers drafted op-eds, which we helped place in the media. Education Chancellor Dennis Walcott came to speak to about one hundred and sixty of our members.

Just before New Year's Eve, we shot a series of videos of teachers sharing their greatest challenges from 2012, and their resolutions for 2013, and then communicating how a meaningful teacher evaluation was necessary for them to realize their resolutions for 2013.

As we were coming into the last couple weeks of the negotiations, especially over the holiday break, we started rolling these videos out. In the worst of it, right before and immediately following the Christmas to New Year's week, the mayor and the president of the teacher's union were throwing punches at each other constantly. These videos started rolling out and created the third voice in the debate, which was the voice of teachers saying, "We want an evaluation. We don't want the bickering. We don't want the fighting. We want an evaluation system so we can get the feedback and support we need to become exceptional."

Leech: How were these videos being delivered?

Schleifer: Through social media. And then we knew that if we got an interesting product out there, we wouldn't have to pay to get airtime. The media would pick up on it. *The Daily News* ran one of the videos on its online site. *Capital New York* wrote about it, and so did a lot of blogs. *Capital New York* described it as "politically smart," because we were providing the voice of teachers and making it very clear to the public.

Unfortunately, the city and union failed to come to an agreement by the January 17 deadline and the state is going to take back $300 million in school funding from the city budget. Our teachers refused to stop there. Our city schools can't do without that money. And if the city doesn't have an evaluation agreement by this coming September we'll lose even more funding. Teachers want meaningful feedback to improve their teaching. Evaluation is a critical component of elevating the profession of teaching so that teachers can deliver to their students an education worthy of them.

We shifted our focus to Albany and called on Governor Cuomo to get involved. Returning to an idea we had floated over a year ago, our teachers called on him to establish a "backstop evaluation" – a default that would kick in if the city and union continued to fail to reach a deal. We had a two-prong approach: a grassroots petition and a TV ad buy. We collected over 2,000 signatures and aired a TV ad featuring three of our teachers calling on Albany to step in. Within days Governor Cuomo announced an amendment to the budget that would establish this backstop, written by the Commissioner of Education in New York State. Come September teachers will have an evaluation and hopefully it'll provide them the support and feedback want.

Leech: The teachers can, in turn, also talk to their unions, I'm assuming?

Schleifer: Yes, absolutely. That's certainly part of it. We encourage our members to be active leaders within their schools and the union.

Leech: Let's shift gears a little bit and talk about what it's like to be a policy advocate or a lobbyist from a personal perspective. Is it a good job to have in terms of work, life, and family balance?

Schleifer: I would say yes, in that it's such fulfilling work. When you're advocating for something, or when you're lobbying for something that you know is going to affect people's lives for the better, and you start to see even small victories affect people's lives for the better, then you go home feeling fulfilled. I think that's something that translates wonderfully to having a healthy work/life balance. You go home tired. I'm exhausted. You're fulfilled at the same time, which I think is wonderful. It's one of the things that I liked most about being in DC. Everyone there is doing something for a cause, usually for a cause that they believe in, to realize a vision of some sort. Most people there are passionate and excited about the work that they do.

It's never the same thing from one day to the next, so it's a great space for people who like to always be thinking on their feet and like a dynamic, unpredictable environment. I also think you have to like people, in terms of wanting to help them, if you're an advocate for a constituency. Liking people is also important because an advocate is constantly communicating. Whether it's through e-mail, or the phone, or meetings, an advocate is constantly talking to people. To do that, you have to be honestly interested in who they are, how they've come to be where they are, what they think, and what they believe. Strategically, it'll make you a better communicator, and, practically, if you don't, you'll burn out. You have to thrive on the interactions with other people, because you'll be having them all the time.

I think advocates also have to be confident enough in what they're fighting for that they can keep asking for things. You have to be strategic enough and thoughtful enough to be sure you're building your relationships carefully and thoughtfully, and thinking through the way you speak and communicate with people. Relationships are your currency. They're the opportunity for being able to do what you want to do for the constituencies that you're serving.

Leech: In what you've just said, there's implicit advice for people who might want to go into public advocacy as a career. But more directly, what advice would you have for them in terms of getting in the door?

Schleifer: The earlier you can start, the better. There is a trajectory of experiences that advocates tend to have. There will be an internship, and then there will be an entry-level position. Throughout that, advocates-to-be should always be looking for mentors, people who will recognize their passion, capacity, and intellect, and who will recognize the value of those new advocates to the movement or the cause. A mentor will want to invest in that potential to help those new advocates get the next position.

Building a network is important but that network should be built thoughtfully, in a way that leads to meaningful relationships with people, where they can count on you and you can count on them. It's helpful to build a broad network so that you can be fluid as opportunities arise. It also is valuable to work on a campaign. Campaign workers develop very robust skill sets and have their mettles tested as they work insane hours for nine months straight, seven days a week, with the principle goal of getting one person, one decision maker, elected to office.

Learning some of this through the academic route was really valuable for me—especially my economic and statistical training, and even some of the soft skills like negotiation. Getting those through a university degree can be valuable, but you don't have to go that route.

Leech: You don't have to have a master's degree in public policy to be an advocate?

Schleifer: No, you don't. I don't think there is one right answer, one singular path into advocacy work. I found my master's degree incredibly valuable because it allowed me to go from my experience teaching into policy and politics, filling in many gaps. The real-life exposure and experience with the communities, and the people, and the issues that you're going to be advocating for grounds you in their reality. A person also certainly could go straight from college and build a career in advocacy, especially with the right mentorship.

CHAPTER

14

Angela Guo

Intern, Center for American Progress Action Fund

Faith Shapiro

Intern, ACLU

***Angela Guo** is a junior at Rice University in Houston. At the time of the interview, she was a summer intern at ThinkProgress, an award-winning political blog founded in 2005. ThinkProgress is a project of the Center for American Progress Action Fund. Guo is also a research intern at the James A. Baker III Institute for Public Policy at Rice and is vice president of Rice's Pre-Law Society. She previously had internships with the U.S. Department of Justice and with From the Top, a National Public Radio program that showcases young musicians. She is from Johns Creek, Georgia, a suburb of Atlanta.*

***Faith Shapiro** is a junior at Rice University, where she is majoring in philosophy and policy studies, with a minor in poverty, justice, and human capabilities. At the time of the interview, she was a legislative intern in the American Civil Liberties Union's Washington Legislative Office. She has been president of the Rice University ACLU chapter and has held internships with a community organization in New Orleans,* the Journal of Feminist Economics, *and a Houston-based literacy organization—in addition to her ongoing involvement in a college-based community service organization. She is from Tenafly, New Jersey.*

An estimated 20,000 interns descend on Washington, DC, each summer to work for members of Congress, federal agencies, the White House, and, of course, interest groups. All are there to learn and get the experience needed to build their résumés for a future job. In this chapter, Shapiro and Guo talk about why they chose an internship that involved political advocacy.

Beth Leech: Angela, this summer you are working as an intern for the Center for American Progress [CAP], right?

Angela Guo: Yes. Although to be more specific, because they like to differentiate between the two, I am working at CAP's sister organization, the Center for American Progress Action Fund, not the Center for American Progress per se. But they're both under the same umbrella.

Leech: And how is CAP Action different?

Guo: CAP Action has more of a political agenda than CAP itself. CAP itself is just a progressive think tank. They promote progressive values. They do not openly support one party or another. Whereas at CAP Action, we are allowed to do a lot more grassroots, actually advocating for something—a party, a side, a specific candidate, anything like that.

Leech: How did you end up there? How did you get interested in doing such a thing in Washington?

Guo: I am here through the Baker Institute for Political Policy, which is Rice's think tank. It is a nonpartisan think tank in Houston that sends twelve students to DC every summer and funds them to be here. It is a blast. And as part of that, we have to find our own full-time internships.

And so for me, I have always been really interested in progressive politics in the Democratic Party, basically. At school, I am really involved with Young Democrats. So I thought coming to DC would be a good option, where I would be doing something that I would personally want to do and where I agree with the message.

I knew that CAP is a big liberal think tank. And I had a couple of friends who did work with ThinkProgress in years past, and they told me that they thought I would really like the environment there.

Leech: So the Baker Institute pays your expenses and also pays you a stipend?

Guo: They pay us a stipend that goes toward our expenses. It covers all of our living expenses, and food, and transportation, and whatnot.

Leech: That is great. You are much luckier than many interns. Most of them aren't paid at all. So how about you, Faith?

Faith Shapiro: I am here through Rice's ACLU club. I am also technically a paid intern through a stipend from a Rice alumnus who is very involved with the ACLU. She funds one Rice student to intern at the Washington Legislative Office every summer.

Leech: How did you get involved with the ACLU on campus in the first place, and what do you do for them?

Shapiro: Community service is actually a big part of my life, and I am very interested in public policy in terms of advocacy for marginalized communities or populations. So my interests are very much in line with the ACLU. I know my boss once said that the people whose rights we have to work hardest to protect are the minority, because they are the ones who are often subject to the whims of the majority, even though that is not supposed to be the case. And so my personal values are very closely in line with the ACLU.

Leech: How many Rice interns are there this summer all over DC? Do you know?

Guo: This year I think we have twenty-five-ish.

Shapiro: Right. But there are also other interns not necessarily affiliated with politics or policy, who have business- or research-related internships.

Leech: And so do you end up seeing these other Rice interns and/or other interns who are not from Rice?

Shapiro: All the time. Obviously, DC has a huge intern culture, especially over the summer. I am living in the dorms at George Washington University, and it has a lot of other interns living there, so I have met interns from not only different universities within the United States, but from all over the world. My suitemate goes to Trinity College in Ireland.

Leech: Besides in the dorms, how do you meet other interns?

Shapiro: At work. So, for instance, here at the ACLU office, although there are not a lot of undergraduate interns, there are a couple. And if you meet them at your office, you probably also share common interests, and so that lends a feeling of camaraderie as well.

Guo: Under the whole CAP umbrella, we have about eighty to ninety interns. And they are all undergrads. And it is a blast because we have an intern softball team, various intern events, happy hours—things like that that we are consistently invited to. It's a great way to meet people, just being at CAP, because there are so many other people who share the same interests. And they are all from a variety of different schools. And then in my dorm suite at GW [George Washington University], I have four roommates from various schools. Two of my roommates are from Princeton, one is from Yale, and two of us are from Rice.

Leech: My impression was that most political interns in DC were not funded. Some of them are even paying tuition.

Shapiro: Well, in my experience, a lot of the people I have spoken to actually are funded. I find that, oftentimes, a lot of Hill interns are not funded. So a lot of the "Hillterns" working for congressmen or senators are not funded. But their internships also tend to be shorter. I know a typical Hill internship is about six weeks.

Leech: Are these people with funding almost always like you, bringing in their money from outside, or are there still organizations in DC that are paying their interns?

Guo: Actually, CAP pays interns pretty well, I would say, compared to most other organizations around. "Hillterns" do not generally get funded unless it is by some outside source. But at CAP, they do pay their interns. If you come in with a stipend, they pay you a little bit less. They give you another stipend. But if you come in with no funding at all, they pay you by the hour.

Leech: That is good to know. So what are your backgrounds? How did you get interested in policy advocacy? Faith, I know you were in the ACLU already, but what about in terms of what you are studying at school and that sort of thing?

Shapiro: So like I said, I had a strong background in community service when I came in to Rice and I want to pursue a career in the public sector, doing public policy or advocacy for a nonprofit organization or an NGO [nongovernmental organization]. At Rice, I am a philosophy and policy studies major, and my minor is in poverty, justice, and human capabilities.

Leech: Is that a set minor or did you get to make up your own?

Shapiro: No, it is a set minor. It is new. We call it PJHC for short but no one knows what it stands for. It is a lot of global development study and poverty studies. It is through the Center for the Study of Women, Gender, and Sexuality, so it does have a gender component. But generally speaking, it is essentially our version of poverty studies. And all of that, hopefully, will culminate in some sort of career in terms of social justice or poverty reduction.

In particular, I am really interested in refugee populations and immigrant rights, and also immigration reform in this country, which also relates very well to the ACLU's mission and some of their projects. So that is how I got interested in public policy, but it started from a community service background where I saw the marginalization of impoverished populations.

I did a lot of work in New Orleans post-Katrina. And as much as Katrina was a natural disaster, I think it was also a disaster of public policy and poor advocacy. And so that is what ultimately got me interested. And then, as I continued at Rice, all of the things that I have been studying have fueled that fire.

Leech: Who were you working with in New Orleans?

Shapiro: I have been there three times now. Originally, I went there on a Mitzvah Corps trip, and we worked with Common Ground Relief, which is a very small grassroots organization. We also worked with the St. Bernard Project and a couple of other nonprofits there. We worked with a lot of different organizations. It was like each day we would work with a different one. When I returned there, it was on an alternative winter break program.

Leech: Through Rice?

Shapiro: No. This one was actually through Young Judaea, which is a Jewish youth movement. Again, we worked with Common Ground through my suggestion because I liked working with them a lot, and a couple of other similar organizations. We worked at soup kitchens.

And then the third time I was there was through Rice Alternative Spring Break, which is a big program through our Community Involvement Center. I worked in schools. It was not rebuilding. It was working within the community. It was great because I got the opportunity to view the community through a different lens—through children. We worked at Head Start schools. I worked at Mahalia Jackson Elementary School, which had just recently been founded. I love New Orleans. New Orleans is a big part of my life. It was the reason I decided to go in the direction I did.

Leech: How about you, Angela?

Guo: I have a very odd path. Growing up in the South, I was always surrounded by conservative ideology. The county I live in is one of the biggest Republican strongholds in the country, and the school that I went to is very, very conservative. I think I started seeing politics and being unhappy with some of the decisions people thought were right. Growing up in that kind of environment, I rebelled against conservative politics and got involved in Young Democrats in middle school. Then I was involved in debate in high school, which I think was a very liberal group.

But then in college, I took a different turn. I started as a music major at Rice in the conservatory. I was a piano performance major and I was really interested in arts advocacy and specifically the fact that many arts organizations are always getting their funding taken away. It really pained me to see it, because I know music is such a big part of my life. So I decided to come to Rice because it had both a solid conservatory and a solid academic setting. But then at Rice, I decided that the direction I thought I wanted to go in was much more public sector—not performance per se for music, but arts advocacy.

When I was looking for internships, I was thinking about applying to both arts advocacy internships and politically active internships. And I think I ended up at ThinkProgress because they told me I could also write with their cultural writer, who does a lot of entertainment and cultural advocacy, which I thought was interesting, while doing social justice issues.

I am a history and public policy major now, but I have always stayed really involved in the arts field. And I think, eventually, I would like to go to law school and potentially work as maybe an arts activist or an arts lobbyist.

Leech: Do you get a chance to play while you are here in DC?

Guo: A little bit. George Washington has a music wing building, so we go there sometimes and hang out. But I think for now, I am definitely much more interested in the reading, writing, and advocating part than the performance.

Leech: Now I am going to ask you each to walk me through an average day. I know average days are sometimes hard to generalize, so maybe you could just tell me what you were doing yesterday, with annotations along the way to let me know how that was weird or usual. Faith, do you want to go first?

Shapiro: Sure. So I come in around nine thirty and check my e-mails. Because I am interning for our director, my internship is a little bit different than maybe some of the other people who work here. I will come in the morning, find out if anything went down after I left the day before—so check my e-mail, check my schedule, check the director's schedule. Most weeks, I will attend a meeting, either a strategy meeting or a general office meeting, where we discuss the different things that are going on. We also have a number of update e-mails that go out.

And we have the *WLO [Washington Legislative Office] Update*, which goes out biweekly to all of our affiliates. It talks about what each of our lobbyists is working on that week and the issues that are maybe going up for a vote or hearings that are happening on the Hill that pertain to our issues.

Leech: What comes next in your day?

Shapiro: I help to compile and distribute the *WLO Update* and I also do some research if we have a particular issue that we are working on as an office. Sometimes, I will be assigned to do research, let's say, on a pertinent member of the committee that an issue is going to, or someone who has been in the media a lot. With immigration, I may be asked to do background research on someone from the Department of Homeland Security. Or if my boss is speaking on a panel and she needs to be briefed on a certain issue that maybe does not pertain directly to what the ACLU has been working on, but that would be important for her to be well-informed in. So those are ongoing projects that have deadlines peppered throughout. And then otherwise, of course, I also have some general intern duties.

Leech: Describe them. What would your typical intern duties be?

Shapiro: Documents—printing them, sending them out, photocopying them, sorting them. I would not say that that is the majority of the work that I do. I do get a lot of substantive work to do here as well.

Leech: What do you think the thing is that you spend the most time on?

Shapiro: It is hard to say. My tasks are very varied, and I think that probably each day I spend equal amounts of time doing all of those things. I would say though the most time is taken when I am asked to either compile reports or to do writing. So I have assisted in ghostwriting some blog posts on our web site and also in compiling the *WLO Update*.

Leech: And when you are doing the research, where is most of this information coming from? Where are you going to get the information?

Shapiro: A lot of it does just come generally from the Internet. A lot of it comes from news articles, which I compile together—as I did, for example, when the Supreme Court ruling was expected about SB 1070, the Arizona immigration law, since the ACLU had a stake in that. So I was compiling a lot of news reports on the issue, and analyzing the different sides and developments, and things like that.

Leech: So you collect them and then summarize them?

Shapiro: Yes. Sometimes it will just be collecting them and sending them out saying, "Here is what was reported today." And sometimes, I will do summaries, depending on the sources. I often do summaries from more DC-based media, like *Congressional Quarterly* and *The Hill*, because they will be a lot longer and more esoteric. And then usually news articles are a lot shorter and do not take everyone as long to read. So usually that is just a compilation of articles.

Leech: Angela, tell me about you.

Guo: Well, my internship is very different from most of the interns at CAP or CAP Action. Since I am working on ThinkProgress, which is the liberal blog and the primary media outlet of CAP Action, I get in at eight a.m. every single day. Then all of us in the office—thirty reporters, writers, and editors, and five interns—start going through Google News, *Huffington Post*, *Politico*, *The Washington Post*, and *The New York Times*. We have thirty to forty tabs open, and we go through and look for all the articles that would be relevant, that we think might be able to go out on our blog. We pull it. We send it on something called PR Core. It is like a listserv except it just goes out to everybody in ThinkProgress. And PR Core moves every other second almost, especially in the mornings when we are compiling and sending, compiling and sending. And then everyone reads all the e-mails that go out through PR Core.

So from about eight to nine a.m. is when we gather all this information and start sending it out. And then at about nine a.m., the editors start going through the articles. They pick up on certain articles and say, "Okay, well, that is really interesting. Why don't you write that up?" The way it is done in the office is if you found it, you get to write it.

Leech: Nice.

Guo: So it is cool. The interns get to write at least one long blog post a day, and usually a couple of short news flashes as well. Today, I have done two already since it was an interesting news day. What we do is write the news from a progressive standpoint that we feel will be of interest to our progressive readers. A lot of times, we take issues from local newspapers or journals, and we publicize them. For example, sometimes there is a crime that we find completely heinous that has not gotten enough attention, and we will write about it and send it out to our readers.

Leech: So you summarize the story and comment on it? And link to it?

Guo: We will comment and link. A lot of times, what we write gets picked up by a lot of the news sources. MSNBC in particular really likes to pull from ThinkProgress. And they always cite us, which is good. The other thing is the new Aaron Sorkin show, *Newsroom*, actually admitted to us that they use a ton of ThinkProgress's materials and they go through our archives and look for things that would go on their show. They recently mentioned us on-air.

We also have very big Twitter and Facebook presences, and so people come for updates all the time throughout the day. So I think the biggest part of the interns' job at ThinkProgress is going through news articles and constantly being really up-to-date in the news and then writing. We do a lot of writing. So what happens after we draft a post is that it gets sent to the editors, who will look through and make any changes they see fit. Usually, they will not make that many changes. They will just tell us, "Oh, could you write a little bit more about that? Could you give us a little bit more information about that?" And we go back and put in the edits, and then it gets sent out and scheduled to post throughout the week.

So it is really fun. And I work until six or six thirty every single day. So it is a long workday. I know the typical intern at CAP usually works from nine to five or nine to six. But since we have to be there and constantly looking through the news, we go a little bit longer.

Leech: And you are producing every day, right?

Guo: Yes. Usually on Fridays we have to write for the weekend as well. Then on the weekend, we get shifts watching the news. So Friday your job is to watch CNN that night or Saturday.

Leech: You can do that from home, but in case there is something big, you need to be watching. So what happens if there is something big? What do you do?

Guo: If there is something big, PR Core still exists over the weekend. So we are still constantly checking our e-mails over the weekend to see if there any news stories. But usually the editors will take charge of that and they will write something up. Also, something else that is cool: they like to send interns along with a reporter to different interviews or press conferences or events. And that is just something that I think CAP does a lot in general.

The day the health care decision came out, they sent a bunch of interns. ThinkProgress sent two of their interns to go outside the Supreme Court to just talk to people, see why they were there, what they wanted out of the decision. And then later, we were able to join Campus Progress, which is the student wing of CAP Action, in a big rally. So we were holding signs, screaming, chanting. A lot of us actually got on the news, so that was interesting. And I have gone with one of our senior reporters to interview the Democratic whip, Representative Steny Hoyer. We also went to the press conference to interview Jose Antonio Vargas the day the Supreme Court's Arizona decision was made.

There is another event that CAP has sent all of its interns to. We had to go lobby on the Hill the first week we were here on behalf of student debt. We were able to schedule meetings with our home senator or our home legislative assistant, and we were able to just go and talk to them, and give them packets and tell them why they needed to keep our student debt rates low. So we spent an entire day doing that just on the Hill. It was a lot of fun and we were able to have a rally, too, where there were a lot of senators who did support keeping the student debt rate the way it was.

Leech: That is great that you get to do that. So now that we have heard about both of your days. And Angela, you have pretty much told us the answer to what you spend most of your time doing. What is a short blog post and what is a long one? How long is long and how short is short?

Guo: Short would be about two hundred to two hundred fifty words. We also do things called news flashes, which are very simple—three, four sentences—summarizing something that just came out. We send those out a lot, too. But usually, a longer blog post or a normal post will have a summary of the events and facts—usually a block quote from somebody important affiliated with the story—and then a little bit of commentary at the end. The longer ones can run up to four hundred or five hundred words, but they do not go more than that.

Leech: Faith, what would you say is the most interesting thing you get to do? What is your favorite thing?

Shapiro: There are two things. I do really enjoy the research that I do. I think that because the ACLU is so well versed in the issues they deal with, the research that I get to do is usually sometimes off the beaten path.

Like I said, I was asked to do a profile on someone. And it was interesting because I learned so much about a public figure. I do not think that I would ever have delved so deeply otherwise. So a lot of times, my research is just really interesting because it involves looking at these issues from a different viewpoint and much more thoroughly than I ever would get from the news.

Also, I am really lucky to work with Laura Murphy. First of all, she is an incredible boss and she is so kind and warm to me and everyone in the office. Second, I get to see firsthand what it is like to be such a high-ranking individual in a company or an organization that does so much, since I get to work with her directly day to day. And also other people. Chris Calabrese, who is down the hall from me and gave me a Band-Aid last week, was quoted in *The New York Times* and interviewed on NBC. So it also is really cool to get to meet these people on a personal level, and then to see them out there doing their job—and be in awe of the work they do.

Leech: So your job is very definitely advocacy. As part of it, have you ever been involved in or been brought along on any formal direct lobbying?

Shapiro: I have not, just because I think that a lot of the lobbying that we do, being that we are a very well-connected organization, is pretty high-level. And sometimes it involves sensitive information. I have been privy to press conferences. We had one here when the Supreme Court decision on the Arizona SB 1070 came out. Our executive director stopped by and a bunch of leaders from the civil rights and immigrant communities also stopped by.

We also had a thirtieth anniversary event for *Plyler v. Doe*, the Supreme Court case that allowed access to public education for undocumented children. Assistant Attorney General Tom Perez and Assistant Secretary for Civil Rights Russlynn Ali spoke at that event. Actually, I was in charge of doing the time cards for the speakers in that event, so I got to sit in the front row.

Leech: You showed a time card to let them know that their time was almost up. I think you mentioned earlier that this event also led to your least favorite internship chore. What was your least favorite internship chore?

Shapiro: Well, everyone helped out. This office is very communally oriented. But I was in charge, at least for a portion of the time, for ushering people in and providing my elevator fob to let the people up.

Leech: So it is hard to get into the building? You have security.

Shapiro: You need to use an elevator fob in order to get to certain floors. And you scan it when you walk into the elevator, so that if you do not have a fob, you cannot go to any floors except for the first floor. You need it at the front door and you need it to operate the elevators. So when we had a large event here on the eighth floor, we needed people to essentially use their fobs to let people up and down while they were all coming in. And we had over a hundred people at this event. So I was in charge of standing next to the elevator and telling people where they were going and swiping my fob and letting them up and then doing it again. People showed up late. But I got relieved from that duty because I was also time card girl. So I had to be at the event, which was nice, because some people had to do elevator duty throughout the entire event. Because one thing about DC is that not everyone is on time.

Leech: So how many interns are there in the office?

Shapiro: I want to say there are probably about fifteen of us. It is not a huge number. I would say we probably have about anywhere from eight to ten main lobbyists, so each of them has an intern or two. And then there are a couple of interns working for National Prison Project, which is a separate ACLU division that is based here.

Leech: You were mentioning that most of the interns are not undergraduates.

Shapiro: I would say probably eighty percent of the interns in this office are second-year law students. There is one first-year law student, but it is primarily 2Ls. When I first got here, I didn't know that 2L meant second-year law student. But I soon found out. I am one of only two undergraduate interns for the Washington Legislative Office.

Leech: Angela, does your office mostly have undergraduate interns?

Guo: Yes. We have a couple of grad students, but mostly undergraduate interns.

Leech: What have you learned during this summer as an intern?

Guo: Oh, my gosh! I have actually learned so much from this experience. Just reading the news every single day and being constantly up to date with the news has taught me so much just about public policy. The other thing the ThinkProgress interns have definitely learned is recognizing names and faces. We write up a lot about politicians, and so this is the first time that we have really been able to put names with faces and what they actually do and who they represent, and what their opinions and policy choices are, which is really cool. It has been a crash course in public policy and in government.

The other thing that we have learned is how to write under pressure, lots and lots of pressure, and under varied timed conditions. And we have learned how to write blog-style. It is not the same as writing a research paper. It is succinct: you get to the point. And people actually want to read blog-style papers as opposed to research papers.

Leech: Did you have any news background before?

Guo: I write for *The Thresher*, Rice University's student newspaper, occasionally. I also have written research papers for the Baker Institute's public policy journal—but very little blogging. Last summer, I worked for an NPR program and did a little bit of blogging, but not even close to this. And so I have learned a lot about blogging.

I also have been able to learn a lot from the people around me at CAP. We have a ton of senior researchers, and senior fellows, and other editors there. At ThinkProgress, it is a very young office. A lot of them are thinking about running for office. A lot of them have worked on the Hill. I think the oldest person there is probably thirty-five. Maybe that is even pushing it. They are within our generation and they have helped us a lot with career advice for the future. Overall, it has been a great atmosphere.

We have also learned a lot from going to events that CAP sends us to. We were able to see President Obama speak at the White House. We were able to be in the East Room, so that was really cool.

Leech: Faith is jealous.

Shapiro: I have a lot of friends working at CAP. They were very excited about seeing Obama. They got to go bowling at the White House, too.

Guo: Yes, we also got to go bowling at the White House. But CAP's motive in sending us someplace is not just to have fun. There is also a purpose. So when we went to go bowling, it was actually called The White House Brief and Bowl, so we got briefed on student debt issues and other education issues by the education officials at the White House. They talked to us and then they brought us bowling. For the student debt day, we had to talk to various news outlets about how we personally felt about student debt and how it was affecting us, or our friends, or our families. And we also had to go lobby on the Hill before we saw Obama. There is always a purpose and we always learn something from it.

Leech: How about you, Faith? What do feel you have learned over the course of the summer?

Shapiro: I have learned a lot, especially about how DC works. I visited here as a child, but only by working with an organization like the ACLU Washington Legislative Office did I began to realize how many different influences go into certain policies, and how strategic it is who supports what, and who you need to speak to and who it has to go through, and how having a history on the Hill is really important for lobbying.

We have brownbag lunches with a lot of our lobbyists. So they tell us how they came to work for the ACLU. A lot of them have experience working for members of Congress on Capitol Hill, and that is a big part of how they got their jobs here. That was something that I had never really even thought about, the possibility of working on the Hill. Also, I have learned so much about the issues that we advocate by being immersed in DC—actually being here and reading *CQ*, and *The Hill*, and *Politico*, and the e-mailed news flashes that go out to our office. Just being in the heart of it gives you a much more comprehensive view of the issues.

I especially have learned a lot connected to the Supreme Court's recent decisions relating to immigration—which is great because I am so interested in refugee and immigrant populations, and human rights as it relates to them. It has been really incredible for me to see it all unfold and to get to go to the press conference that we had when the decision upholding the Arizona anti-immigrant law came out, and to get to talk to our lobbyists who work on that issue.

It has really been a fantastic opportunity to get really well-acquainted with the issues. I have learned what it is like to have a career, and that it is possible to have a career in the nonprofit sector in a public policy capacity. I have learned a lot about positions that I did not know existed, and companies and organizations that are in DC that I could potentially work for as an adult. So it has been very eye-opening in that way.

Leech: Where do you go from here? How about you, Faith? What will you do after your internship is over?

Shapiro: Well, ultimately I would like to pursue a career in social justice. If the ACLU would have me, I would love to work for them. This internship has been an incredible experience. This coming year, I will be president of the ACLU club at Rice, so, hopefully, I can apply what I learned here about national issues more locally.

Long term, I am interested in going to law school, as just about everyone in this office is in law school if they are not already a lawyer. But I would want to keep a strong focus on social justice issues, in particular the problems that surround refugee populations, human rights, and immigration reform. I would love to work on immigration reform in the future. I hope to get into a law program that focuses on issues like that so that I ultimately can pursue a career similar to the lobbyists in this office.

Leech: So would your plan be to go to law school right after you graduate, or do you not know yet?

Shapiro: One thing about working with a bunch of law students as interns is that the overwhelming response to that is I will hopefully take a year or two off—maybe to work, if I can get a job. I also plan to apply for different fellowships and scholarships: the Fulbright, things of that nature, maybe to do some research abroad. As a result of this summer, my plans have broadened a little bit. I would be really interested in working in DC as a legislative assistant for the ACLU, or a similar organization, or on the Hill. I think that would be a very valuable experience, and a lot of the law students advised me that it is really important that you pinpoint exactly why you want to go to law school before you do it, because it makes the first year a lot more bearable.

Leech: How about you, Angela?

Guo: All of the Baker Institute interns are required to do a research project after we return to campus, and in the first week of school, we give a presentation in front of all of the Baker Institute fellows at Rice on some issue that we have researched throughout the summer. I think my topic is going to be bias in political journalism. It will be something that I have seen a lot of, so that will be interesting. We write a paper, we give a presentation, and we defend it in front of a lot of these fellows. So that will be a little bit intimidating.

In terms of the long run, I am also really interested in going to law school. I think a lot of people in DC are. It is either that or public policy school. I have had such a good experience in DC that I think I do want to come back. Something else that I want to do is work on a campaign. Having done all of this writing this past summer on sort of campaign issues, I think it would be really cool if I took a year off, maybe in 2016, and went to Iowa and worked on a Democratic campaign. I think that would be a great experience and that might lead to a lot of open doors.

The other thing that the Baker Institute program specifically provides us is a really good broad alumni network. We are the ninth cohort of interns funded by the institute, and a lot of the alums now have pretty high-level positions. Those former interns from the Baker Institute have been really good about helping us and telling us what to do from here. And so I hope I can return to DC someday to get involved in arts lobbying or arts advocacy. In the near future, I am definitely looking to go to law school.

Leech: Very good. What advice do you have for future interns or people who want to be interns?

Shapiro: Have a good résumé. Have good interview skills. No, I am kidding. I think my advice would be to come to DC with an open mind. Every organization is different. I know I worked for a local nonprofit in Houston last summer, and this summer could not be more different. I think there is nothing like a nonprofit that functions in DC. I have worked from the grassroots perspective. I worked for a literacy organization last summer. And this summer, to see how an organization can impact public policy and affect the legislation that goes out is incredible. But if I had come here close-minded and said, "Only grassroots!" and was not open to learning new things, I think that I would have had not nearly as incredible of an experience.

It is also very important to take every opportunity you get. There are tons of intern events. You get invited to one hundred and one lunches, such as the brownbag lunches here. There are outside organizations that will have issue briefings on all kinds of things, things that the ACLU is not involved with but I will get invited to because I am part of the DC intern culture. And some of my most incredible experiences here have come out of saying, "Okay, you know what? I'm going to go this briefing on the Israeli-Palestinian conflict." And that is not something that the ACLU deals with, but it is something I was interested in, and I went and it was incredible. I met incredible people. I learned about an issue that I was not as well-versed on as I would like. DC has tons of opportunities, both within your organization and outside in the community.

Leech: How do you get on the intern list so that you get all of those invitations?

Shapiro: The invitations just go out. They find you. I do not even know. We will have someone from our office say that one of their friends passed this on to them and said, "Hey, let the interns in your office know." Most of mine do come from the office, even if they are not ACLU-affiliated. It is just people saying, "Hey, you're an intern. Either you're interested in this topic or you need free food." You attend these things.

I went to a happy hour for people who are interested in getting a master's in international policy. And going in there, I was not really sure if I was interested in getting a master's for international policy. But after leaving, I may be very interested in getting a master's in international policy. Before, I did not know enough about it to make an informed decision. It actually relates really well to my interest in human rights and refugee populations. The university has joint master's degree programs with their law degree programs, which I did not know either. So I think that you have to be open to learning and having new experiences while you are here, especially in a community of such driven individuals.

All of the interns I meet here are incredible. I am floored, not only by the people who I work with, but by the people that I meet. Because everyone here is just really driven, dedicated to what they are doing, and wants to make a difference.

Leech: Okay, good. And Angela?

Guo: One piece of advice that I would give is that you never know who you are going to run into, or who you are going to meet, or what you are going to see in DC. And that is really important. I think the networking opportunities here are amazing, and every intern should take advantage of them. We saw US Treasury Secretary Tim Geithner walking down the street. We run into senators. One of my friends who works at Brookings ran into Bill Clinton in the hallway.

Leech: Bill Clinton.

Guo: Yes. You just never know what is going to happen. And I would say take advantage of it, and also be on your best behavior all the time, because you also never know what is going to come out of an awkward meeting with somebody who just happened to be there. So it does offer a lot of outstanding networking opportunities.

And I would agree with Faith: take advantage of every little invite that you get, every little event that you get invited to. Actually, two sources that I use a lot are Linktank and Weekbook, online sites that list events in Washington. They compile a list of all the talks, and all the lunches, and all the free events that you can go to that week. At CAP, almost every day there is some lunch or some person coming to talk. Some of the interns say, "I would rather just stay at my desk for lunch hour." But you really shouldn't. You should absolutely go down there.

A couple of weeks ago, I went to a talk by Maryland Governor Martin O'Malley with one of the girls I work with. We were able to get ten minutes alone with O'Malley, and that was insane. Because he might actually be a presidential candidate in the next four or eight years. So it is cool the amount of opportunities DC has and that they are open to all the interns. Everyone should take advantage of these kinds of opportunities. You never know what is going to happen or what's going to come out of it.

Shapiro: You're right, Angela. When I went to the intern event on the Israeli-Palestinian conflict that I mentioned earlier, I met someone who then invited me to the intern happy hour about the master's in public policy. And then at that happy hour, I met someone who was organizing a reception at the Indian ambassador's house for a retiring senator. So I got to go to that reception as well, which was incredible. There were tons of members of Congress there, and I met all of these really interesting people. That is a memory I am going to have for the rest of my life. And it was an opportunity that I would have missed out on if I had ever at some point said, "I prefer to stay at my desk for this event," or, "I would rather go home for dinner than have dinner at this intern summit." I think that is how those things work. One opportunity leads to another.

Guo: I was thinking about two other things that were really important for the summer. One is reaching out to your alumni network. I know that for me and for a lot of Rice students here, this summer has just been made all the more of a positive experience because we have reached out to alumni. Actually, this afternoon at four thirty, we are going over to the White House because one alumnus, Josh Ernest, is the Deputy Press Secretary to President Obama. He said, "Oh, of course I want to meet with you Rice students." And he cleared his schedule.

Leech: You called him and said, "Will you meet with us?"

Guo: I met him at a Baker Institute event a couple of months ago at Rice. And he said, "Obviously, I will be in DC over the summer. Just give me a call." And so a couple of us are going over later today to meet with him at the White House, and he is going to walk us around and tell us how he got from Rice to this position. We have three congressmen in the House who are alums from Rice, and they have been more than happy to just go around talking to

Rice interns, which I think is fantastic. So that is another little piece of advice: definitely reach out to your alumni network.

And the last thing I can think of is picking random roommates was honestly the best decision I made. I am living with one other Rice student, but I am in a suite with three people who I adore after spending the summer with them. And we all work in different places. I am very liberal, but one of my roommates is working for the Republican National Committee and she is in their legal office. It is amazing just to talk with her and see what she thinks and what I think, and talk about it. We do not argue, but politics are just broadened once you are able to listen to the other side.

And the other advantage to having roommates who are all interns is that we get to go to a ton of different events. If my roommates hear about something at their office, they can invite me to come with them. I was able to go to a couple of talks at the Council on Foreign Relations because one of my roommates works there. Get out of your comfort zone and live with people that you do not know.

Leech: Did you two manage to get to all of your talking points by the end of this interview? Faith, did your boss, Laura Murphy, give you advice about the best way to interview?

Shapiro: No.

Leech: She knew I was easy, right?

Shapiro: I think she very much respects my personal autonomy. I think that is one thing that is really fantastic about working for her. So she trusts me, I think, to do the interview. And she gets to see a transcript.

Leech: Good point.

CHAPTER

15

Craig Holman

Government Affairs Lobbyist

Public Citizen

***Craig Holman** is the government affairs lobbyist for Public Citizen, a national consumer advocacy organization whose mission is to "serve as the people's voice in the nation's capital." He holds a PhD in political science from the University of Southern California and has conducted extensive research related to campaign finance and lobbying reforms. In addition to his work in Washington, Holman is working with European governmental and nongovernmental organizations to develop a lobbyist registration system for the European Union.*

Working for a nonprofit watchdog organization puts Holman in a very different position in terms of resources compared with lobbyists at the for-profit lobbying firms that line Washington's K Street. Nonprofits are far less likely to have affiliated political action committees (PACs) and their lobbying expenditures are on average less than one-fifth of what corporations in Washington spend. Public Citizen reported spending about $200,000 in 2011 on lobbying.

Before coming to Public Citizen ten years ago, Holman was a senior policy analyst at the Brennan Center for Justice at New York University's School of Law and he worked as a senior researcher for the Center for Governmental Studies in Los Angeles. In addition to his PhD, he has a BA in political science and philosophy from the University of Wisconsin.

Beth Leech: How did you become a lobbyist?

Craig Holman: Well, I come from academia, actually. I was working at New York University at the Brennan Center for Justice, and had just completed a study that served as the primary evidentiary record for the McCain-Feingold law that fundamentally reformed campaign finance in 2002. Once we got that law passed, Public Citizen contacted me and asked if I wanted to come to DC to serve as a lobbyist on campaign finance matters. It was a transition I found intriguing.

In academia you never quite see the results of your work—not very often anyway. As a lobbyist, I still get to use my academic expertise, but I apply it in concrete, specific, results-oriented situations of trying to get specific legislation through. Serving as a lobbyist affords me a different and interesting dynamic for applying my skills.

Leech: What was the study that you worked on related to the McCain-Feingold reform?

Holman: The study is known as *Buying Time 2000*. Through the Campaign Media Analysis Group [CMAG], a conglomeration of academic institutions literally rented an old Navy satellite that used to spy on submarines during the Cold War, but is now just flying around in space not doing much, and we used it to monitor television commercials around the country during the 2000 presidential election.

Leech: Before that, there wasn't any record of politically related commercials?

Holman: No, there was no record of most of these commercials. Not unless they were directly connected to a formal candidate or party campaign. Commercials that were financed by groups that claimed they're only sponsoring "issue" ads rather than campaign ads were not recorded anywhere, and there was no disclosure of how much was being spent on these issue ads, or who's behind them or the content of the ads.

In the *Buckley v. Valeo* decision back in 1976, the Supreme Court tried to figure out the difference between issue ads and campaign ads. Issue ads are not subject to regulation and disclosure, but campaign ads are subject to the contribution limits and the disclosure requirements of the Federal Election Campaign Act. The Supreme Court just made up the legal difference in a footnote. Footnote 52 in the Buckley decision says that the difference is whether the ad uses one of eight magic words: "Vote for," "vote against," "elect," "support," "cast your ballot for," "Smith for Congress," "defeat," "reject." If it had one of those eight words or phrases, then it was a campaign ad, subject to disclosure requirements. If it didn't use one of those magic words, then it was not subject to any kind of regulation or disclosure. That's how the campaign finance system operated from 1976 up until the McCain-Feingold law, so groups that avoided the magic words did not register with the Federal Election Commission and did not disclose what they were doing.

To test whether the magic words test had any basis in reality, we tapped into the CMAG satellite to monitor all these television commercials and take a look at what was happening in the real world of campaign advertising. The satellite sucked in almost a million television commercials in that 2000 campaign, and we had students at the University of Wisconsin and Brigham Young University watch the ads and answer a survey about the content. Most of the survey questions were straightforward and objective, like, "Does the ad use any of the magic words?" The one subjective question we had in the survey was, "In your opinion, is this ad designed to influence how you would vote for or against a candidate?" The results would then be sent to me at NYU's Brennan Center for analysis.

We found that just two percent of the political ads sponsored by outside groups that our students viewed as intending to influence their vote actually used the magic words. Just two percent!

Leech: Wow.

Holman: That means that ninety-eight percent of the campaign ads sponsored by outside groups that were saturating the airwaves were outside the realm of disclosure. Even when we took a look at candidate ads—all candidate ads are regulated, no matter what they say—only ten percent of candidates ever said, "Vote for me," or "Don't vote for my opponent," because that's just a tacky way of doing electioneering. So the campaign ads themselves never said to vote for or vote against anyone.

That study was used to get the McCain-Feingold campaign finance law through Congress. During the Senate debates, I'd be getting the study results in as the law was being debated on the Senate floor. I would do a quick analysis at New York University, design an electronic SPSS chart showing the results, and then e-mail the chart to one of our colleagues on the Senate floor, like Senator Olympia Snow or Senator Susan Collins. I'd be watching on C-SPAN and see, literally an hour later, my chart being brought out in a blown-up format onto the Senate floor.

Leech: You already were very much an advocate.

Holman: Yes. I was serving in that role because the numbers just simply were in support of passing this type of campaign finance law. The numbers showed that Footnote 52 in the Buckley decision was pure myth and we needed something else, and that was the McCain-Feingold law.

Leech: That's fascinating. And you continue that work today at Public Citizen. Public Citizen has a broader mandate than just campaign finance, but you focus primarily on campaign finance?

Holman: I focus on money in politics, generally. Lobby reform became a very big interest of mine once I came to DC and began lobby work. Remember this was in 2002, and I fairly quickly realized that what I viewed as the role of lobbying was not the reality on Capitol Hill.

Leech: How did it differ?

Holman: Well, for me, lobbying was bringing expertise and information to lawmakers so that they could make better-informed decisions and pass better legislation. What I realized was that most lawmakers weren't very interested in information or expertise, but rather were primarily influenced by lobbyists who could provide money, campaign money as well as personal enrichment. This was the era of Jack Abramoff. I soon realized that I wasn't able to get that much done because, as a lobbyist for Public Citizen, I was not a source of money for lawmakers.

Leech: Abramoff was the lobbyist who went to prison as the result of a bribery and fraud scandal.

Holman: Right. Abramoff and most of the lobbying firms along K Street were very involved in influence peddling through monied means. The hired-gun lobbyists rarely had any particular expertise or information to provide. What they did have was money to make direct campaign contributions: networks of business associates whose individual contributions could be bundled together so the lobbyists could provide very large campaign contributions, and connections to campaign contributors who could host major fundraising events. Money for wining and dining. Jack Abramoff even had Table 40 set aside in his Signatures Restaurant to fete lawmakers at will. They could afford paying the large salaries necessary to attract lawmakers and their staff to leave public service and spin through the revolving door as well-connected and well-paid lobbyists themselves. But neither Public Citizen nor any of the citizens' groups had that kind of money or those revolving-door lawmakers on salary.

I began working on lobbying reform, thinking, "This is not how things should be done on Capitol Hill." I proposed some lobby reform legislation that was introduced by friends in Congress, like Senator Russ Feingold and Representative Marty Meehan, but it didn't draw much interest in Congress. As a matter of fact, we couldn't even get hearings for it. I'd be knocking on the doors of members of Congress, making phone calls, trying to get co-sponsors for the legislation. This was in 2004 and 2005, and there was very little interest on Capitol Hill. Most members wouldn't even meet with me to discuss the lobby reform proposal.

Leech: But eventually a reform measure did pass.

Holman: Yes, indeed. All that changed in January 2006, when news suddenly broke that Jack Abramoff had worked out a plea bargain with the Department of Justice in which he agreed to point the finger at all those members of Congress whom he bribed.

As soon as that news broke, my telephone started ringing off the hook. Congressional offices were calling and saying, "You know, that lobby reform legislation sounds pretty interesting—maybe we can sign onto this. And here are some other ideas for other reform legislation." It just spiraled onto the national agenda, onto Capitol Hill's agenda. Groups from the right, from the left, from the mainstream, all got involved in trying to come up with some sort of meaningful lobby reform legislation. We eventually got it passed into law as the Honest Leadership and Open Government Act of 2007.

Leech: How did that act change things?

Holman: It fundamentally changed the practice of lobbying on Capitol Hill. To give a little background, the House and Senate were under Republican control in 2006, and because of the Jack Abramoff scandal, even the Republicans were joining in on the lobby reform movement. They were the ones that originally started crafting some serious lobby reform legislation, but as it continued through the committee process and then the amendment process, the legislation continued to get watered down.

The Senate approved one version of the bill that was so weak that Public Citizen could no longer even endorse it. Nor could the rest of the reform community. I recall the opening sentence of a coalition statement condemning the Senate-approved legislation: "The United States Senate failed the American people today." The House passed similarly weak legislation, and the entire reform community came out opposing both measures at that point because they were so weak. In the end, both bills went to conference committee, and Tom DeLay and the Republican leadership in the House declined to even appoint conferees. So, the legislation perished in 2006 simply by being ignored by Congress once again.

Public Citizen and others in the reform community decided that we couldn't just let this happen. We organized a huge grassroots effort to try to keep lobby reform on the nation's political agenda as we entered the 2006 elections. One of the campaigns we did was a candidate pledge drive, and it was the most successful candidate pledge drive I've ever participated in. A third of all candidates running for Congress pledged to support serious lobby reform if they were elected.

The candidate pledges helped boost this issue on the nation's political agenda. There were exit polls following the election showing that lobby reform and corruption was the number-one issue that affected voting decisions. The result was that Democrats swept both the Senate and the House, largely on this anticorruption campaign.

Leech: That's impressive.

Holman: With that, Harry Reid, now the Majority Leader in the Senate, and Nancy Pelosi, the Speaker of the House, took this lobby reform legislation, the Honest Leadership and Open Government Act, and introduced it as the very first bill of the new Congress. And it quickly became law.

Now, getting back to your question as to what sort of impact it had: it had a major impact. Prior to the Honest Leadership and Open Government Act, most legislation and lobbying activity was done through influence-peddling tools that involved campaign money—promises of lucrative, high-paying jobs once members of Congress left office through the revolving door, or trips to Scotland to play golf, or gifts of prime seats at sporting events. That was the influence-peddling game on Capitol Hill.

With the Honest Leadership and Open Government Act, we shut down gifts that lobbyists and lobbying organizations could provide to members of Congress or their staffs. Lobbyists, and even organizations and businesses that hire lobbyists, are now banned from providing any gifts to members and staff. This includes a ban on wining and dining. Lobbyists and their employers can no longer take a member of Congress out and buy him or her dinner. Or, for that matter, lobbyists cannot even pay for snacks, or provide free tickets to sporting events or give any other gift.

We restricted travel that could be paid for by lobbying organizations, so if you're an organization that employs a lobbyist, you can only pay for a one-day trip for a member of Congress, just long enough to fly them out to give a speech at your conference, and then fly them back the next day. These trips have to be pre-approved by the Ethics Committee, and the itineraries are posted on the Internet for all to see. Lobbyists cannot even travel with a member of Congress to those types of events.

Accommodations provided to members have to be the same as those provided to everyone else at the function. And members and staff cannot fly to the event in a corporate jet, only via commercial airfare—and that must be business class or less. The days of the Jack Abramoff wining and dining, and trips to Scotland to play golf all came to an end in 2007.

Leech: That's a lot of change.

Holman: A lot of change, but much of the gains came undone later, and I'll get to that.

Leech: Not everything is fixed yet.

Holman: I was also advocating to prohibit lobbyists from being involved in any campaign fundraising, but even the reform-minded 110th Congress wasn't willing to go that far. Congress was willing to have full disclosure of these fundraising events, however, and so we ended up with disclosure of direct as well as bundled campaign contributions by lobbyists, and fundraising events hosted by lobbyists.

Leech: That means that if a lobbyist raises a lot of money from other people for the member of Congress, the lobbyist has to disclose that.

Holman: Yes, the bundling has to be disclosed, and disclosed online, and that's still in effect. We also made it much easier to access information that lobbyists must disclose about their activities because of a phrase that I put into the legislation. Instead of filing paper documents that were not easily searchable, lobbyists now have to file electronically, and those electronic reports are available online in a "searchable, sortable, and downloadable" format. That means these records can now be searched online by any number of criteria, such as lobbyist, organization or client. The records can be sorted by such criteria as amount of expenditure, issues lobbied or date. And if you want to download the data into your own database program, such as SPSS, that can be done, too.

Leech: Researchers everywhere thank you.

Holman: That made a huge difference. Now we have an excellent disclosure system. We also now require lobbyist activity reports to be filed every three months as opposed to twice a year.

Leech: So now the files are more up-to-date. You mentioned that you were the one who inserted that language into that bill. Can you talk a little bit about how a lobbyist would go about doing that?

Holman: Certainly. To get effective legislative reforms, I don't just offer ideas and bullet points that say, "Point: You need to have electronic disclosure. Point: You need to ban wining and dining." I won't offer something that simple, because I've learned that when I am not specific, it will tend to be drafted by staffers in Congress into something that is not at all what I'm working toward.

I will almost always provide a draft version of a bill or sections of the bill. I provide not only the ideas, but also my suggestions on how it should be written in statutory language. Then it goes to staffers and eventually the Office of the Legislative Counsel, and they always rewrite it, of course—but, by providing the initial drafts, at least I'm setting the stage for where this type of legislation is going. I'm a firm believer in providing actual statutory language for a legislative proposal, as well as summary bullet points that outline the objectives.

Leech: You would first give that language to staff of the members of Congress who were interested in proposing such a bill?

Holman: That's right. Then the staff goes over it and they rewrite it, and then it goes to Leg[islative] Counsel in the House and the Senate, and the Leg Counsel will rewrite it. It comes out as a very different bill, but at least I've set the parameters of how the legislation is going to look. I did the same with the Honest Leadership and Open Government Act. It helps keep the focus.

Even in this particular case, there were things that happened in the drafting that caught me by surprise. I was working on revolving-door provisions with then-Senator Barack Obama and Senator Russ Feingold, and we were going to have much stricter revolving-door restrictions on entering lobbying after leaving government service. However, many members of Congress rebelled against that idea, especially the elder chairmen of committees who were planning on retiring soon and taking lucrative lobbying jobs themselves.

They didn't want to see any further restrictions on the revolving door, so that was the one thing that we ended up not getting in this bill that should have been in there.

We had a substitute measure that was offered by Representative Marty Meehan. That was to at least require members of Congress to disclose any job negotiations they were having for future employment, so the public can determine whether there's a conflict of interest going on. Unbeknownst to me—I didn't catch this—the Leg Counsel on the House side wrote that the disclosure reports had to be filed with the House Ethics Committee rather than with the Clerk of the House. Well, the House Ethics Committee does not disclose any of their reports, as opposed to the Clerk of the House, which is a disclosure entity. So now all these disclosure reports get filed through a secret agency and rarely get disclosed to the public. That's what we're stuck with right now. I missed that, so we still have that today.

Leech: You mentioned that some aspects of the Honest Leadership and Open Government Act [HLOGA] have come undone. What happened?

Holman: When we passed that sweeping lobby reform in 2007, we achieved a great deal to help level the playing field between lobbyists who don't have a lot of money, like me, versus K Street lobbyists. We ended the kinds of gifts and travel that moneyed interests could pay for, but citizens' groups could not afford.

It forced all lobbyists, whether you're K Street or a Public Citizen lobbyist, to do your business on Capitol Hill—going into the lawmaker's office instead of taking him out to a golf course. You actually show up in their offices, present your case, provide your information and expertise, and do what lobbying really is supposed to be all about.

Leech: Then decisions are based on the quality of your argument and your evidence rather than on what gifts you have to give.

Holman: That's right. HLOGA elevated merits of the arguments and reduced the role of money. But the Supreme Court's decision in *Citizens United* in 2010 once again elevated the status of money in lobbying.

Leech: That case ruled that it was unconstitutional to limit independent campaign expenditures by corporations and other organizations. What was the effect of all that money?

Holman: It had a direct impact on the integrity of the legislative processes. Suddenly I was up against K Street lobbyists on Capitol Hill who could direct the spending of hundreds of thousands or millions of dollars in campaign funds to support or oppose a lawmaker. Right after the *Citizens United* decision, I was providing a congressional briefing to staffers on the impact of the ruling itself. One staffer asked, "How can I say no to a lobbyist who now has deep pockets to unseat my boss if they don't like us?"

That fear is valid. Lobbyists for corporate clients have always been in the role of directing the corporate PAC campaign contributions based on the company's legislative and political priorities. But campaign contributions from PACs are limited to $5,000 under federal law and fully disclosed to the public. With Citizens United, the same corporations can now make unlimited and undisclosed expenditures for or against candidates—all of which will be directed by the corporate lobbyists. K Street lobbyists are once again elevated to the status of kingmakers in Congress.

Leech: Because they could make a difference in elections.

Holman: Yes. We had two big steps forward with HLOGA, and with Citizens United, we had another big step backward.

Leech: At this point, what are you and Public Citizen doing to address the effects of the *Citizens United* ruling?

Holman: We're trying to make sure that the rules of HLOGA don't get entirely thrown to the wayside. More directly, we have to deal with the *Citizens United* decision. As long as we allow the five justices on the Supreme Court to decree that a corporation shall be treated as a person under the First Amendment, the democratic system—both in terms of elections and the quality of representative government—is going to suffer. We have to do what we can to rein in that damage, if not reverse it altogether.

Leech: What sorts of things is Public Citizen doing?

Holman: We are working around the clock trying to get full disclosure of where all this corporate money is flowing. About half of it does not need to be disclosed under the law. We are supporting the Disclose Act, which was just reintroduced in Congress. We are also encouraging the Securities and Exchange Commission to pass regulations that would require full disclosure of corporate political expenditures, including lobbying expenditures, by publicly owned corporations. The SEC has just announced that it will pick up that topic for rulemaking in April 2013.

At the same time, we're monitoring the compliance to the ethics rules themselves and trying to close some of the loopholes. There's one big loophole that has been poked into the travel rule. Under the pressure of K Street lobbyists, the House and Senate ethics committees have now issued rules saying that if a lobby entity sets up a separate 501(c)3 charitable organization on paper, then that charitable organization can pay for the travel junkets.

Leech: What effect has that change had?

Holman: After 2007, we had reduced the amount of travel junkets by two-thirds. At the end of last year, we reached the same level of travel junkets that we had prior to 2007. We've returned full circle, back to the Abramoff era.

Leech: What sorts of actions can one do to try to address something like that?

Holman: First, we produced numbers to show what's happening, and then I've met with a task force of the House Ethics Committee that is studying the travel rules. I've been pleading with the Ethics Committees to close this loophole, and at the same time, I am going to the public and the press and highlighting the abuses to try to apply pressure on the Ethics Committees to close the loopholes. It would require either an ethics rule change at this point, or a reinterpretation of the rules by the Ethics Committees.

Leech: Public Citizen has suggested in one of its publications that there is an ironic silver lining to the problems created by *Citizens United*. Could you explain that a little bit?

Holman: Most of the reforms that we achieve come out of scandal. What *Citizens United* has created is the environment for scandal. We're seeing huge increases in the amount of money flowing into politics and much of it is secret slush-fund money. That is the pre-Watergate situation, and ideal opportunity for wheeling and dealing, for buying government favors, for corruption and scandal. It's on the heels of scandal that we achieve our greatest reforms. It's like how we achieved HLOGA. We achieved that on the heels of the Jack Abramoff scandal. We now have a situation that is ripe for scandal again. We're ready to move forward with some more sweeping reforms.

Leech: What are you working on at the moment?

Holman: The revolving door is big on my agenda. Jack Abramoff readily admits the revolving door was one of his favorite tools for influence peddling. Once a member of Congress or a congressional staffer thought that they could in a year or so leave Congress and get a very lucrative job in Jack Abramoff's lobbying firm, he said he had them in his pocket. Staffers on their own initiative would call Abramoff to notify him of issues that he might be interested in, just because they thought they were going to get a $300,000 job with him next year. It was one of the very most effective influence-peddling tools employed, back then as well as today.

Public Citizen did a study on the revolving door and found that forty-three percent of all former members of Congress who served in Congress sometime between 1998 and 2006 became registered lobbyists when they left public service. Almost half of Congress is spinning through the revolving door. We wanted to strengthen the revolving-door policy and extend the cooling-off period from one year to two years, and then also prohibit anyone who left Congress from doing any lobbying activity at all during that two-year period.

Under the old law, a retiring member could not make a lobbying contact for one year after leaving Congress. All that meant was the retiring member could not actually pick up the telephone to call his or her old buddies. The former lawmaker could become a registered lobbyist, could manage the entire lobbying team of a lobby shop, organize the entire lobbying campaign, prepare all the lobbying messages, and then have someone else make the phone call. That's all it meant.

During the HLOGA debate, we pressed for extending the cooling-off period from one year to two years, and including "lobbying activity," including strategizing on a lobbying campaign, as part of the prohibited activity during the cooling-off period. We lost nearly all of the strengthening revolving-door provisions in the Honest Leadership and Open Government Act, with the exception that Senators Feingold and Obama prodded the Senate to extend its cooling-off period to two years. Everything else in the ineffective old law was kept intact.

Barack Obama, however, carried the movement for strong revolving-door restrictions with him to the presidency. The very first day he stepped into the White House, he issued an executive order that contained those types of stronger revolving-door restrictions and even went further. That order—Executive Order 13490—can only apply to the executive branch, so it did not apply to Congress. What Obama did get is a mandate for all presidential appointees to agree that they would never lobby the Obama administration, so that ends up being an eight-year ban on lobbying the Obama administration.

Even more importantly, Obama imposed the first-ever reverse revolving-door restriction on the executive branch. Not only is there a problem with members of the government leaving government and becoming lobbyists, but there's just as big a problem with special interests and lobbyists moving into government and capturing the agencies that regulate their companies and clients. It's called regulatory capture. No one had ever tried to address this problem. Obama, in his executive order, set up a policy where all presidential appointees now must sign an ethics pledge declaring that they will not take any official actions that directly affects their former employers or clients, or issues that they had lobbied on, in the past two years.

I would like to see this codified into law, because I know when the Obama administration comes to an end, that reverse revolving-door restriction is going to come to an end. I'd like to see it applied to all subsequent White House administrations. That's one of the big projects I have been working on.

Leech: Are you getting very much good feedback on that?

Holman: I'm getting some feedback on that. There are some members of the Senate who have expressed interest in introducing this type of legislation. About a year ago or so, when I approached the White House about codifying the revolving-door restrictions, they were saying, "Well, let's just see how it works first as an executive order before going to the legislation." Without a green light from the President back then, it's something I have not been pursuing legislatively in the 112th Congress, but I am fully planning on moving ahead with it in this new Congress.

Leech: What do you think about criticisms of Obama's executive order that argue that, as a result, people who are lobbying are simply using loopholes to avoid registering?

Holman: Yeah, I love hearing those arguments from the lobbyists. The argument, by the way, is twofold. The first part of the argument is that all those restrictions do nothing at all—they're meaningless restrictions. Then in the second breath, the argument is: "We've got to get rid of these onerous restrictions." They're either meaningless or they're onerous—one or the other, but they can't be both.

One very popular myth that lobbyists have been spreading around claims that since the White House now records lobbyist visits and puts them on the Internet, now everyone is just meeting in a coffee shop outside the White House to avoid being disclosed. That is a complete myth. There have always been visits to the coffee shops outside the White House. There always were beforehand, there always will be afterward, and that's just because you have to get all this clearance to get into the White House. If I want to meet with someone in the White House this afternoon, I can't get clearance in time. Lobbyists and White House staff will meet in the coffee shops, but that's not in an effort to try to get around lobbying restrictions.

An appropriate solution that Obama should consider is to modify the disclosure of White House "visits" to include any lobbying contacts with executive branch officials, inside or outside the White House.

In a similar vein, the decline in lobbying registrations has been exaggerated. There appears to have been some decline in lobbyist registrations, but not by phenomenal amounts. And that decline began not just because of Obama's revolving-door policies, but because of all the different ethics requirements that we passed in the Honest Leadership and Open Government Act.

Most lobbyists can and have adapted. A few have chosen to risk violating the law and evading the registration requirement. In order to address this problem, a full lobbying contact disclosure system—in which public officials would note and disclose all of their official meetings—would provide the public with the type of record so we could identify those who should be registered as lobbyists. This is another project on my agenda.

Leech: Is there anything else you've been working on recently?

Holman: One of the results of my work with lobby reform on Capitol Hill is that I've become a reform advocate for the European Community as well. After helping get the Honest Leadership and Open Government Act through, I've been invited to Brussels about half a dozen times to testify before the

European Commission, the European Parliament, or advocacy groups on lobby reform, and consulted with them on what to do.

It's been interesting. And because I'm writing for academic publications as well, I've been publishing some studies on lobby reform globally, especially focused on Western and Eastern Europe. It is a small club of people who study and advocate for lobby reform on the international stage.

By the way, one member of that club is Jack Abramoff. Since being released from prison in 2010, after serving nearly four years for various corruption charges, Abramoff has become a strong advocate for lobbying reform, lecturing on what is wrong with the system both at home and abroad, when his parole officer permits. Abramoff knows from personal experience the potential for corruption caused by money in politics. While we disagree on most everything else in politics, he and I both understand the need to break the potentially corrupting nexus of lobbyists, money, and lawmakers—and we are working together toward that end. No one can make the case better than Jack Abramoff. Though I never thought I would say this a few years ago, I consider Jack a friend.

Leech: Let's shift gears for a little bit and talk about you and your workday. What is it like to be you? How would you spend an average day?

Holman: To tell the truth, there really isn't an average day. The days and my paths change radically from day to day, depending on what happens. I develop long-term plans for legislation and reforms I want to see put in place, such as codifying the revolving-door restrictions and increasing enforcement of the Lobbying Disclosure Act, but I also spend a lot of time playing defense. There will suddenly be a new development on Capitol Hill attacking some of the reforms that already are in place or trying to prevent some of the other reforms that I have in mind.

The average day really bounces all over the place. Some days I'm playing defense. Other days I'm drafting legislation in my office. Other days I'm out trying to get sponsors and co-sponsors of those legislative proposals. Other days I'm organizing a coalition of groups to try to defend existing laws that we have on the books. Most days, I am appealing to the public through the press to try to keep the public very involved in what's happening on Capitol Hill. It changes. Every single day is different.

Yesterday, for instance, all the new members of Congress arrived on Capitol Hill, so I spent most of the day going to all the new members' offices, trying to meet them and their staff, getting to know who they are and letting them know who I am. Today, I'm trying to find a lawmaker who will sign on to a complaint that I will be filing with the Federal Election Commission for what I consider illegal fundraising during the election. Next week, I will probably still be looking for a lawmaker to sign on to my complaint, but I will also be trying to make sure the Office of Congressional Ethics gets set up and functioning.

Throughout the course of all of these days, I continue doing media work to try to keep the press and the public informed as to what's happening. The press is very important for my objectives. For K Street lobbyists, money is probably the most significant tool when it comes to influence peddling. As a lobbyist for Public Citizen, that's not an option for me. To counter the effects of money, I have to get the public involved, and I do that largely through the press, as well as through grassroots activities. I try to keep a very high profile in the press in order to carry some weight on Capitol Hill.

Leech: Do you have a usual set of reporters who you tend to work with?

Holman: Well, there is a large number of reporters who I frequently work with, and it's a fairly diverse pool. It ranges from what I consider sort of the campus newspapers, like *Roll Call* and *The Hill*—they tend to be very effective when it comes to insider work on Capitol Hill—to national news outlets like NPR or *60 Minutes*.

A *60 Minutes* story led to one of the things that I was able to achieve in the 112th Congress. Insider stock trading laws had never applied to Congress. Representatives Louise Slaughter and Tim Walz had introduced a bill to apply insider-trading laws to members of Congress and congressional staff, and I was trying to promote that bill. The most I could get was nine co-sponsors on the legislation last year, and clearly it wasn't moving anywhere.

Quite some time before I had gotten a call from Ira Rosen, who is a producer for *60 Minutes*, and he was fishing for ideas, news stories, and I clued him in to this whole congressional insider-trading story. About a half a year later, *60 Minutes* came out with a great television exposé on the topic, and we went from nine co-sponsors to one hundred eighty the next week. That shows the critical power of the press in getting the public involved and trying to shame Congress into doing what's right. That's one of the main tools that I have for trying to be able to influence legislation on Capitol Hill.

Leech: Do you have any advice for young people who are interested in jobs in policy advocacy? What would you suggest they do, if it's something that they think sounds like an interesting career?

Holman: There are some easier ways to go about it than to get a PhD. When I was an undergrad, I debated whether to pursue my doctorate or take the easier route and go to law school, which is three years of schooling and a multiple-choice exam, and you're out. I love academia so I chose the political science route, which was a very long and difficult path. You're probably familiar with it.

Leech: Indeed.

Holman: I find that the PhD doesn't make a whole lot of difference when it comes to credentials in this line of work. Much to my surprise, people on

Capitol Hill tend to have higher respect for law degrees than they do for doctorates or PhDs.

Leech: Why do you think that is?

Holman: Probably because law degrees bring in more money than PhDs. Being a lawyer is a high-paying profession. A doctorate, even though far more academic and with far more expertise, brings in much less money than lawyers do, and I suspect that may be the reason. By the way, I don't mean to suggest that I regret getting my PhD. I would have done it anyway.

Leech: What do you think makes someone a good lobbyist? What characteristics make someone good at being a policy advocate or being a lobbyist?

Holman: There are different traits for different types of lobbyists. If you're going to be more like a hired-gun lobbyist, representing whoever employs you, the principal trait for effectiveness is networking—having that outgoing personality where you establish all these connections and you're constantly working with coalitions and groups of people and insiders. If you're a lobbyist who's pursuing a particular agenda, such as I am at Public Citizen, expertise is the principal component, though the ability to network runs a close second.

Leech: You seem to do a lot of networking as well. Obviously, you have to know a lot of people to be able to approach them and suggest things to them and get them to help you.

Holman: Yes, networking is always essential for all types of lobbyists. But for a hired-gun lobbyist, it is the one trait that is most important. For my style of lobbying, it's really the expertise that is the most important trait. But in order to get my ideas and my legislative proposals out there, I have to do the networking as well. I do a lot of it through the press. Quite a few people on Capitol Hill know who I am, even if they haven't met me, and that's because they frequently read about me, or see me on television, or hear me on the radio. Much of the networking can be done through that sort of media work.

Leech: What do you like the best about your job?

Holman: Quite a bit. I believe in what I'm doing. I'm not a hired-gun lobbyist who will pursue an agenda for anyone who pays me. Instead, I'm actually doing what I really want to do, and for some reason unbeknownst to me, a group named Public Citizen pays me to do what I want to do.

One thing that I really do appreciate—serving as a professional lobbyist as opposed to just an academic career—is that I get to see my ideas put in practice. I put them down on paper, try to get them passed as legislation and public policy, and actually see the final outcome of my ideas materialize in the form of legislation, regulations, and public policy. That's something quite exciting.

Leech: Is there anything you don't like about your job?

Holman: There's much that angers me. Serving as a lobbyist for the past two years has been very frustrating. The Republican caucus in both the House and the Senate decided that as an electoral strategy, they would defeat any legislative proposal that the Obama administration supported, to try to make Obama look like a do-nothing president, in the hope that that would help them win the White House in 2012.

For the last two years, it's been like hitting my head against a wall, trying to find Republicans to sign on to some of this important reform legislation. It was one of the main reasons why I couldn't pursue the revolving-door proposal in the 112th Congress. You had to get Republicans on board or nothing would happen. They controlled the House and had a filibuster-proof minority in the Senate.

It's been a very fruitless two years, with the sole exception of the congressional insider-trading bill. I'm hoping, as we move into the 113th Congress, now that the White House is off the table, that Republicans and Democrats will realize that their role is not just to try to get elected and to win the White House, but actually to govern, and we'll see some more bipartisan support happening on the Hill in the next year.

Leech: How does being a lobbyist, especially a lobbyist for an organization like Public Citizen, work in terms of personal life and balance between personal and professional? Are you working all the time, or do you find time for outside things?

Holman: I mostly work. It's an uphill struggle here on many of the battles that I'm pursuing. There aren't that many people who have the means to be able to dedicate their activities toward these battles, so it's a small group of reformers that are pushing many of these lobbying and campaign finance reforms. As a small group, we've got to put in a whole lot of work on this. I really do spend most of my time in the office or on Capitol Hill. To tell the truth, I enjoy it. I believe in what I'm doing. And because I spend most of my time pursuing what I believe in, I don't even see it as work.

I

Index

B

C

D

E

G

H, I, J, K, L

M

N

O

P, Q